The Man
Who Created
the Middle East

The Man
Who Created
the Middle East

A Story of Empire, Conflict and the Sykes–Picot Agreement

CHRISTOPHER SIMON SYKES

WILLIAM
COLLINS

William Collins
An imprint of HarperCollins*Publishers*
1 London Bridge Street
London SE1 9GF
WilliamCollinsBooks.com

First published in Great Britain by William Collins in 2016

1 3 5 7 9 8 6 4 2

Copyright © Christopher Simon Sykes 2016

Christopher Simon Sykes asserts the moral
right to be identified as the author of this work

A catalogue record for this book is
available from the British Library

ISBN 978-0-00-812190-7

Printed and bound in Great Britain by
Clays Ltd, St Ives plc

MIX
Paper from
responsible sources
FSC www.fsc.org   FSC® C007454

FSC™ is a non-profit international organisation established to promote
the responsible management of the world's forests. Products carrying the
FSC label are independently certified to assure consumers that they come
from forests that are managed to meet the social, economic and
ecological needs of present and future generations,
and other controlled sources.

Find out more about HarperCollins and the environment at
www.harpercollins.co.uk/green

I dedicate this book to the memory of my grandfather, Mark Sykes, whom I would so love to have known.

'… of this I am sure, we shall never in our lives meet anyone like him.'
(F. E. Smith. 1st Earl Birkenhead)

The Man
Who Created
the Middle East

Contents

Introduction

It is extraordinary to think that my grandfather, Sir Mark Sykes, was only thirty-six years old when he found himself signatory to one of the most controversial treaties of the twentieth century, the Sykes–Picot Agreement. This was the secret pact arranged between the Allies in the First World War, in 1916, to divide up the Ottoman Empire in the event of their victory. It was a piece of typical diplomacy in which each side tried its best not to tell the other exactly what it was that it wanted, while making the vaguest promises to various Arab tribes that they would have their own kingdom in return for fighting on the Allied side. None of these promises materialised in the aftermath of the War, Arab aspirations being dashed during the subsequent Peace Conference in which the rivalries and clashes of the great powers, all eager to make the best deals for themselves in the aftermath of victory, dominated the proceedings, and pushed the issue of the rights of small nations into the background. This was the cause of bad blood, which has survived to the present day.

Perhaps it is because my grandfather's name is placed before that of his fellow signatory that history has tended to make him the villain of the piece rather than Monsieur Georges-Picot. 'You're writing about that arsehole?' commented an Italian historian in Rome last year, while even my publisher suggested that a good title for the book might be 'The Man Who Fucked Up the Middle East'. These kinds of comment only strengthened my resolve to find out the truth about a man of whom I had no romantic perceptions, since he died nearly thirty years before I was born. I felt this meant I could be objective.

I also knew that there was much more to him than his involvement in the division of the Ottoman Empire, which occupied only the last four years of his life. Before that he had led a life filled with adventures and experiences. As a boy he had travelled to Egypt and India, explored the Arabian desert and visited Mexico. He had been to school in Monte Carlo, where he had befriended the croupiers in the Casino, before attending Cambridge under the tutorship of M. R. James. His first book, an account of his travels through Turkey, was published when he was twenty, before he went off to fight in the Boer War. He travelled extensively throughout the Ottoman Empire, mapping areas that cartographers had never before visited. He was generally recognised as a talented cartoonist, whose drawings appeared regularly in *Vanity Fair*, as well as being an excellent mimic and amateur actor, gifts that, when he eventually entered the House of Commons, ensured a full house whenever he spoke. All this against a background of a difficult and lonely childhood that he rose above to make a happy marriage and become the father of six children.

I decided to tell his story largely through his correspondence with his wife, Edith, a collection of 463 letters written from the time they met till a year before his death. As well as chronicling his daily activities, they provide a fascinating insight into his emotional state, since he never held back from expressing his innermost feelings, pouring his emotions onto the page, whether anger embodied in huge capital letters and exclamation marks, humour represented by a charming cartoon, or occasionally despair characterised by long monologues of self-pity. They are also filled with expressions of deep love for Edith, with whom he shared profound spiritual beliefs. Sadly, almost none of her letters have survived.

Needless to say his writings also often embody the attitudes regarding race that were common among members of his class in a world which was largely ruled by Great Britain. Though they are anathema to us today it was considered quite normal in the nineteenth century to refer to Jews as 'Semites', the peoples of the East as 'Orientals', and the South African blacks as 'Kaffirs'. With this in mind I decided not to sanitise these terms when I came across them. I was also mindful of the fact that while Mark expressed many racist views about the Jews when he was a young man, he radically changed his mind after meeting the celebrated journalist Nahum Sokolow and embraced Zionism.

When I was growing up my father rarely talked about my grandfather, and when he did so he always referred to him as 'Sir Mark'. I think growing up in his shadow had been too much for him. Certainly his former governess, Fanny Ludovici, known in the family as 'Mouselle', who worked as his secretary, endlessly regaled us with stories of what a wonderful man our grandfather had been and what a loss it was to the world that he had died so young. My aunts and uncles also expressed this view, though when I actually interviewed my Aunt Freya, Mark's firstborn, about her father for a book I was writing, *The Big House*, she had very little to say about him, and I suddenly realised that the reason for this was that she scarcely knew him as he was hardly ever at home. My interest was aroused, however, and when the Arab Spring sparked off a series of revolutions that spiralled into the situation we see today, with the Middle East seemingly on the point of disintegration, and the words Sykes–Picot regularly on the front pages, the time seemed right to tell the story of the 35-year-old junior official who was one of the men behind it.

An Exhumation

In the early hours of 17 September 2008, a bizarre scene took place in the graveyard of St Mary's Church, Sledmere, high up on the Yorkshire Wolds. In a corner of the cemetery hidden by yew trees were two tents illuminated by floodlights, from which there would occasionally emerge figures dressed in full biochemical warfare suits, their shapes creating eerie shadows on the outer walls of the church. But this was no science-fiction movie. It was an exhumation, of a man who had died nearly 100 years previously, and it was hoped that his remains might provide evidence that in the future could save the lives of billions.

The grave that was being opened up on that early autumn morning was that of Sir Mark Sykes, 1st Baronet of Sledmere, and MP for East Hull. He had passed away on 16 February 1919, aged thirty-nine, a victim of the Spanish flu, a particularly deadly strain of influenza that had swept across the world towards the end of the First World War, killing 10 per cent of all those it infected. At the time of his demise, Sykes was staying in Paris, where he had been attending the Peace Conference. Had he been a poor man he would have been buried at once nearby, the custom having been to bury victims of the flu as quickly as possible to avoid the further danger of spreading the virus by moving them. However, if a family could afford to pay for the body to be sealed in a lead coffin, a very expensive process, then it could be shipped home for burial, which is how Sykes came to lie in rest in a quiet corner of East Yorkshire rather than in a far-off Paris cemetery.

Though there have been many other strains of influenza in the intervening years, none have been as toxic as the Spanish flu, so called because Spain was the first country to report news of large numbers of fatalities. A Type-A virus classified as H1N1, and thought to have originated in poultry, it broke out in 1918, probably in America, and spread like wildfire partly owing to the movement of troops at the end of the war. Its symptoms were exceptionally severe, and it had an extremely high infection rate, which was the cause of the huge death toll. What made it exceptional, however, was that unlike most strains of influenza, which are normally deadly to the very young and the very old, more than half the people killed by H1N1 were young adults aged between twenty and forty. By the time any of the therapeutic measures employed gave a hint of being successful, the virus was on the wane and between 50 million and 100 million people had already died. It was a death toll that has haunted virologists ever since.

To this day, the great, unanswered question about H1N1 is how this dangerous strain of 'avian flu' made the leap to humans, one that has become even more urgent since the emergence in the 1990s of a yet more highly pathogenic virus, H5N1, first documented in Hong Kong in 1997. Using isolated viral fragments from H1N1 flu victims, of which there were only five examples known worldwide, mostly from bodies preserved in permafrost, scientists were able to reconstruct a key protein from the 1918 virus. Called *haemagglutinin*, it adopts a shape that allows it readily to latch on to human cells, and its discovery went a long way to helping virologists understand how such viruses adapt to new species. It struck one of them, Professor John Oxford, of Queen Mary University of London, that if modern methods of extracting DNA could derive so much information from frozen samples, then a great deal more could be extracted from soft tissue, such as might be found in a well-preserved body that had been sealed in a lead-lined coffin. He knew exactly the condition in which such a body might be found from photographs he had been shown of the freshly exhumed body of a woman who had been interred in a lead casket in the eighteenth century in a cemetery in Smithfield. 'This lady was lying back in the lead coffin,' he said, 'with blue eyes. She was wrapped in silks, and had been in that coffin for two hundred years. She was perfectly preserved.'

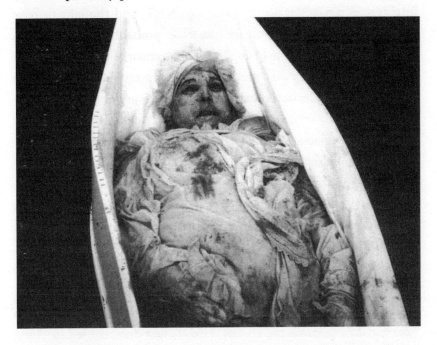

Oxford knew that 'We could take for example a big piece of lung, work on it, do the pathology and find out exactly how that person died, so in the next pandemic we would know to be especially careful about certain things.'[1] Ian Cundall, a contact in the BBC, told him the story of Sir Mark Sykes, and he decided to contact the living relatives, who all gave their permission for the project to go ahead. This included moving the coffin of Sykes's wife, who had died eleven years after him and had been buried in the same grave. After the Home Office and the Health and Safety Executive had been satisfied that the operation would involve absolutely no risk to the public, all that was left was for the local Bishop and Rural Dean to give their assent.

The exhumation team dug until they reached the remains of the coffin of Sykes's wife, Edith, which, being made of wood, had disintegrated, leaving only the bones. These were carefully moved aside before the dig was continued, the utmost care being taken until one end of Sir Mark's lead coffin was exposed. At first this looked to be in good condition, until it was noticed that there was a four-inch split in the lid. 'That didn't bode well,' reflected Oxford. They pulled back the coffin's lead covering, to find that, as Oxford had suspected when he saw the split, the body was not in the perfect condition they had so prayed for. The clothes had disintegrated and the remains were entirely skeletal. The team managed to recover some hair, however, which was important as that would possibly include the root and some skin, and, as usually happens, the lungs had collapsed onto the spinal cord, allowing the anatomist to remove some dark, hard tissue. Finally they extracted what might have been brain tissue from within the skull. With the exhumation at an end, prayers were recited, and then the team stood round the re-closed grave and sang 'Roses of Picardy', the song that soldiers used to sing on the way to the front. When the news of the exhumation finally reached the ears of the Press, there followed a rash of headlines such as 'Dead Toff May Hold Bird Flu Clue'.

Though the samples removed from Sykes's grave have revealed nothing so far, there is always hope that they may in the future. New advances in technology have allowed scientists to take DNA samples from dinosaurs that died thousands of years ago, and it is known that even in circumstances where it has been poorly preserved, a virus can leave a genetic footprint. So the chance exists that in the future a vaccine may be created that has its origins in tissue taken from the body of Mark Sykes, and which would protect the world from an H5N1 pandemic that could, with intercontinental travel as common as it is today, kill billions. If that were to happen it would be a great posthumous legacy for a man who has been reviled for what he achieved in his lifetime, namely the creation of what is known today as the Middle East through the Sykes–Picot Agreement. When he signed his name in 1916 to this piece of diplomacy, which has been since derided as 'iniquitous', 'unjust' and 'nefarious', he was only thirty-six years old.

Chapter 1

The Parents

On 21 April 1900, the eve of his departure for South Africa to fight in the Boer War, the 21-year-old Mark Sykes paid a visit to his former tutor, Alfred Dowling, who told him: 'How it is that you are no worse than you are, I cannot imagine.'[1] These may have seemed harsh words spoken to a man who was facing possible death on the battlefield, but they were intended as a compliment from a friend who knew only too well what Sykes had had to overcome: a childhood that had left him filled with bitterness and of which he had written, only four days earlier: 'I hate my kind, I hate, I detest human beings, their deformities, their cheating, their cunning, all fill me with savage rage, their filthiness, their very stench appalls [*sic*] me ... The stupidity of the wise, the wickedness of the ignorant, but you must forgive, remember that I have never had a childhood. Remember that I have always had the worst side of everything under my very nose.'[2] The childhood, or lack of it, of which Sykes spoke in this letter to his future fiancée, Edith Gorst, had been a strange and lonely one, spent in a large isolated house that stood high up on the Yorkshire Wolds. Sledmere House had been the home of the Sykes family since the early eighteenth century, when it had come into their possession through marriage. In the succeeding decades, as the ambitions and fortunes of the family had increased, along with their ennoblement to the Baronetcy, so had the size of the house, which had grown from a modest gentleman's residence of the kind that might have been built in the Queen Anne period to a grand mansion, the design of which had its origins in schemes drawn up by some of the great architects of the day, such as John Carr and Samuel Wyatt. Built in the very latest neo-classical style, it had a central staircase hall, off which, on the ground floor, were a Library, Drawing Room, Music Room and Dining Room, all with the finest decoration by Joseph Rose, while much of the first floor was taken up by a Long Gallery doubling as a second Library that was as fine as any room in England.

This was the house in which Mark Sykes was brought up, as an only child, the progeny of an unlikely couple, both of whom were damaged by their upbringing. His father, Sir Tatton Sykes, had been a sickly boy, a disappointment to his own father, also named Tatton, an old-fashioned country squire, of the type represented in literature by characters such as Fielding's Squire Western and Goldsmith's Squire Thornhill. He was hardy in the extreme, and Tatton, his firstborn, lived in constant fear of a father who had no time for weakness, and was only too free with both the whip and his fists, believing that the first precept of bringing up children was 'Break your child's will early or he will break yours later on.' This principle, better suited to a horse or dog, was followed exactly by Tatton, who imposed it upon his own offspring, six girls and two boys, in no uncertain terms.

The young Tatton despised everything his father stood for, and grew up a neurotic, introverted child who developed strong religious beliefs and could not wait to get away as soon as he was of age. As it happened he reached adulthood at a time in history when the world was opening up to would-be travellers. The railways were expanding at great speed. Brunel had just built the SS *Great Western*, the largest passenger ship in the world, to revolutionize the Atlantic crossing. Steamships regularly travelled to and from India, and on the huge American tea clippers it was possible for a passenger to sail from Liverpool all the way to China. For someone as painfully shy and who valued solitude as much as him, travel to a distant place was the perfect escape, and in the years between his leaving Oxford and the eventual death of his father in 1863, Tatton visited India, America, China, Egypt, Europe, Russia, Mexico and Japan, making him one of the most travelled men of his generation. But of all the places he visited, none struck him as forcibly as the lands that made up the Ottoman Empire, stretching from North Africa to the Black and Caspian Seas, where he was particularly fascinated by the myriad religious sites and shrines, which appealed to his own powerful spiritual beliefs.

Tatton was in Egypt when, on 21 March 1863, he was brought the news of his father's death. 'Oh indeed! Oh indeed!' was all he could manage to mutter.[3] He returned home with only one thing in mind: to take a new broom to the whole place He sold all his father's horses, and his pack of hounds, and had all the gardens dug up and raked over. These had been his mother's domain and he set about destroying them with relish, demolishing a beautiful orangery and dismantling all the hothouses in the walled garden, no doubt in revenge for her not having been more protective of her children. When all was done he embarked upon his own passion, one that had grown out of his early travels through the Ottoman Empire, when he had been astonished by the religious fervour he had encountered amongst the large number of pilgrims to the holy cities. The considerable quantity of crosses and memorials which had been erected along the roads as reminders of these journeys had made a deep and lasting impression upon him, and he had returned home determined that some similar demonstration of the people's faith should be made in the East Riding of Yorkshire. He therefore decided that he would use some of his immense wealth to build churches where none stood, building and restoring seventeen during his lifetime.

As the owner of a beautiful house and a great estate, now scattered with fine churches, it soon became clear that Tatton would need someone to hand them all on to, especially since he was nearing fifty. His introverted character, however, did not make the path of finding a wife a smooth one, and when he did finally get married it was to a girl who was thrust upon him. Christina Anne Jessica Cavendish-Bentinck was the daughter of George 'Little Ben'[4] Cavendish-Bentinck, Tory MP for Whitehaven, and a younger son of the fourth Duke of Portland. Though Jessie, as she was known, was no beauty, having too square a jaw, she was certainly handsome, with large, dark eyes, a sensual mouth and curly hair which she wore up. She was intelligent and high-spirited, and had political opinions, which at once set her apart from the average upper-class girl. She also loved art, a passion that may have had its roots in her having sat aged five for George Frederick Watts's painting *Mrs George Augustus Frederick Cavendish-Bentinck and Her Children*. She later developed a talent for drawing, and her hero was John Ruskin, whom she had met and become infatuated with, while travelling with her family in Italy in 1869.

Jessie's mother, Prudence Penelope Cavendish-Bentinck, was a formidable woman of Irish descent who went by the nickname of 'Britannia'. From the very moment Jessie had become of marriageable age, she was determined to net her daughter a rich and influential husband. According to family legend the pair of them were travelling through Europe in the spring of 1874 when, as they were passing through Bavaria, Jessie became mysteriously separated from the party. Faced with the unwelcome prospect of spending the night alone, she was obliged to turn for help to the middle-aged bachelor they had just befriended, Sir Tatton Sykes. He, quite correctly, made sure that she was looked after, and, the following morning, escorted her to the station to catch the train to join up with her family. However, when she finally met up with them, her mother feigned horror at the very thought of her daughter having been left unchaperoned overnight in the company of a man they barely knew. As soon as she was back in London, Britannia summoned the hapless Tatton to the family house at no. 3 Grafton Street and accused him of compromising her daughter. It was a shrewd move, for Tatton, to whom the idea of any kind of scandal was anathema, agreed at once to an engagement, to be followed by the earliest possible wedding.

The nuptials, which took place on 3 August 1874, in Westminster Abbey, were as splendid an occasion as any bride could have wished for, with a full choral service officiated by the Archbishop of York, assisted by the Dean of Westminster. It was, wrote one columnist, 'impossible for a masculine pen to do justice to such a scene of dazzling brilliancy'.[5] There were those, however, who considered it the height of vulgarity. 'The Prince of Wales,' wrote Tatton's younger brother, Christopher, from the Royal Yacht *Castle*, to which he had conveniently escaped in order to avoid the celebrations, 'is so disgusted with the account of the wedding in the *Morning Post*. He says if it had been his there could not have been more fuss.'[6]

'You looked such a darling and behaved so beautifully,' Britannia wrote to Jessie. 'I can dream and think of nothing else.' She attempted to allay any fears her daughter might have had by heaping praise upon her new husband, whom she described as a man of worth and excellence of whom she had heard praises on all sides. 'He has won a great prize,' she told Jessie, continuing, 'I believe firmly he knows its worth and you will be prized and valued as you will deserve. All your great qualities will now have a free scope.'[7]

Jessie arrived at Sledmere on 15 August 1874, to find the sixteen household servants all gathered together to greet her. At the head of the line-up was the housekeeper, Mary Baines, an elderly spinster aged sixty-six, who had begun her life in service under Tatton's father. She ruled over two housemaids, three laundry maids and two stillroom maids, and was responsible for the cleaning of the house, overseeing the linen, laying and lighting the fires, and the contents of the still-room. The other senior female servant was Ann Beckley, the cook, who was on equal terms with the housekeeper, and who had under her a scullery maid and a dairymaid. The butler, Arthur Hewland, was in charge of the male servants, consisting of a pantry boy and two footmen. Tatton's personal valet was Richard Wrigglesworth. The servants were housed in the domestic wing, enlarged and improved by Sir Christopher in 1784, and they welcomed the young mistress to Sledmere.

Her younger sister, Venetia, bombarded Jessie with questions about Sledmere. 'Is the Park large?' she asked. 'Have you a farm? What is the garden like, is there any produce? Have you any neighbours? What sort of Church have you. Where is it and who is the Clergyman high or low? What sort of bedrooms?'[8] In fact the Sledmere at which Jessie had arrived was badly in need of a facelift. Virtually nothing had been done to the house since it was built, and as four of Tatton's sisters had left home to be married, the last in 1863, he had lived there with only his spinster sister, Mary, to look after the place. She had had little opportunity to decorate and imbue the house with a woman's touch, since Tatton was extremely careful with his money and was abroad for six months of the year On arriving at Sledmere, Jessie made up her mind to change all this, but her determination to renovate the house met a major stumbling block in that trying to get money out of Tatton to carry out her schemes was like trying to get blood out of a stone. 'It has been practically impossible,' she was on one occasion to write in a letter to her lawyer, 'to persuade Sir Tatton to pay any comparatively small sums of money, nor to induce him to contribute to the keeping of our ... establishment in town and country.'⁹

After years of living with the introverted Sir Tatton, Jessie's extravagant and outgoing nature came to most of the household as a breath of fresh air, and she worked hard to breathe life into the house. In *Algernon Casterton*, one of three semi-autobiographical novels she was to write later in her life, Jessie described her methods of decoration through the eyes of Lady Florence Hazleton, recently wed and attempting to instil some life into her new home, Hazleton Hall. 'She had made it a very charming place – it was in every sense of the word an English home. She found beautiful old furniture in the garrets and basements, to which it had been relegated in those early Victorian days when eighteenth century taste was considered hideous and archaic. She hung the Indian draperies she had collected over screens and couches; she spread her Persian rugs over the old oak boards. The old pictures were cleaned and renovated, and among the Chippendale and Sheraton tables and chairs many a luxurious modern couch and arm-chair made the rooms as comfortable as they were picturesque.'¹⁰ This could well have been a description of the Library at Sledmere, which was the first room on which Jessie made her mark. She plundered the house for furniture and artefacts of every kind, and soon the vast empty space in which her father-in-law had taken his daily exercise was filled to overflowing with chairs, tables, day-beds, china, pictures, screens, oriental rugs, bric-a-brac from Tatton's travels and masses and masses of potted palms.

For the first two years of her marriage, Jessie threw herself into the role of being the mistress of a great house. She organized the servants, she breathed life into the rooms, she attended church and took up her deceased mother-in-law's interest in good works and education, she read, wrote and hunted. She also tried hard to be a good wife, accompanying Tatton on his travels abroad, and to the many race meetings he attended when he was back home. But it was an uphill struggle. Twenty years later she was to say that she had never been to a party or out to dine with him since their marriage. She could never have guessed, when she took the fatal decision to bow to her mother's wishes, the life that was in store for her with Tatton. Their characters were simply poles apart. While she had a longing for gaiety and company, he wished wherever possible to avoid the society of others.

Like his father, he seldom varied his routine. Each day he rose at six, and after taking a long walk in the park he would eat a large breakfast, before attending church. He spent the mornings dealing with business in the estate office, before returning to the house at noon for a plain lunch, which always featured a milk pudding. After lunch he would snooze, then return to the office for further business.

He took a light supper and was in bed by eight. He did not smoke and the only alcohol that passed his lips was a wine glass of whisky diluted with a pint of Apollinaris water, which he drank every day after lunch. This was hardly a life that was going to keep a young wife happy for long, and her frustration and boredom were reflected in a pencil sketch she secretly made on the fly-leaf of a manuscript book. It depicts an old man lying stretched out asleep in a chair, snores coming out of his nose. Above him are written the poignant words 'My evenings October 1876 – Quel rêve pour une jeune femme. J.S.'[11]

What changed life for Jessie was the eventual arrival of a child, though many years later she was to confide to her daughter-in-law that it had taken her husband six months to consummate the marriage, only with the utmost clumsiness, and when drunk. In spite of the rarity of their unions, however, she managed to get pregnant, and in August 1878 announced that she was expecting a child. The news was the cause of great rejoicing in Sledmere, all the more so when the child was born, on 6 March 1879, revealing itself to be the longed-for heir, a fact that must have delighted his father, who knew that his duty was now done. Though born in London, where his birth was registered in the district of St George's Hanover Square, within a month he was brought up to Sledmere to be christened by the local vicar, the Rev. Newton Mant.

The ceremony, a full choral christening, took place in St Mary's, the simple Georgian village church, its box pews filled to capacity with tenant farmers and workers and their families, all come to welcome the next-in-line, and each one of whom was presented with a special book printed to mark the occasion. The infant was traditionally named Tatton and Mark after his forefathers, while Jessie's contribution was the insertion of Benvenuto as his middle name, an affirmation of her great joy at his arrival as well as a nod towards her love of Italy. When the ceremony was over, the doors of the big house were thrown open to one and all to partake of a christening banquet in the library, where tables laden with food were laid out end to end. Jessie was presented with the gift of a pearl necklace, and Mark, as he was always to be known, was cooed over and passed round by the village women.

Needless to say, Jessie's mother was thrilled by the arrival of her grandson, as were Jessie's friends and admirers. In one quarter only was there a singular lack of rejoicing at the birth of a new heir. Christopher Sykes, Tatton's younger brother, was a sensitive, intelligent and charming bachelor of fifty-one who was MP for the East Riding, and a leading member of the Marlborough House set that revolved round Edward, Prince of Wales. He had been relying on his older brother to bail him out of his financial difficulties, which were the result of the constant and lavish entertaining of his Royal friend, both at his house in London, 1 Seamore Place, and at Brantingham Thorpe, his country home near Hull. The notion that his Tatton would ever marry, let alone sire a son, had never entered his mind, and when he managed both, the first came as a surprise, the second as a shock. 'C.S.,' wrote Sir George Wombwell, a Yorkshire neighbour, 'don't like it at all.'[12]

Though producing a son and heir had strengthened Jessie's position immeasurably, she was as restless as ever and the next couple of years saw her indulging in a number of liaisons which set tongues wagging, beginning in 1880 with the dashing Captain George 'Bay' Middleton, one of England's finest riders to hounds. When this flirtation ended, at the end of 1881, she took up with a German Baron called Heugelmüller, a serial womanizer who eventually ran off with her cousin Blanche, Lady Waterford. 'Oh Blanche, how you have spoilt my life,' she wrote miserably in her diary in August 1883. 'He is selfish poor ugly and a foreigner, and yet I like him better than anyone or anything.'[13] Her unhappiness was compounded by the fact that in the summer of 1881 she also suffered a miscarriage. 'That walk on Saturday, the consequence of so much quarrelling,' wrote Captain Middleton in August 1881, 'must have been too much for you, and am very sorry your second born should have come to such an untimely end. Altho' the little beggar was very highly tried ... Goodbye and hoping this will find you strong, but don't play the fool too soon.'[14]

Jessie's state of mind was noticed by a new acquaintance she had made, George Gilbert Scott Junior, a young Catholic architect who was working on the restoration of a local Yorkshire church at Driffield. Intrigued by the Sykeses' strange marriage, and having strong links to the hierarchy of the Catholic Church, he saw them as perfect subjects for conversion. 'The Baronet is a serious, taciturn, melancholy man, who has no hobby or occupation but church-building,' he wrote to Father Neville, secretary to Cardinal Newman at Birmingham Oratory. 'It is his craze and he grudges no money upon it and yet he is not happy. With everything to make life sweet, abundant wealth, fair health, a keen enjoyment of open-air exercise, a splendid house, a noble library, a clever luxuriously beautiful wife, and a promising healthy young son, he is one of the most miserable of men, neglects his wife, his relations, his fellow-creatures generally, lavish in church-building, he is parsimonious to a degree in everything else, leaves his wife, whose vivacity and healthy sensuous temperament throw every possible temptation in the way of such a woman, moving in the highest society, exposed within his protection to the dangers of a disastrous faux pas and all this for want of direction ... I want to interest yourself, and through you the Cardinal, in these two. The securance to the Catholic Church in England <u>of a great name</u>, a great estate, a great fortune, is in itself worth an effort ... But to save from a <u>miserable decadence</u> two such characters (as I am convinced nothing but the Catholic Faith can do) is a still higher motive and venture respectfully to ask your prayers for their conversion ...'[15]

It was in fact a road down which Jessie had been considering going. 'You have not forgotten that many years ago I told you that I was in heart a Catholic,' she wrote in a letter to an old friend and Yorkshire neighbour, Angela, Lady Herries, 'only I had not the moral courage to change my religion.' After 'many struggles and many misgivings', she told her, she was at last ready to embrace the faith, adding, 'and I shall have the happiness of bringing my little child with me'.[16] It was a brave move considering that the Sykeses had been Anglicans since time immemorial, the six churches so recently built by her husband being monuments to their faith. She would have liked to persuade Tatton to join her, but he was reluctant to take the step for fear of offending the Protestant and Methodist villagers of Sledmere, even if he gave her the impression that he would consider doing so. 'Sir Tatton, who as you know is of a nervous and retiring temperament and who dreads extremely publicity, has decided to wait to make his final profession when he intends he will be at Rome in the end of February.'[17]

Angela Herries, sister-in-law to the Duke of Norfolk, the head of England's leading Catholic family, was delighted to hear the news of the conversion. It was through her family connections that Jessie had been given an introduction to the Cardinal Archbishop of Westminster, Henry Edward Manning, and she was pleased that he had not wasted the opportunity of adding another wayward soul to his flock. He had indeed taken a very personal interest in Jessie, who bared her soul to him in her letters. 'Since I returned from London,' she wrote to him in November 1882, 'I have thought much and sadly of all the wasted opportunities and the useless and worthless life I have led up to the present time, thinking of nothing but my own amusement, and living without any religion at all for so many years. I sometimes fear that the voice of conscience and power of repentance has died away from me and that I shall never be able to lead a good or Christian life. I feel too how terribly imperfect up till now my attempts at a Confession have been, and how many and grave sins I have from shame omitted to mention ...'[18]

With Lady Herries and Lord Norreys acting as her godparents, and Lady Gwendolyn Talbot and the Duke of Norfolk as Mark's, Jessie and her son were received into the Catholic Church at the end of November. The conversion caused some upset in Sledmere, as Tatton had predicted it would, and in an attempt to soften the blow Cardinal Manning wrote a 'long and eloquent' exposition on the subject for the vicar of Sledmere, the Rev. Mr Pattenhorne. Nevertheless, Jessie was riddled with guilt at the unhappiness she had caused to him and his congregation. Her inner struggles continued, and she was devastatingly self-critical in her letters to Manning. 'I ... fear steady everyday useful commonplace goodness is beyond my reach,' she told him. 'Honestly I am sorry for this – I have alas! no deep enthusiasm, no burning longings for perfection, no terrible fears of Hell – I am wanting in all the moral qualities and sensations which I have been led to believe were the first tokens and messages of God the Holy Spirit working in the Human heart.'[19]

In taking Mark with her into the Catholic Church, Jessie well and truly staked her claim on him, and there is no doubt that she was the overwhelming influence upon him as he grew up. To her, children were simply small adults who should quickly learn how to stand on their own two feet. As soon as Mark had started to master the most basic principles of language, she began to share with him her great love of literature and the theatre. As well as the children's books of the day – the fairy tales of Grimm, Hans Andersen and George Macdonald, the stories of Charles Kingsley and Lewis Carroll, the tales of adventure of Sir Walter Scott, James Fenimore Cooper and Robert Louis Stevenson – she read him her own favourites, Swift, Dickens and Shakespeare, much of which she could quote from memory. She encouraged him to dress up and act out plays, and she was delighted when he began to develop a talent for mimicry and caricature.

By regaling him with tales of her travels across the world, and of all the people she had met and the strange sights she had seen, Jessie also gave Mark a sense of place and of history. She described to him the architectural wonders of medieval Christendom, and told him of the important ideas and ideals which grew out of the Renaissance. Fascinated by politics since childhood, she brought to life for him all the great statesmen and prominent figures of the past, heaping scorn on modern politicians, bureaucrats and businessmen, none of whom had any romance. She also passed on to him her hatred of humbug. The result of all this was that by the age of seven he was thoroughly precocious.

With Tatton away so much of the year on his travels, if anyone was a father to Mark, it was old Tom Grayson, the retired stud groom, who had been at Sledmere since the days of his grandfather. A tall, white-haired old man in his eighties, with a strong weather-beaten face and a kindly smile, he was an inseparable companion to his young master, a friendship that brought great happiness to his declining years.

He taught him to ride – 'this is t'thod generation Ah've taught ti'ride,' he loved to boast, – and helped him look after his pride and joy, an ever-growing pack of fox terriers. He also contributed greatly to his education, sharing with him his great knowledge of nature and the countryside, and inspiring his imagination with tales of local folklore and legend, which gave him a strong sense of locality and of his origins.

Grayson was like a rock to his charge. As a highly intelligent and sensitive child Mark could hardly have failed to be affected by the worsening relations between his parents, and when things got bad he always knew he could escape to the kennels or the stables. By the mid-1880s, Tatton was getting increasingly parsimonious and difficult, while Jessie had taken a lover, a young German Jew of her own age, Lucien de Hirsch, whom she had met some time in 1884, and with whom she had discovered a mutual fascination with the civilization of the Ancient Greeks. In a sizeable correspondence, she shared with him details of the tribulations she was forced to suffer at the hands of 'the Alte Herr', the old man, which was the nickname they gave Tatton: 'that vile old Alte,' she wrote in the summer of 1885, 'has been simply too devilish – last night when I got back from hunting – very tired and very cold – he saluted me with the news that he had spent the afternoon going to the Bank and playing me some tricks, and after dinner, when I remonstrated with him and told him this kind of thing could not continue. He pulled my hair and kicked me, and told me if I had not such an ugly face, I might get someone to pay my bills instead of himself ... I was afraid to hit him back because I am so much stronger I might hurt him.'[20]

The times Jessie dreaded most were the trips abroad with Tatton, taken during the winter months, long journeys of three months or more which separated her from her son as well as her lover. 'Je suis excessivement malheureuse,' she wrote to Lucien from Paris on 4 November, en route to India, 'de quitter mon enfant – qui est vraiment le seul être au monde excepté toi que je desire ardemment revoir.'[21] On these trips Tatton would become obsessed about his health, exhibiting a hypochondria that often bordered on the edge of insanity. 'We mounted on board our Wagon Lits', she wrote, 'and passed a singularly unpleasant night. He had a cabin all to himself, and my maid and I shared the next one. I took as I always do the top bed and was just going to sleep when the Alte roused us and everyone on the car with the news his bed was hard and uncomfortable. We made him alright, as we thought, and all went to sleep. In about 2 hours, tremendous knocking and cries of Help! Help! proceeded from Sir T's cabin. It then appeared he had turned the bolt in his lock and could not get out. Such a performance – shrieks and cries – it was nearly an hour before we got his door open and then he was in a pitiable state.'[22]

His extraordinary habits also drove Jessie to distraction. He had for example a mania about food. He would not eat at regular hours, forcing her to eat alone, while his own mealtimes were often erratic. Every two hours or so he would devour large quantities of half-raw mutton chops, accompanied by cold rice pudding, all prepared by his own personal cook and eaten in the privacy of his bedchamber. 'He has also adopted an unpleasing habit,' wrote Jessie, 'of chewing the half-raw mutton, but not swallowing it, a process the witnessing of which is more curious than pleasant.'[23] He took no exercise, and when not driving about in his carriage lay on his bed 'in a sort of coma'.[24] At night he would often call Jessie to his room as much as eight times, leaving her frazzled from lack of sleep.

Of all his obsessive whims, however, the most worrying was his fixation that he was going to die. 'The Alte is a sad trial,' she wrote to Lucien on 20 December, from Spence's Hotel in Calcutta. 'About 2 this morning Gotherd and I were woken by loud shrieks and the words "I am dying, dying, dying (crescendo)". We both jumped up thinking at least he had broken a blood vessel – We found absolutely nothing was the matter … We were nearly two hours trying to pacify him. He clutched us … and went on soliloquising to this effect, "Oh dear! I am dying, I shall never see Sledmere again, oh you wicked woman. Why don't you cry? Some wives would be in hysterics – to see your poor husband dropping to pieces before your eyes – oh God have pity. Oh Jessie my bowels are gone, Oh Gotherd my stomach is quite decayed, my knees have given way, Oh Jessie Jessie – Oh Lord have mercy."[25] 'This is not a bit exaggerated,' she added, 'quite the contrary', concluding, 'My darling, I think of you every day, I dream of you every night …'[26]

In January 1887, Jessie was at Sledmere and beside herself with fury because of the latest of Tatton's outrages. She loved to sit in the Library, which she had filled with palms and various potted plants. 'I am very fond of them,' she wrote to Lucien, 'and when quite or so much alone there is a certain companionship in seeing them.' The room being so large, however, and having eleven windows, it was only made habitable by having two fires lit in it. Having gone away for a few days, she had instructed the servants to keep a small fire burning in one of the grates until she returned. 'After my departure,' she wrote, 'the Alte in one of his economical fits ordered no fires to be made till my return. The frost was terribly severe – the gardener knew nothing of the retrenchment of fuel and when he came three days later to look round the plants he found them all dead or dying from the cold.'[27] Morale throughout the household appears to have been at a very low ebb. 'The confusion here is dreadful, everyone is so cross, all the servants quite demoralized. Broadway leaves Monday – I am very sorry for him – The coachman cries all day – I can do nothing! Gotherd is in a fiendish temper – and the Alte is in his most worrying state.'[28]

However snobbish and scheming Jessie's mother may have been, she had a soft spot for her grandson, and was increasingly worried about the effect that both the general atmosphere at Sledmere, and his parents' frequent absences abroad might be having on him. They were often away for months at a time, and she saw how he was left in a household with eleven female servants, and only three males, around whom he apparently ran rings: 'if he remains for much longer surrounded by a pack of admiring servants,' continued his grandmother, 'and with no refined well-educated person to look after him … and check him if he is not civil in his manners, he will become completely unbearable … When he goes to Sledmere he is made the Toy and idol of the place and each servant indulges him as they please.'[29] His burgeoning ego needed stemming, and she felt strongly that the way to achieve this was to engage a tutor for him. She made her feelings known to Jessie. 'He is a charming child and most intelligent and precocious, which under the circumstances makes one tremble, for there is no doubt that he is now quite beyond the control of women.'[30] For a start, engaging a tutor for Mark would give him a male companion other than the elderly Grayson, to ease the loneliness of his life at Sledmere. Jessica herself admitted this in a letter to Lucien, on the eve of another trip abroad, this time to Jerusalem. 'The house is to be quite shut up, all the servants that are left to be on board-wages, the horse turned out, and poor little Mark left by himself … and not a soul in whom I have any confidence in the neighbourhood to look after him.'[31] She set out on her travels having even forgotten to buy him a birthday present, writing to Lucien in February, from Jerusalem, 'March 16th is Mark's birthday – it would be very kind of you if you would send him a little toy from Paris for it – as I fear the poor child will get no presents, and he would be so delighted.'[32]

Up till now, the elementary part of Mark's education had taken place at Sledmere village school. Here he had learned to write and spell under the worthy schoolmaster, Mr Thelwell, but had shown little aptitude for other studies: 'he was not a diligent scholar,' commented Thelwell; 'book-work was drudgery; but having great powers of observation and a splendid memory, he stored a mass of information'.[33] Almost everything else he had learned, he had done so at his mother's knee, so in 1887 Jessie gave in to her mother and hired a young tutor, Alfred Dowling, whom Mark nicknamed 'Doolis'. No sooner had he arrived than his new charge had dragged him up to see the Library, which he said was the only 'schoolroom' he ever loved. 'I wish you could see the library here,' he was later to write to his fiancée, Edith Gorst, 'it is really very interesting. Going into a library that has stopped in the year 1796 is like going back a hundred years. Everything is there of the time. In the drawers is the correspondence dated for that year. In the cupboards are the ledgers and rent rolls of the last century. If I stayed in it long I, too, would be of the last century, because everything there is of the same date, from fishing rods to the newspapers.'[34]

'I enjoyed an advantage over most of my age,' he was to write in a memoir, 'in having access to the very large library at Sledmere, and, before I was twelve, I was quite familiar with the volumes of *Punch* and the *Illustrated London News* for many years back.'[35] He was particularly fascinated by military history, inspired no doubt by the large collection of old uniforms and muskets which lay about the house, a reminder of the days when his ancestor Sir Christopher Sykes had, in 1798, raised a troop of yeomanry to defend the Wolds against the French, and amongst his favourite books were Marshal Saxe's *Reveries on the Art of War* and Vauban's seventeenth-century treatise *New Methods of Fortification*. There were other rarer and more forbidden books too, such as Richard Burton's translation of the Arabian Nights, the footnotes of which, with their anthropological observations on Arab sexual practices such as bestiality, sodomy, eunuchism, clitoridectomy and miscegenation, all contributed to his sexual education.

It was a bout of illness at this time that heralded the beginning of what was to be the most important part of Mark's schooling. He was bedridden for a few months with what was diagnosed as 'a congestion of the lungs',[36] and when he recovered it was decided that the damp climate of Yorkshire winters was the worst thing possible for him. From then on he was to spend the winter months abroad travelling, at first with both his parents, and later, when Jessie ceased to accompany Tatton on these journeys, with his father alone. In the autumn of 1888, he made his first trip abroad, to Egypt, where he acquired a fascination for and some knowledge of antiquities from the cicerone of the ruling Sirdar, Lord Grenfell, to whom Tatton had been given an introduction. This elderly guide later recalled him as having been 'the most intelligent boy I had ever met. Mark took the greatest possible interest in my growing museum; he very soon mastered the rudiments of the study; he could read the cartouches containing the names of various kings, and, with me, studied … hieroglyphics.'[37]

In Cairo, Mark made a new friend in George Bowles, the son of an old admirer of Jessie, Thomas Bowles, who was staying with his family at Shepheard's Hotel. They accompanied the Sykeses on a trip up the Nile, and the two boys became inseparable. Soon they were exploring on their own and Mark passed on to George his new passion for ancient artefacts. At Thebes the two boys bought themselves a genuine mummified head. 'That it will one day find its way into the soup,' wrote Thomas in his diary, 'unless it soon gets thrown overboard I feel little doubt.' They were nicknamed 'the two English baby-boys by the Arabs' and 'distinguished themselves by winning two donkey races at the local Gymkhana, Mark having carried off the race with saddles, and George the bare-backed race; but two days ago they fell out, and proceeded to settle their differences by having a fight according to the rules of the British prize ring, in the ruins of Karnak – a battle which much astonished the donkey-boys. Having shaken hands, however, at the end of their little mill, they are now faster friends than ever, and are at present, I understand, organising a deep-laid plot to get hold of an entire mummy and take it to England for the benefit of their friends and the greater glory of what they call their museum.'[38]

This was the first of many trips that Mark was to make over the next ten years, which were to contribute more to his general development and education than anything he ever learned at school. 'Before I was fifteen,' he later wrote, 'I visited Assouan, which was then almost the Dervish frontier ... Then I went to India when Lord Lansdowne was Viceroy. I did some exploration in the Arabian desert, enjoying myself bare-footed amongst the Arabs, and I paid a trip to Mexico, reaching there just when Porfirio Diaz was attaining the zenith of his power.'[39]

In the spring of 1890, aged eleven, Mark returned from a trip with his father to the Lebanon to find that, against the wishes of his father, who would have preferred Harrow, he had been enrolled by his mother as a junior student at Beaumont College, Windsor, a Roman Catholic school often called 'the Catholic Eton'. She chose the school, which stood on rising ground near the Thames at Old Windsor, bordering the Great Park, not for religious reasons, but because it was more likely to nurture an unorthodox character such as Mark's. The Rector, Father William Heathcote, was a known libertarian who believed that qualities such as humour and loyalty should be encouraged. She also approved of the emphasis placed by the school on theatre.

Having been exposed to far more than most boys of his age, and with his precocious and rather rebellious nature, Mark was an object of curiosity from the very moment he arrived at his new school. 'He was quite unlike any other boy,' wrote a contemporary, Wilfred Bowring, 'and most of the boys certainly thought him eccentric. He took no part in the games, but soon gathered round him and under him all the loiterers and loafers in playroom and playground.'[40] Instead of organized games, he devised elaborate war games and could often be seen charging across the playground, perhaps in the guise of an Arab warrior, or a Red Indian chief. 'I can recollect him now', continued Bowring, 'at the head of a motley gang, all waving roughly made tomahawks, charging across the playground to meet an opposing band.'[41] He kept a stock of stag beetles, with which he amused people by getting them intoxicated on the school beer, and was also the subject of much hilarity on account of his haphazard manner of dressing and his scruffy appearance, a trait shared by his close friend Cedric Dickens. 'I can see the two of them,' recalled Cedric's brother Henry, 'wandering into a certain catechism class ... on Saturday afternoons, always dishevelled and invariably steeped in ink to the very bone. It must have taken years to get that ink out ... I can see him too pretending to hang himself by the neck in a roller towel in the lavatory, and precious nearly succeeding too, by an accident! It was my hand that liberated him. So far as my observation went, never doing a stroke of school work.'[42]

It is a tribute to the monks of Beaumont that they made no attempt to force Mark into a mould into which he was not going to fit. Accepting that he would never have to earn a living, they seemed instead content with teaching him his religion. They made little attempt to ensure he did his school work, and his exercise books, rather than being crammed with Latin vocabulary and translations, were filled with entertaining histories based on Virgil and Cicero, illustrated with witty caricatures, a talent he had inherited from his mother. When Jessie, as she did from time to time, swooped down on the school to remove him to far-off places, the authorities simply turned a blind eye. 'On several occasions,' remembered Wilfred Bowring, 'Lady Sykes, generally half-way through term, announced that she proposed to take Mark on a journey of indefinite length. Mark vanished from our ken for about six months, when he reappeared laden with curios from the countries he had visited. These curios nearly always took the shape of lethal weapons, most welcome gifts for his school cronies. He returned from these trips with a smattering of strange tongues ... full of the habits, customs, history and folk-lore of the countries he had visited.'[43] Most boys, one might expect, would have been spoiled by this kind of upbringing. 'Not so Mark,' wrote one of his teachers, Father Cuthbert Elwes. 'Though he was undoubtedly a remarkably intelligent and intensely amusing boy, his chief charm was his great simplicity and openness of character and entire freedom from human respect.'[44]

On his return to school, he invariably attracted a large crowd around him to listen to the extraordinary stories he had to tell. Sitting cross-legged and often puffing on a hubble-bubble, he regaled them with tales of being taken by his father to a mountain in the desert that was home to 'the weird Druses of Lebanon', whom few schoolboys could name, let alone place; of sleeping in tents on the edge of the Sea of Galilee; and of the dreadful scenes he witnessed in the lunatic asylum in Damascus, where wretched madmen imprisoned in tiny kennels, each six feet by five, 'clamoured and howled the lifelong day; over their ankles in their own ordure, naked save for their chains, these wretched beings shrieked and jibbered! Happy were those who, completely insane, laughed and sang in this inferno.'[45]

'He was a consummate actor,' wrote Father Elwes. 'On a wet day, when all the boys were assembled together in the playroom, he would stand on the table and entertain his schoolfellows with a stump speech which would go on indefinitely.'[46] His talents for acting and story-telling found their truest expression when he went up to the senior school in 1892, and they gained him the only award he was ever to win at school, the elocution prize for a play he wrote and directed himself, 'A Hyde Park Demonstration', in which he took the leading role of the orator. He also published his first piece of writing, an article for the first issue of the *Beaumont Review*, entitled 'Night in a Mexican Station', which was an account of an incident that had taken place during a trip to Mexico he had made with his father during the winter of 1891–2. They had taken an overnight train to the north of the country, and Mark demonstrated his powers of observation in his amusing descriptions of some of the passengers in the different carriages. Those in the 'Palace on Wheels', for example, included 'The Yankeeized Mexican – viz, a Mexican in frock coat and top hat; the "Rurales" officer, a gorgeous combination of leather, silver and revolvers, etc; the American "drummer", a commercial traveller ...; and lastly, the conductor – a lantern-jawed U.S. franchised Citizen, a voice several degrees sharper than a steam saw.'[47]

One boy who fell under Mark's spell during this period was his cousin, Tom Ellis, who had left Eton to enroll at Beaumont, a move that had been engineered by Jessie, who considered him a perfect companion for her son. 'About 1894,' he later wrote, 'I was enveloped in one of her whirlwind moods by Jessica and flung into the society of a large, round, amiable boy of my own age. Three years of Cheam and one of Eton had produced a sort of palaeolithic cave-boy in me with a crust of classical education. Even so I think it took me about three minutes to succumb completely to Mark's charm, even though he opened the conversation by demanding my opinion on the Fourth Dimension ... I think Mark was as lonely as I was, for he adopted me and added me to the retinue which he employed for his romantic purposes.'[48]

Ellis often spent his holidays at Sledmere, which, he later recalled, 'was to a boy of my age remarkably like fairyland. That is, anything might happen at any moment, and strange things did happen at odd moments … Strangest of all were the queer evenings when theoretically Mark and I were both abed and asleep. I would wander alone to Mark's room, and whilst the elders played poker savagely Mark would talk high and disposedly of everything in the world and often of things not even discussed in public. It was my great good fortune to be introduced to the vile and ignoble things of the world by the only soul I have known who seemed to be completely proved against them. All those sexual matters, that are hinted at, boggled, hatched and evaded until the boy is initiated into a mystery in the grubby way of experience, were for Mark either dreary commonplace or subjects suited to Homeric laughter. At the same time Mark maintained that high matters should be gravely discussed with the aid of a two-stemmed hubble-bubble.'[49]

Mark was fifteen now and driven by an insatiable curiosity about the world. Everything he read about he was keen to put into practice. Military history was still one of his passions and he eagerly introduced his new friend to Vauban's *New Methods of Fortification*. No longer satisfied with merely looking at the diagrams, he decided they should bring them to life: 'nothing would satisfy Mark but a model siege upon the lawn,' recalled Ellis, 'so shortly there rose a fortress about ten foot square, laid out strictly according to Vauban, bastions, lunettes, redans and all else. Guns were represented by door bolts, and I was told off to invest the fortress scientifically. With a saloon rifle apiece, we fired alternate shots, but any digging involved the loss of a shot. This meant that I dug madly while Mark shot … By the third day of the siege the lawn was a nightmare. I had closed upon the doomed fortress, and, joy of joys, I looked like beating Mark at one of his own games. About this moment Sir Tatton glanced at what had once been a fair lawn and was now a mole's Walpurgis night. I faded into the horizon, but Mark came out of the situation manfully. Sir Tatton was then ploughing up the park "to sweeten the ground". And Mark maintained that our performance was doing the same for the lawn!'[50]

These military games became more and more elaborate, with Mark calling on children from the village to play the part of troops, which he, being the young master, could command without opposition. He devised complicated battles in the park and paddocks, in which he devoted great attention to the working out of tactics and the designing of fortifications. Poor old Grayson often found himself drawn into these. 'Witness the battle of Sledmere Church,' remembered Tom Ellis, 'which nearly brought about the death of Grayson … Mark ordained that the church was to stand the onslaught of the heretics, represented by old Grayson and the twins of Jones, the jockey. After a prolonged siege the heretics attempted to take the outer palisades of the church by escalade, and were repulsed with one casualty. Old Grayson, being eighty, was not of an age to stand a fall from a fifteen-foot ladder.'[51]

But not all was fun and games in Mark's life, far from it. Tom Ellis wrote of 'nightmare scenes amongst the grown-ups that faded as strangely as they began … Through these Mark walked quite steadily, with myself trailing dutifully in pursuit.'[52] The fact is that his mother's behaviour was steadily deteriorating, and had been since the spring of 1887, when her lover, Lucien de Hirsch, had died suddenly in Paris of pneumonia, while she was in Damascus with Tatton. It had broken her heart, for in the short time she had spent with him she had had a glimpse of what life could have been like for her had she married a man of her own age and with her own interests. Both the knowledge of this and the loss of him proved too much to bear and she began to lose control. As part of a deal she had struck with Tatton before setting out on their last trip to the Middle East, that she would stay with him in Palestine as long as he wished, he had agreed to take a lease on a London house for her, 46 Grosvenor St. This is where she retreated when she returned home and where she was to spend more and more time in the years to come. Away from 'the Alte' and with a healthy disrespect for the conventions of society, she attempted to drown her sorrows in a hedonistic lifestyle. Soon the grand ground-floor rooms of this impressive Mayfair house were filled with the scent of cigarette smoke – smoking was a habit forbidden at Sledmere – and the sounds of merry-making, dominated by the rattle of the dice and the clink of the bottle, two vices to which Jessie was to become increasingly addicted.

There were more lovers too, mostly dashing army officers who took advantage of her generosity and did nothing to improve her state of mind. As her drinking increased, so did her indiscretions, until the vicious gossips and jealous spinsters of London drawing-rooms were whispering in each other's ears with undisguised pleasure the new name coined for her by one of the wittier amongst them. To them she was no longer Lady Tatton Sykes, but Lady Satin Tights. 'Nevertheless,' she had written to Cardinal Manning in 1882, 'I have … a real reverence for goodness and wisdom … and a desire … to try and utterly abandon my sinful and useless life.'[53] She did not give up the struggle. Society may have laughed at her behind her back, but amongst the poor and needy she was revered and blessed with a kinder nickname – 'Lady Bountiful'. When she was at Sledmere, much of her time was spent in daily visits to dispense food, clothing or money to families in need, while in Hull, where slum housing and conditions for the poor were particularly bad, she was something of a heroine. She was known particularly for her work on behalf of poor children, and Lady Sykes's Christmas Treat, for the Catholic children of Prynne Street, had become an important annual event. 'I gave a Tea in Hull for the children of the Catholic School,' she had written to Lucien on 31 December 1886, 'which lasted from midday till 6.30 … There were 520 children, and I was carving meat for three hours. I think they enjoyed themselves poor things. Certainly they were very poor and 21 boys and 1 girl amongst them had *no* shoes or stockings, and in this bitter weather too. We made a huge sandwich for each child and gave them besides various mince pies and cakes. It was a great pleasure to me.'[54]

Nor was her charity confined to Sledmere. She lived at a time when philanthropy was almost a social imperative and in London there was no shortage of directions in which she might turn her attention. Her particular interest was the Catholic poor in the East End, mostly Irish immigrants who were flooding in to look for jobs which were better paid than back home, or at least thought to be so. In they swarmed into the cheapest and already most overcrowded districts, creating appalling slum ghettoes from which it was difficult for them to escape. 'Whilst we have been building our churches,' thundered the author of a pamphlet entitled *The Bitter Cry of Outcast London*, 'and solacing ourselves with our religion and dreaming that the millennium was coming, the poor have been growing poorer, the wretched more miserable, and the immoral more corrupt.'[55] It was typical of Jessie to combine her social life and her charity work in a flamboyant style and she would often astonish people by leaving a party in full swing and going straight to the East End to dispense soup. Still dressed in her ball gown and sparkling jewels, she appeared to the homeless like a fairytale princess.

Though she now led a life which was increasingly independent from her husband, Jessie was still Lady Sykes and she continued to play that role as she was needed, acting, for example, as Tatton's travelling companion. She accompanied him to Russia in 1887, India in 1888 and Egypt in 1889. Her powers of flirtation remained undiminished and each trip netted her new admirers. In Russia a General Churchyard fell under her spell. In India, two young men, Richard Braithwaite and David Wallace, were rivals for her love, but it was in Egypt that she came closest to finding again the happiness she had felt with Lucien when she embarked on an affair with Eldon Gorst, a young diplomat and rising star in the Foreign Office who had been assigned to the British Consulate-General in Cairo. For two years they conducted a passionate relationship with periods of great happiness interspersed with the heartbreak of separation. There could be no future in their union, which, when it finally broke up, left them both heartbroken. Jessie was inconsolable.

Aged thirty-six, her sadness compounded in April 1891 by the death of her beloved father, she felt her life was beginning to cave in on her. Over the next two years, her drinking became heavier, her promiscuity more flagrant, and she began to haunt bookmakers' shops and the premises of money-lenders, while those who cared for her looked on in horror, powerless to help, foremost amongst them her fifteen-year-old son.

Chapter 2

Trials and Tribulations

Watching his mother's slow deterioration was extremely difficult for Mark, and for the first time in his life, he began to dread her visits to Beaumont, fearing that she would be begging him to intervene on her behalf with his father, or, worse still, that she would be drunk. 'I can still see Lady Sykes,' recalled Henry Dickens, 'descending on Beaumont like a thunderbolt, entering into tremendous fights with Father Heathcote, the then and equally pugnacious rector.'[1] At home he felt increasingly isolated, having no one to whom he could really turn. His tutor, 'Doolis', had left, as had his replacement, Mr Beresford, and his worries about Jessie were not the kind of thing he would have discussed with Grayson or any of the house servants. He began to spend more and more time with his terriers, the pack of which numbered six, and he took comfort in eating, which caused his weight to balloon. Then just at a time when he was at his most vulnerable, he formed a new friendship, in the form of the nineteen-year-old daughter of his father's coachman, Tom Carter. Alice Carter, whose father had come to Sledmere from the neighbouring estate of Castle Howard, was anything but the 'village maiden'. Tall, good-looking and stylishly dressed, she had a job as a teacher in the village school, and when she met Mark up at the house stables, he immediately captivated her. To an intelligent and literate girl such as her, who had seen little of the world, he was a romantic figure, fascinating her with tales of his travels through the Ottoman Empire, and impressing her with his fluency in Oriental languages. She also saw that he was very lonely.

Mark took Alice for walks with the dogs, rode with her, showed her all his favourite places in the park and in the house, and they spent many happy hours in the Library, where he showed her his best-loved books and read her stories from the Arabian Nights. He gave her a present of an inkwell made from the hoof of a favourite pony he had had as a child. A strong attraction soon developed between them, the eventual outcome of which was the consummation of their affair, in Alice's recollection, on the floor of the Farm Dairy.[2] The romance lasted long enough for them to plan to elope to London, which they managed to accomplish for a short while. To keep such an affair secret in a tight-knit community such as Sledmere was, however, impossible, and gossip meant that they were soon tracked down by Jessie and forcibly separated, leaving them both distraught.

The repercussions of this affair were far-reaching. The Carter family had to leave Sledmere and were sent to London, where employment was found for them in Grosvenor Street, while Alice was set up in a house round the corner in Mount Street. Tatton was angry enough to threaten to disinherit his son, a step which Jessie somehow managed to dissuade him from. Instead, he was immediately removed from Beaumont School and forbidden from accompanying his father on his annual trip to the East. Instead he spent the winter of 1894 alone at Sledmere with his terriers, from whom he could not bear to be separated, and with a new tutor, a young Catholic called Egerton Beck, who was widely read and already the author of a number of papers on monastic history. A man of impeccable dress and manners, with a fascination for the past, he hit it off at once with his new charge, of whom he was to become a lifelong friend. Mark could not wait to take Beck into the Library, where they spent hours studying the papers of the Sykes ancestors, poring over the wonderful folios of engravings by Piranesi, and devouring the military histories that Mark loved so much.

In the spring of 1895, at the age of sixteen, Mark was sent abroad, to an Italian Jesuit school in Monaco, an unusual choice inspired by his mother's friendship with the then Princess of Monaco, the former

Alice, Duchess of Richelieu, whom Jessie had met in Paris, at one of her celebrated salons in the Faubourg Saint-Honoré. Jessie, Beck and three of his terriers accompanied him there, and they moved into a rented house, the terriers living out on the flat roof. 'The atmosphere at Monte Carlo,' Mark later wrote, 'was a peculiar one for a boy of my years. It is quite natural to think of people going there for pleasure, but for study seems rather curious. I knew everything about the inner workings of the tables and knew most of the croupiers.' Not as well as Jessie, however, who haunted the tables while her son was at school. One day word got out that she had disgraced herself by flinging her hat down on the table in fury after sustaining a particularly large loss.

As for the school itself, which Mark attended as a day-boy, he found the discipline stifling after the relaxed atmosphere of Beaumont, and much of his time was taken up with his terriers, whose number had grown to eight by the time they returned to England in July. Sadly in the autumn he had to leave them behind when he left for Brussels to undergo the final part of his education before going up to university, a stint at the Institut de Saint-Louis, a slightly less rigid school than the one in Monaco, but where the boys were still 'very much overworked'. He was to take lodgings in a hotel during the term-time, which unfortunately forbade pets, so he had to bid farewell to his little family, with whom he was eventually reunited at Christmas.

Amongst the guests staying in the house that December was Jessie's former admirer Thomas Gibson Bowles, with his daughters, Sydney and Dorothy, who was nicknamed 'Weenie'. Sydney wrote an account of the stay in her diary. They arrived on Christmas Eve. It was snowing heavily and the Sykeses were giving a Christmas party in the house for the tenants. 'Two whole cows [were] cut up, and the mince pies were without number. There were ... fifty or sixty people come for the beef and we were struck by their good-looking, well-fed appearance.' At dinner, Jessie gave presents to the two girls, a 'lovely little box' to Sydney and 'a handsome writing desk' to Weenie. 'Lady Sykes is *very nice* and *extremely kind-hearted*,' she noted.

On Christmas Day, which was 'all snow and glitter', a 'great number of Carol singers came round all day, beginning as soon as we got down to breakfast', but there was no church since Tatton had demolished the existing one in order to build a much grander Gothic church. Instead 'Father Theodore and Mark and I and Grayson *and* the dogs (an ugly little crew of ten fox terriers) went for a long walk through the wood.' She later noted, 'Mark keeps ten together in order to observe their habits when living in lots. One of their habits is that when their *leader* gets old, they kill and eat him!' At lunch they had the nicest crackers she had ever seen. 'There was one I should think quite a yard and a half long, which Mark and I pulled. It went off with such a bang that Tap was quite frightened.'

Sydney found Tatton very kind, but also thought him rather silly. 'It is impossible to help laughing at him,' she wrote. 'For instance, Mark is still very fat, too fat really, though not so bad as he used to be. But Sir Tatton, seeing him a trifle thinner than when he last saw him, said "Ah Yes! Yes! Wasting away, wasting away." I roared. I simply couldn't help it.' There were more crackers at dinner, after which they played charades 'which were very funny,' noted Sydney. 'One word was "Preposterous", another "Drunk-ard", another "Dyna-mite", etc, etc. Mark seems to have a great talent for acting among his other accomplishments.'[3]

This was to be the last happy Christmas that Mark was to spend at Sledmere for many years to come, for life was about to take a terrible downward spiral. To begin with, the relationship between his parents had reached a new low. His mother's drinking had reached the point where her faithful maid, Gotherd, had on several occasions to hide her scent to prevent her drinking that too, as well as resorting, when her mistress was in a particularly bad state, to such tactics as hiding her stays so that she could not go out and disgrace herself on the street. She was also severely in debt. As early as 1890, for example, she had owed as much as £10,000, a staggering sum equivalent to over £1,000,000 at today's values, and, when pressed for the money by the Union Bank, had given them a letter purporting to be a guarantee for that amount signed by Tatton. When the bank had asked him to confirm this, he had denied that the signature was his. Jessie told him he was mad to suggest that she would commit such a fraud, and to avoid a scandal Tatton had paid up, but the incident had shaken him.

At 46 Grosvenor Street, the bills were piling up. To pay them, Jessie was borrowing money from unscrupulous moneylenders – a Mr Sam Lewis was one, a Signor Sanguinetti another – at the most exorbitant interest rates, and she was speculating on the stock market. She often found herself borrowing from one person merely to pay back another. She even sank to asking Mark to lend her money from his allowance. This time Tatton, supported by the bank, put his foot down and refused to help her, a decision in which he was also backed up by his new land-agent, his nephew, Henry Cholmondeley. In the winter of 1896, Tatton's advisers, in particular a ruthless lawyer called Thomas Gardiner, Deputy Sheriff to the City of London, persuaded him to go one step further. A recent amendment to the Married Women's Property Act of 1882 stipulated that a husband would be declared free from all debts subsequently incurred by his wife if he advertised his refusal to pay up in a daily newspaper. In spite of his abject horror of the impending publicity, and the fact that this was hardly a gentlemanly thing to do, Tatton went ahead and became the first man ever to publish such a notice. It appeared in various newspapers on the morning of 7 December.

I, SIR TATTON SYKES, Baronet, of Sledmere, in the County of York, and No. 46 Grosvenor Street in the County of London, hereby give notice that I will NOT be RESPONSIBLE for any DEBTS or ENGAGEMENTS which my wife, LADY JESSICA CHRISTINA SYKES, may contract, whether purporting to be on my behalf or by my authority or otherwise.

In desperation Jessie now took to gambling and was soon losing sums as high as £530 a week at the tables and in the bookmakers' shops. Her behaviour began to lose her friends, including Blanche Howard de Walden, the mother of Mark's friend Tom Ellis. A nervous and delicate woman, she became afraid of Jessie, and put an end to the friendship between their sons. 'I must admit,' Tom later wrote, 'that Jessica, partially caged and embittered, was terrifying. At last Mark and I saw that our friendship could not continue. Mark had been more than a friend. He had been a sort of miraculous Philistine striding through the difficult age of adolescence and bowling over the conventions that I could only blindly resent. We had never talked of religion and we had never discussed our mothers. These two things we kept sacred. We knew what was putting us apart, and I think it was bad for both of us. The parting had to come, and Mark shook hands with me a little ruefully and said suddenly "If we meet again we shall smile at this. If not, then was this parting well made."'[4]

It is hard to believe that this enforced separation would not have left some ice in Mark's heart, though what happened next was far worse, and may have inspired his former tutor, 'Doolis', to warn him, 'Unless you strive and fight against circumstances, you will grow up a worthless, cruel, hard-hearted, frivolous man.'[5] He returned from Brussels for the Easter holidays, and instead of his terriers racing out of the house to greet him, barking wildly, tails wagging and tongues eager to lick his face, there was no sign of them. There was silence. The servants would not look him in the eye. Then, under instruction from his father, one of the grooms took him down Sylvia's Grove, a long carriage drive named after his great-grandfather's favourite dog. There, beneath a tall beech tree by an iron gate, he met with a dreadful sight; the bodies of his beloved dogs, suspended from a branch, hanged to death on the orders of his father.

The fit of blind rage on his father's behalf that inspired such a vicious and cruel act was the result of him having found out that Alice Carter had given birth to Mark's child, a boy she had named George. It was a fact of which Mark was ignorant and was to remain so for the rest of his life. Though Jessie had succeeded in keeping the pregnancy a secret from Tatton, it had been impossible to prevent him finding out once the child was born, as she felt strongly that she had to persuade him to take financial responsibility, and it is a tribute to her strength of character that she managed to achieve this. She then arranged for Alice's cousin, Mary Page, and her husband, Frederick Lott, to adopt the baby. George was brought up in Sheerness, where Frederick worked in the docks, and here Alice was allowed to visit him in the guise of his aunt. Jessie impressed it upon her that on no account was she to attempt to make any contact with Mark, whose interests and honour were not to be compromised. 'She totally accepted this,' her granddaughter, Veronica Roberts, later confirmed. 'I imagine that Jessica must have been very persuasive and very forceful too. Alice also probably had a great feeling of guilt. She no doubt felt that she had misled this boy and was now paying for it. She always held this strong belief that nothing whatsoever should damage Mark's reputation.'[6]

What saved Mark from being completely dragged down by the hideous events being played out around him was going up to Cambridge University, in the Easter term of 1897. He was accompanied by Beck and an Irish valet, MacEwen, an old servant of his mother's. Jessie had chosen Jesus College, for reasons thoroughly typical of her. She had originally intended him to go to Trinity, but on arriving late for her appointment with the Master had given as her excuse, 'I'm sorry to be late, but I've been at the Cesarewitch.' When he replied 'Oh, and where may that be?' she interpreted his ignorance of turf affairs as stupidity, turned tail and headed to the neighbouring college, which happened to be Jesus, to put her son's name down there. 'I was going to make sure,' she said later, 'that my son was not put in the charge of a lunatic!'[7]

Mark was hardly the run-of-the-mill Cambridge student. 'I must say I was not impressed by him when he first came,' wrote one of the dons, Dr Foakes Jackson. 'He struck me as a rather undeveloped youth whose education had been neglected. I considered that he would soon vanish from the scene and be no more heard of. By slow degrees I realized that Sykes was a man of exceptional powers. I discovered that he was one of those people who really understand the traveller's art and can educate themselves by observation … [He] showed even as a lad an extraordinary grasp of all that was really important in the countries he visited and surprised those who knew him by the breadth of his interests.'[8] His evident charm and intelligence allowed him, just like his mother, to get away with murder. 'About once a week,' recalled Foakes, 'his man McEwen appeared in his place with a message to the effect that Mr Sykes regretted that he "could not attend upon my instructions that day", the words being evidently those of McEwen.'[9] His tutor, the Rev. E. G. Swain of King's, soon realized that his new charge had little, if any, interest in the tasks ahead of him, such as passing exams, but was, on the other hand, head and shoulders above most of his fellow students when it came to knowledge of the world and of the important things in life, and was also excellent company. 'He never failed to be unobtrusively amusing,' he recalled, 'and, since none of us had had experiences like his, he was always interesting. His experiences of travel, acute observation, retentive memory and great powers of mimicry supplied him with means of entertainment such as no one else possessed …' He was impressed too by how unspoiled he was. 'It would be hard to find,' he wrote, 'another instance of a wealthy young man, completely his own master, who lived so simply or held so firmly to high principles.'[10]

The most important friendship that Mark struck up in his first term at Cambridge was with the distinguished scholar Dr Montague Rhodes James, then Dean of King's. He was a historian, amateur archaeologist, expert on medieval manuscripts, writer of ghost stories and an excellent mimic, and it was his habit to hold open house each evening in his rooms on the top floor of Wilkins' Buildings in King's College and he would leave his door ajar for any student who wished to visit. 'To a very large number of them,' wrote a contemporary, 'he was the centre of their Cambridge life. It is safe to say that not one of them ever found him too busy to talk to them, play games with them, make music with them on that very clangy piano, and entertain them with his vast stores of knowledge, his inexhaustible humour and his unique power of mimicry. The tables were piled deep with books and papers, with perhaps a whisky bottle and siphon standing among them.'[11] Mark and James were made for one another. 'On many an evening,' James later wrote in his autobiography, 'he would appear at nine and stay till midnight: I might be the only company, but that was no deterrent. Mark would keep me amused – more than amused – hysterical – for the whole three hours. It might be dialogues with a pessimistic tenant in Holderness, or speeches of his Palestine drago-man Isa [sic] ... or the whole of a melodrama he had seen lately, in which he acted all the parts at once with amazing skill. Whatever it was there was genius in it.'[12]

Acting was one part of his life at Cambridge to which he gave one hundred per cent, becoming a leading member of the Cambridge Amateur Dramatic Club, acting in and directing productions such as Sheridan's *The Critic*, as well as designing and drawing the posters that advertised them. It was a good way of temporarily forgetting the prob-lems that overshadowed his life. His mother was now in deeper trou-ble than ever. The effect of his father's advertisement had been to bring all her creditors out into the open, each one clamouring for payment. Since no one would now lend her any money, she could no longer resort to the expedient of borrowing from one to pay off another. In a last-ditch attempt to settle the matter once and for all, Tatton's lawyers drew up an agreement under which, in return for her promise 'not to speculate any more on the Stock Exchange or to bet for credit on the Turf', she would receive a lump sum of £12,000 to discharge her existing liabilities, and a guarantee of a future allowance of £5,000 per year plus 'pin money' out of which she would pay all the household and stable accounts in London. The signing of this might have solved the problem had it not been for the fact that, paying exorbitant inter-est rates of 60 per cent, the true sum borrowed by Jessie since 1890 was £126,000, meaning there were still massive debts which she had kept secret, and by the spring of 1897 the creditors were once again banging at the door. They were led by one Mr Daniel Jay, of 90 Jermyn

Street, a moneylender with the telegraphic address 'BLUSHINGLY, LONDON', whom Mark was later to refer to as 'the biggest shark in London'.[13]

Tatton's lawyer, Gardiner, advised him to stand firm and not pay his wife a penny more. He arranged for him to leave the country for three months and, in the meantime, put the house in Grosvenor Street up for sale and gave notice to all the servants. He also made it his business to collect any information he could which might be eventually used against Jessie. He sent his men to Yorkshire, for example, to collect statements from people willing to testify as to her drinking. One such affidavit, from the second coachman at Sledmere, James Tovell, told how he had collected her one morning in July 1894. 'I could not understand her orders,' he said, 'and she kept me driving her about from about 10 until 3 o'clock and was unable to tell me where she wished to go.' He went on to state that 'her conduct was so notorious that onlookers frequently chaffed me on her condition'. Robert Young, the assistant stationmaster at Malton, said, 'her conduct was the subject of conversation amongst the men'.[14]

Seeing that he was getting nowhere, Jay now decided to take his case to court to force the payment of the debts. His case was straightforward; that he had consistently lent money to Lady Sykes, and, as evidence of this, the court would see five promissory notes all signed in 1896 by both Sir Tatton and Lady Sykes, for sums ranging from £1,200 up to £5,000. He had made repeated requests for their repayment, but to no avail. There was also an important letter, apparently signed at Grosvenor Street, on 2 January 1897, asking Jay to accept security for payment until the return of Sir Tatton from the West Indies in March. The problem was that Tatton denied that the signatures on the notes and the letter were his.

After an initial delay of one month, owing to Tatton having fallen victim to a bout of bronchial pneumonia, the case finally opened in the Queen's Bench on 12 January 1898. Heard before the Lord Chief Justice, Lord Russell of Killowen, it was loudly trumpeted and closely followed by an eager pack of journalists from all the daily papers. It is easy to imagine how the ears of the press must have pricked up when they heard the opening address of Mr J. Lawson Walton QC, acting for Jay, for he did not understate 'the eccentricities of character which marked the defendant in the knowledge and estimation of his friends'.[15] He described a man of great wealth who had few outside pursuits other than church-building and horse-breeding and who, though he never betted himself, had sowed the seeds of such an interest in his young wife by expecting her to accompany him to racecourses all over England. As a result of this, he told the court, she 'engaged to a considerable extent in that form of excitement'. Sir Tatton was also parsimonious to a degree that he was prepared to allow an overdraft of £20,000 to permanently exist at his bank, in spite of the heavy interest, because he could not bear to call up the cash to pay it off. In addition to this, the jury were told, he was a recluse who never went out into society – since they were married, she had never once been out to a party or out to dine with him – and who shirked responsibility for the payment of almost all expenses necessary for the upkeep of two houses.

After giving a brief account of the charges, he called Jessie to the stand, and in his cross-examination of her enlarged the picture of the extraordinary Sykes marriage. Nominally, she told the jury, she was to have £1,000 a year, but it was always a fight to get it. She had found herself living in a house 'as large as Devonshire House'[16] to which very little had been done since 1801 and which then had no drains. Sir Tatton paid for nothing, and whenever she applied to him for money he was very tiresome. At one point, before the birth of her son, she had even been obliged to sue him for her pin money. As a result of this attitude, she had, with his knowledge, begun to borrow money, and had been doing so for eighteen years. Her debts had consequently increased like a snowball 'and time did not improve them'. She knew, she claimed, it was 'an idiotic thing'[17] to do, and would never have done it had she been able to get the money elsewhere.

Cross-examined by Tatton's junior QC, Mr Bucknill, she elicited laughter from the court when, in answer to his question as to whether she considered her husband was a sound business man, she replied that in her opinion he was 'as capable of managing his own affairs as most women'.[18] As an example, she cited the fact that instead of reading his letters, many of which contained share dividends, he often just threw them in the wastepaper basket. She had once found, she recalled, a warrant for a very large sum from Spiers and Paul in the bin, and had asked him to give it to her as a reward. She also intimated to the court that Tatton knew about her betting and was very proud when she won. He would tell everybody he saw about it, and always wanted £100 out of her winnings. When asked if she was angry after he had placed the advertisement in the newspapers, she replied, 'You are not angry with people who are like children … He is like a child in many ways … Yes, like a naughty child.'[19]

Most of the notes in question, she told Mr Bucknill, were signed in Grosvenor Street, and she had explained to Tatton that she wanted him to sign them in order for her to get money. It was unlikely, she had assured him, that he would ever have to pay up. When questioned closely about the times and dates of the various notes, she became vague, saying Tatton 'did not mind what he signed' and repeating, 'He would not give me any money, so I had to borrow.' As Bucknill piled on the pressure she was reduced to repeating the defence that 'Sir Tatton knew all about it, but he had a bad memory.'[20]

Re-examined by Mr Walton, Jessie reiterated that all the signatures purporting to be Sir Tatton's were made by him, in her presence. These included those on two cheques for £1,000 signed in 1895 in Monte Carlo, and cashed at Smith and Co.'s Bank, which Tatton subsequently claimed to be forgeries. 'Sometimes he used to say he had signed guarantees, sometimes that he had not,' Jessie rambled on, her testimony having become rather disconnected. 'It never made any difference to our way of living. He never treated me as having been guilty of a great crime. I do not think he realized what forgery meant. I have never had a cross word with him about it. I went over to Paris last October and lunched with him, and he said "Oh, it's all the lawyers. It's not my fault."'[21] Laughter filled the court room.

Two of Mark's tutors were now called. Robert Beresford, who succeeded Doolis, told Mr Walton that, in his opinion, the signatures were those of Sir Tatton, though in cross-examination by his defence counsel, Sir Edward Clarke, he admitted that the last document he had seen him sign had been as far back as 1892, and that the more recent signatures 'were blurred and unlike his normal signature'. When asked by Lord Russell if he considered Sir Tatton an intelligent man, he caused a stir by answering that he had always thought him to be suffering from incipient insanity. 'He would go about in ten coats,' he told a surprised court. 'You don't mean that literally?' asked Lord Russell, adding, 'You mean two or three.' 'No I don't,' he replied. 'I mean seven or eight overcoats one over the other … I can swear to that distinctly, because there were five covert coats, and one or two silk coats.' When Egerton Beck was called to the stand and told the court that, in spite of Sir Tatton being 'habitually a sober man', one signature did not look as if it were written by a very sober person, Sir Edward asked, 'That observation as to sobriety does not apply to Lady Sykes?'[22] Luckily for Jessie, Lord Russell forbade that line of questioning.

The third day of the trial began with Lord Russell asking Tatton to make two copies of the letter of 2 January, with two different pens. While he was doing this, Sir Edward Clarke opened the case for the defence. The question before the jury, he said, was a simple, if serious, one. Did Sir Tatton sign the notes, or were they forgeries by Lady Sykes? 'A case more painful to an English gentleman,' he continued, 'could not be imagined.' Called to the stand, Tatton 'gave his evidence in a low voice with a slow, nervous, hesitating manner, and kept repeating his answers over and over again, repeatedly fingering the Bible which lay on the desk before him, and occasionally raising it and striking the woodwork sharply to emphasise what he said.' He had never seen the notes and he had never signed them, and he had certainly not written the letter of 2 January. He had never had any need to borrow money, he said, preferring to keep an overdraft at the bank, which could run to any amount, since the bank had securities.

After the advertisement had appeared, he had agreed to make a final payment of his wife's liabilities 'to avoid scandal! To avoid scandal! To avoid scandal!'[23]

Cross-examined by Mr Walton, Tatton caused much amusement by asking if his lawyers could 'refresh his memory' about the details of the alleged Monte Carlo forgeries. So great in fact was the laughter when Mr Walton said 'No!', that Lord Russell had to threaten to empty the courtroom. Walton then did his best to try and show that Tatton really had very little memory of what he had signed and what he had not, but he could not sway him from the basic fact that when it came to the Jay notes, he was adamant that he had nothing to do with them. The copies he had made earlier of the 2 January letter were then shown to the jury, Tatton complaining that the pens he had had to write with were too thin. When Mr Walton said that that was because the original was written with a quill pen, Tatton stated, 'Well, I have not used a quill pen for 40 years,'[24] leaving his interrogator floundering.

Mr Walton, who saw his case collapsing, now revealed that Mark was in court, and, though he realized that 'it was a painful thing to ask him to give evidence on the one side or the other',[25] he invited Lord Russell to call him onto the stand so that he might be questioned as to the veracity of these dates. This the Lord Chief Justice refused to do, though he told him that he could do so himself if he so wished. Though at first Walton decided against this course of action, on the morning of the following day, destined to be the last of the trial, he changed his mind.

It was a devastating experience for Mark to be forced into the witness box to testify that one of his parents was a liar, and, as Sir Edward Clarke told the jury in his summing up, his evidence was so vague and therefore so inconclusive that he might have been spared the ordeal. It was given in a barely audible whisper. In his final address, Sir Edward gave no quarter to Jessie, whom he described as a woman of 'discreditable character', for whom there could be 'no sympathy and perhaps no credence'. When it came to the turn of the counsel for the plaintiff, Mr Walton accused Tatton of being a man without honour.

'The disaster of victory,' he told the jury, 'would be infinitely greater than the disaster of defeat. To himself, if he won the case, there would be the degradation of the wife of twenty five years, to Mr Mark Sykes the dishonour of his mother, and to Lady Sykes, it might be, other proceedings in a criminal court. At present Sir Tatton might wish to win this case, but in the evening of his days would he wish his name to be clouded with the dishonour of his wife?'[26]

In the end the jury took only forty-five minutes to decide that 'The letter of 2 January, 1897, was not in the hand of Sir Tatton Sykes.' As the newspapers were quick to point out, this verdict left Jessie in an unenviable position. 'The person upon whom the verdict of the jury fell with such crushing force last week,' commented *The World*, 'stands arraigned by that verdict, on a double charge of forgery and perjury; and any shrinking from the natural sequel of such arraignment will certainly be interpreted as a sign of partiality in the administration of justice.'[27] Luckily for Jessie, there was never any criminal prosecution brought against her, because of the problems arising from the fact that the main witness against her would have been her husband. The horrendous publicity was punishment enough, and the fact that public sympathy lay with Tatton. 'Sir Tatton Sykes may not have been the most judicious of men in the management of his household,' commented the *Times*' Leader of 19 January, 'but if his evidence is to be believed, as the jury believed it, he has shown great forbearance for a long time.'[28] A few days later Sydney Bowles wrote in her diary, 'The verdict in the Sykes case was for Sir Tatton, which has hit Lady Sykes and Mark very hard. The latter told George he is not ever going to speak to or see his father again, and he will never go to Sledmere again so long as Sir Tatton lives.'[29]

Chapter 3

Through Five
Turkish Provinces

Devastated by the outcome of the trial, and simmering with anger, Mark made plans to travel abroad for a few months. He needed to get away from the lawyers, a profession he would despise for the rest of his life, and to put as much distance as possible between himself and his parents. His education had suffered from the stress of the trial, the result being that he had failed the 'Little-Go' exam that all Cambridge students were required to take in their second year. Luckily for him, the Rev. Swain attached little importance to this. 'He could have taken the ordinary degree easily enough,' he noted, 'if he had set himself to do it, but it never seemed to him worth doing. He seemed to be always looking round the University to see how it might best serve him, and to follow his own conclusions without considering the views of other people or whether his practice were usual or unusual. He seemed to me to do this with great sagacity … The power of close application to what did not immediately interest him, if he ever had it, was lost before he appeared at Cambridge.'[1]

His plan, supported by his tutors, who understood how much both he and they would get out of the trip, was to return to Palestine and Syria, scene of many of his childhood travels. With the help of *A Handbook for Travellers in Syria and Palestine*, first published in 1858 by the London publishers John Murray, he mapped out a journey that would take him as far east of the river Jordan as was possible, before striking north to Damascus through the remote and mountainous

Druse country of the Haurân. In preparation he also persuaded the distinguished lecturer in Persian Professor Edward Granville Browne to give him some basic instruction in Arabic, and though Mark was soon reporting to Henry Cholmondeley that his lessons were progressing well, Browne let it be known that he considered his new pupil to have 'the greatest capacity for not learning he had ever met!'[2] Unfortunately for Mark, scarcely was he set to leave for the East than his mother got wind of his intentions and tried to attach conditions to her parental blessing. 'I forgot to tell you,' he wrote from Cambridge to his first cousin, Henry Cholmondeley, the Sledmere agent, '… my mother was quite willing for me to go if I took the maid and herself with me, which is of course ridiculous'. Barely concealing his anger he added, 'The only object of having me here is to come down and extort a few shillings or pounds as the case may be, to read all the letters she may find in the rooms and return to London …'[3]

He left without her, accompanied only by his servant, McEwen, travelling first to Paris, and from there taking the Orient Express to Constantinople, a journey of three and a half days. He arrived at the Pera Palace Hotel, however, only to find three telegrams from his mother that had reached there before him.

(1) Return at once important.
(2) Must return at once father will not settle.
(3) Absolutely necessary your return will explain on arrival.

'Having read these,' he wrote to Henry Cholmondeley, 'I replied that I could not return and proceeded to the Custom House where I was delayed some two hours. At length I proved in different ways viz (by 20 francs) that I was neither an Armenian travelling on a forged passe-porte [sic], or an English conspirator or an importer of Dynamite …' He then boarded a Russian steamer bound for Jaffa, carrying 800 Russian pilgrims in the hold: 'when I went into the hovel that does duty for a Saloon,' he told Cholmondeley, 'I found the Russian Skipper blind drunk with two lady friends from the shore'.

He did not, he continued, expect it to be 'a pleasant voyage as I am the only other passenger'.[4]

On arrival in Jaffa Mark took the daily train to Jerusalem, operated by the French company Société du Chemin de Fer Ottoman de Jaffa à Jérusalem et Prolongements. It was an uneventful journey, bar one incident, which both amused and impressed him: 'when the train reached a station called Ramleh,' he reported to Cholmondeley, 'a shot was fired, and presently a man appeared tied up like this (drawing),

he was a Turkish cavalryman. It turned out that he had had a quarrel with a farmer two years ago, he had been looking for him ever since, found out where he was, obtained leave to go to Ramleh and shot him in the station. He then gave himself up saying he had done what he wanted and they might do what they liked.'[5]

In Jerusalem, Mark was greeted by an old friend, Sheik Fellah, a Bedouin of the Adwan Tribe in Ottoman Syria, whom he had previously met on his travels with his father: 'the old Sheikh recognized me,' he told Cholmondeley, 'and shouted to the crowd that I was his son'.[6]

They then set off north-east for Jericho, close to the river Jordan, where on 10 March they picked up the rest of the party, consisting of a dragoman, the traditional Ottoman guide, a cook, a native servant, five muleteers and an Armenian photographer who was to spend one day with them photographing Sheikh Fellah's camp at El Hammam. 'The people were wild and interesting,' wrote Mark. 'The Arabs, every man of whom carried a weapon of some sort, struck terror into the heart of the Armenian. They dug him in the ribs with a pistol, whereat he wept, upset his camera, and remembered he had pressing business at Jericho. He wanted to return at once, but I persuaded him to take four photographs.'[7]

Sheikh Fellah's nephew, Sheikh 'Ali, invited them for lunch. 'The food consisted of a huge bowl of meat and rice,' Mark recorded, 'into which I and another guest, who was a holy dervish, first dipped our hands. The holy man showed no dislike to eating with so ill-omened a kafir as myself, but told my dragoman that he had known an Englishman with a long beard who spoke Arabic, had read all Arabic books and wrote night and day without eating or sleeping, and whom he had nursed at Salt during an illness. His name was Richard Burton. In return that evening I invited the two Sheikhs to dine with me. Fellah is a great friend of the Franciscans, having a room of his own in their convent in Jerusalem, and so had learnt the use of knife and fork, but 'Ali, true son of the desert, was much puzzled by the Frankish eating tools, and invariably took the spoon from the dish for his own use.'[8]

Mark's travels progressed smoothly until, on 13 March, he reached 'Ammân, today the capital of Jordan, the site of which is described in the 1903 edition of Murray's *Handbook* as being 'weird and desolate ... The place is offensive too from its filth. The abundant waters attract the vast flocks that roam over the neighbouring plains, and the deserted palaces and temples afford shelter to them during the noon-day heat; so that most of the buildings have something of the aspect and stench of an ill-kept farm-yard.'[9] Here the Circassian military caused problems for Mark's party, insisting that he did not hold the correct travel permits, and though he managed to get as far as Jerash, a ten-hour ride away, he was held up there for a number of days. On 19 March, when he was finally able to continue his journey towards the ancient biblical city of Bosrah, he was lucky enough to meet the Hajj pilgrimage on its way to Mecca, an experience that very few Westerners would then have had.

'It was an extraordinary sight,' he wrote, '... miles it seemed to be of tents of every shape and form: military bell tents; black Bedawîn tents; enormous square tabernacles of green, red, and white cloth; tiny *tentes d'abri*, some only being cotton sheets on poles three feet high. The gathering of people would be almost impossible to describe. In one place I saw a family of wealthy Turks in frock coats, all talking French; close by, a green-turbaned Dervish reading the Korân; a little further on, the Pasha of the Hajj, in a fur-trimmed overcoat, giving orders to a dashing young Turkish subaltern; here, two men who owned a most gorgeous palanquin which they were in hopes of letting to some rich lady from Cairo, were fighting over the fodder of the two splendid camels that carried it; there, Arab stallions were squealing and kicking at the mules of the mounted infantry contingent ... There were at least 10,000 civilians in the pilgrimage. Among them were many whole families of hajis, children and women being in almost as great numbers as men ... The enormous procession, at least four miles long, glittering with red, green and gold saddles and ornaments, was an impressive sight that I shall never forget; for every animal had at least four bells on its saddle or neck. I could hear it like that sound of the sea ...'[10]

For Mark, the country of the Haurân was the most interesting part of his trip, known as it was for the number, extent and beauty of its ruins. It was the home of the Druses, a monotheistic religious and social tribe whose sheikhs formed a hereditary nobility that preserved with tenacity all the pride and state of their order. The correct letters of introduction were vital for the progress of a traveller through their lands, but once obtained they would be received with the greatest hospitality, with no requirement of compensation. 'When I arrived at Radeimeh,' he wrote, 'the Sheikh was particularly hospitable, not only giving me dinner but feeding all my muleteers and servants. The sight of McEwen sitting between two Druse Sheikhs and being solemnly crammed by them with rice and bread dipped in oil and pieces of mutton was, to say the least, quaint. After … the Sheikh took my dragoman aside and told him that there was a certain place in the desert named Heberieh, where there were many arms, legs and fingers sticking in the stones.'[11] No European had yet visited this strange place, which he said was a long ride away and would need an escort of at least fifteen men. 'I decided to visit the place the next day,' wrote Mark, 'visions of some ancient quarry or isolated sculpture rising before me, and as there was no mention of anything of the sort in Murrays Handbook, I had great hopes of making a discovery.'[12]

At four the following morning, the party set off and after two hours' riding found themselves in country which Mark described as being some of the most extraordinary he had ever seen in the course of his extensive travels in four continents. He wrote of it as 'a fireless hell; nothing else could look so horrible as that place. Enormous blocks of black shining stones were lying in every direction; in places we passed great ridges some 20 feet high and split down the centre. One of these stretched over a mile and looked like a gigantic railway cutting. There was neither a living thing in sight, nor the least scrub to relieve the eye from the monotony of the slippery black rocks. My dragoman said to me "I tink one devil he live here."' After four hours' hard riding through this inferno, the party reached an open space in the centre of which was a hill. The Druses announced that they had reached their destination.

'At first I thought the hill was only a mass of lava and sand,' Mark wrote in his report, 'but on closer examination I found that it was a huge mass of bones and lava caked with bones. It was infested with snakes; I myself saw four gliding through the bones. When I had taken some photographs and secured some specimens of the rock and bones, we started on our return … I can say on excellent authority that I am the first European who has visited this place.'[13] When Mark eventually submitted his findings to the Palestine Exploration Fund, they concluded that the bones were probably the remains of a herd of domestic animals that had been caught in a volcanic eruption.

To have travelled to places where few Westerners have ever set foot and to have made a 'discovery' must have seemed the greatest of excitements for a young man of twenty, and it was undoubtedly one of the catalysts that gave Mark a life-long fascination with what would come to be generally known as the Middle East. He returned to Cambridge with a large supply of Turkish cigarettes, a Damascus pariah dog named Gneiss, an assorted array of Oriental headgear and a desire to share his experiences with anyone who would join him in his rooms, usually sitting cross-legged on the floor puffing away at a *hookah*. He lectured to the Fisher Society, and to the Cambridge Society of Antiquaries, as well as writing up an account of his travels for the Palestine Exploration Fund. He was planning his next trip when he received an important letter. 'I have just heard from the Royal Geographical Society,' he wrote to Henry Cholmondeley in the autumn, 'to tell me that my discovery in Syria is of the greatest importance. My tutor has in consequence given me leave to stay down next term if I go abroad. I have every reason to believe that I shall find some extraordinary things in the Safah, the place where I discovered the "Hill of Bones". I am the first person who ever entered the place. This was merely because for some reason the natives like me.'[14]

Mark was in high spirits when around this time he received an invitation to lunch at Howes Close, the Cambridge home on the Huntingdon Road of the local Conservative MP, Sir John Eldon Gorst. Gorst, who served as Vice-Chairman of the Education

Committee in Lord Salisbury's government, was the father of Jessie's former lover, Jack, as well as another son, Harold, and five daughters, Constance, Edith, Eva, Gwendolyn and Hylda. This large and affectionate family welcomed in Mark, who, as an only child, was quite unused to the warm and friendly atmosphere they generated with their in-jokes and humorous banter, but he quickly fell under their spell. He too entranced them, regaling them with tales of his adventures, acting the part of the individual characters in each story.

Sunday lunch at Howes Close became a regular outing for Mark, not least because he found himself increasingly attracted to Edith, the middle of the five girls. Twenty-six years old, tall and handsome, with soft features and thick chestnut-coloured hair, she was, like him, a convert to Roman Catholicism, and their mutual devotion to their religion became the basis for, first, a firm friendship, and then a growing attraction. She was also an accomplished horsewoman and since Mark also had a horse stabled in Cambridge, they took to going riding together. After the intrigues and machinations of his mother, Edith's down-to-earth approach to life came like a breath of fresh air. 'I really like [you],' he told her, 'really and truly and not in any way tinged with that ridiculous, maudlin, drivelling, perverse folly that idiots call "being in love". I like you because you are honest and unselfish, because you are the only truly straightforward person I have ever met.'[15]

Edith's emotional support was doubly important in the light of his mother's situation. She was at her lowest ebb. Her friends had all dropped her. She could not approach her brothers, who were all respectably married with families, while her younger sister Venetia, married to an American millionaire, Arthur James, and one of Society's leading hostesses, considered that she had disgraced herself beyond measure and would have nothing to do with her. She had been turned out of the house in Grosvenor Street and, to cap it all, in December 1898 she suffered the death of her beloved brother-in-law, Christopher, who had been one of the few people to stand by her through all her troubles. Mark decided that before he left on his next journey, he would make one more effort to persuade his father and his lawyers to reach a final settlement with Jessie. 'Dear Cousin Henry,' he wrote to Cholmondeley, '… would you try & get a meeting arranged between yourself, my father, Gardener [*sic*] and I at Gardner's [*sic*] office, this is the last chance of a settlement, & worth trying, my mother is really broken and would accept any reasonable terms. I hope I can trust you to arrange this meeting as after that I should feel quite unresponsible for any further disgraces & that I had done all possible to stop it …'[16]

Confident that he had set the wheels in motion to try and help his mother, he prepared to set out for Syria. On the eve of his departure he went to mass in Cambridge to take one last look at Edith, an event which reinforced his feelings for her. 'If you knew the agony of mind I went through,' he wrote to her on his return, '… when I saw you leave the church and I went away without a word, if you knew how I felt that day, how I shook as if with an ague, with dry mouth and trembling steps, how I watched you go away further and further, and by quickening my steps I could have caught you up and didn't for fear that you might have some small inkling what was in my mind before I chose you should, because I thought to myself, perhaps I am only in love …'[17]

Mark left for Syria on 14 December, intending to return to the Haurân in the hope of making more discoveries, but things did not work out quite the way he had hoped. The country was divided into three districts, or *Wilayets*: Aleppo in the north, Beirut in the west and south, and Damascus, which embraced the whole country east of the river Jordan. Each of these was governed by a Wâli, and was in turn divided into districts which themselves were governed by more officials. No progress could be made by the traveller without a series of permissions, the issue of which was by no means certain, often leading to days or even weeks of delays. For some reason, 'difficulties arose' and Mark was refused a permit by Nazim Pasha, the Wâli of Damascus, to visit the Haurân. Instead, he decided to travel to Baghdad by way of Aleppo.

The party left Damascus on 17 January. 'I took with me,' wrote Mark, 'a dragoman, a cook, a waiter, four muleteers, and a groom;

seven Syrian mules ... two good country horses for myself and one each for the cook and the waiter; a Persian pony for the dragoman; and last, though not least, a Kurdish sheepdog that answered to the name of Barud, i.e Gunpowder, and not only attended the pitching and striking of the camp but after nightfall undertook the entire responsibility of guarding it.'[18] Of the attendants, including Michael Sala, the cook, and Jacob Arab, the waiter, by far the most important was the dragoman, a Cypriot Christian called Isá Kubrusli, whose job was to act as interpreter and guide. A striking-looking man with piercing eyes, he had worked as a dragoman for forty years, in which time he had served a number of important Englishmen, notably Sir Charles Wilson on his expedition to locate Mount Sinai in 1865, and Frederick Thesiger in the Abyssinian Campaign of 1867–8, 'Thirty years ago,' Mark wrote, 'a dragoman was a person of importance; a man similar in character to the confidential courier who in the last century accompanied young noblemen on the Grand Tour. But he has degenerated and for the most part is now simply a bear leader, to hoards [sic] of English and Americans who invade Syria during the touring season.'[19]

Isá, who worked for the Jerusalem office of Thomas Cook, had a very poor opinion of most of his clients. Unlike the rich and cultured gentlemen he had encountered in the old days, who wore beards, could ride and shoot beautifully, and were liberal with 'baksheesh', 'Now everything very different,' he used to say. 'Many very fat and wear rubbish clotheses; many very old men; many very meselable; some ride like monkeys; and some I see afraid from the horses. Den noder kind of Henglish he not believe notin; he laugh for everything and everybody; he call us poor meselable black; he say everything is nonsense and was no God and notin ...'[20]

In the first week of their journey, the weather deteriorated by the day, with constant rain and hail storms, and eventually turning to snow, which got heavier and heavier until 'the weather was too cold for camping, so I telegraphed to Damascus for a carriage to take me to Aleppo'. Eventually an 'antique monstrosity' arrived, drawn by four horses abreast. It was 'enormously broad, with a rumble for baggage behind' and 'had the appearance of a decayed bandbox on a brewer's dray; and, as I found to my cost, was extraordinarily uncomfortable'.[21] Their first stop was at the village of Hasieh, 'the most desolate and filthy little village that it has ever been my luck to visit'. The guest house consisted 'of a large heap of offal with four rooms leading off it: the first and best was occupied by the cow; the second which was not quite so clean, was given to me; in the other two most of the villagers were gathered together to watch my cook preparing what he called "roast whale and potted hyæna", that is roast veal and potted ham'.[22]

It was a miracle that they ever reached Aleppo, considering that, in the early hours of one morning, the troublesome coachman made an attempt to sabotage the journey by deliberately overturning the coach. 'The carriage fell on its side with a fearful thud,' recalled Mark, 'which was accompanied by a howl of terror from both the dragoman and the cook. The ensuing scene was not without a humorous side. The carriage opened and spat out a curious assortment of men and things on the scrub of the Syrian desert, and it was only when the cook, the bath, the medicine chest and the dragoman had been lifted off me that I was able to survey the scene of the accident. Its appearance reminded me exactly of those admirable pictures drawn in Christmas numbers of illustrated papers of Gretna Green elopements coming to grief in a ditch; luckily however no lady was present, for the language made use of, whether in Arabic or in English, was neither that of the Koran nor Sunday-at-Home.' When they did finally reach their destination, he found it 'not altogether a pleasant town'. The natives had a penchant for throwing stones at the hats of foreigners, and often had faces disfigured by 'Delhi Boils', which gave them 'a most sinister expression'. Almost everyone he met, he wrote, who was not a native, 'seemed to be trying to get away from the place, without success'.[23]

Six days in Aleppo was quite enough. The party then struck out for Baghdad. Not a day went by without Mark being either amused or frustrated by the character of local people. 'Their ideas of time and space are *nil*,' he noted. 'If you ask how far away a certain village is, you may be told "one hour", be the real distance anything from five minutes to twelve hours; or, when you are beginning to feel tired, everyone you ask during the space of a couple of hours may tell you that you are only "seven hours" from your destination. This is really … most annoying.' At Meskeneh he got his first view of the Euphrates, which did not greatly impress him. 'Its water is so muddy,' he noted, 'that it is impossible to see through a wine-glass filled with it.'[24]

Meskeneh was the first of a series of military outposts, manned by police or mounted infantry, which lined the high road from Aleppo to Baghdad. They were intended to help keep order in the valley, and to prevent the Anezeh Arabs from crossing the Euphrates, and it was at one of these that Mark now spent each night. When he finally reached the first bridge across the river at Falúja, the final stop before Baghdad, he was amused by what he found there. 'There is a telegraph wire which crosses the river but there is no telegraph office; the only official in the place is the collector of tolls who dozes most of the day on the bridge; there are no troops; and there is no police station within twenty miles of the bridge. There is therefore nothing to prevent any number of people crossing it … Truly the ways of the Unspeakable are inscrutable.'[25]

After days of trekking through the desert, the approaching minarets of Baghdad were a wondrous sight: 'the golden mosque appeared in the distance in the midst of a cluster of palm trees, and … the effect was very beautiful and inspiring'. Once within the city walls, however, although he was impressed by its cleanliness, Mark found little to inspire him, and after spending an enjoyable week staying with the English Resident, he was keen to be on his way to Mosul. Before leaving he penned a letter to Henry Cholmondeley. 'I have had the most trying weather on my trip, the thermometer has varied in one month from 5° below zero to 90° in the shade, including fogs, snows, sandstorms + 1 week's incessant rain am going up to Mossoul [sic] and thence to Batoum or Trabzionde [sic] but my route will depend on the state of the country Climactic & Political, it is useless to tell you all that has happened as it fills at least 30 pages of a diary, I can show you the faces of the people tho' …

He signed the letter with his Arabic signature, adding the question, 'How would this do as a check [*sic*] signature?'[26]

The journey from Baghdad up to the Russian border turned out to be full of incident, beginning with an encounter with some robbers north-east of Kerkúk. At the time he was travelling with a local governor, or *Kaimakám*, and his military escort, when they came under fire from some robbers: 'just as we entered a kind of natural amphitheatre, about two thousand yards broad,' he recalled, 'I was handing him my cigarette case, when I was startled by the buzzing of a bullet somewhere overhead followed by the faint "plop" of a rifle on the hill side. I looked round but the kaimakám took a cigarette out of my case and lit it without saying a word. Two other bullets passed overhead and I made some remark about them; he merely said *Sont des voleurs*

Monsieur, and it was only after five more shots had been fired that he took any further notice.' Mark was impressed by the coolness of the man, 'who seemed to think no more of the matter than a farm-boy would of crow-scaring'.[27]

Approaching the town of Mosul, Mark was able to give further rein to his love of underlining the comic and exaggerating the grotesque. 'The first thing that struck me,' he wrote, '… was a splendid bridge. It is a fine piece of workmanship and has only one fault; it does not cross the river. The engineer commenced building it about a hundred and seventy yards from the bank; he built twenty-four piers, and at the twenty-fourth came to the water. Then after due consideration he thought that he would build the bridge with boats, and these he chained to the end of the masonry. Though this structure is useless as a bridge, it makes an excellent rendezvous for beggars, lepers and sweetmeat vendors.'[28]

The hardships of the journey increased after Mosul. They were constantly on the lookout for brigands, often mule-rustlers, and as they began to climb up into the mountains, the terrain became more treacherous, with rushing rivers and streams, non-existent roads and tracks that were impassable to anything but mules. It was bitterly cold, but the scenery was magnificent. 'Overhead was a blue sky, below, the vegetation, such as it was, was green as an emerald,' wrote Mark. 'We were among high mountains, whose ruggedness was relieved here and there by clumps of stunted trees. There was snow on the peaks, and down the sides of the mountains streams rushed frantically … In one place we had to pass a very rickety patched-up bridge … Isá when crossing missed his footing and only by the greatest good luck I caught him by the band of his Ulster. Even now it makes me shudder to think of what might have happened to him; for there was a drop of forty feet into a river running like a mill race towards the mass of rocks over which it fell.'[29]

As Mark and his party drew closer to Bitlis, a strategic Armenian town that was to see 15,000 of its inhabitants massacred by the Turks in July 1916, they began to see more and more snow, which soon became so deep that they had to drag their mounts through it. His plan had been to head straight from here to the Black Sea port of Trebizond, and then home, but when this proved impossible he was forced to go to Van instead. This meant abandoning the muleteers in favour of fifteen man-sledges, each of which could carry a hundred pounds weight of baggage. One of them even had the added weight of Isá, who, fearful of getting cold, had drunk a whole bottle of mastic, the local aniseed-flavoured spirit, and had become so drunk that he had to be tied face-down onto his sledge. Mark was astonished at the strength of the men who pulled these sledges. 'They kept up a pace of about three and a half miles an hour,' he noted. 'They mounted steepish hills with only raw hide lashed under the soles of their feet, and they only rested for five minutes or so every three quarters of an hour. The heavy breathing of the sledge-draggers, the gentle zipping of the sledges as they passed over the snow, the occasional moaning of the drunken man, and the stamping of the cold feet had such an effect on me that a couple of hours after leaving Bitlis I was fast asleep. When I awoke I saw a glorious sunrise; the red flush of the sun on the waters of Lake Van … was beautiful indeed.'[30]

Crossing Lake Van, the largest lake in Turkey and seventy-four miles across at its widest point, was a hazardous affair. They hired a fifty-ton fishing boat, the *Jámi*, hired from and captained by its Armenian owner, and though at first all went well, after two hours the wind dropped, and there followed a fearful nocturnal storm during which the sail split, water began to seep in, and the boat began to list alarmingly. The crew, including the skipper, panicked and proved useless, and when Mark tried to get Isá to help him get the ballast straight, he became 'quite childish, and … screamed "Why you bring me to this debil country? I say bad word for the day I came with you; rubbish boat, rubbish captain, rubbish sea; I say bad word for the religion of this lake!" Then as the boat took a particularly heavy roll, he stood on his feet with a cry of "Our God help us!" (the us being prolonged into a perfect scream) and then collapsed on the side of the boat and lay there vomiting and praying.'[31] In the end Mark was reduced to watching over the ballast and bailing by himself. It was, he confessed, 'one of the most dismal vigils I have ever kept',[32] and Mikháil, his cook, later confessed, 'We were as near death as a beggar to poverty.'[33]

The storm had abated by sunrise, and the shore was in sight. Their plight had been noted from the shore by a Kurdish horseman, who galloped along the cliffs and, with the aid of a stout whip, persuaded a group of Armenians to tow the *Jámi* to safety. In Van, Mark spent a week with the British consul, Captain Maunsell, before setting out on the slow and arduous trek to the Russian border. The last part of this journey, over a high mountain pass, was almost too much for Isá, the rarefied air giving him heart palpitations. He 'threw himself on the ground gasping,' wrote Mark, 'unable to walk any farther. I tried to carry him on my back but the result was that we both rolled head over heels in the snow; so I got out the medicine chest and gave him a mixture of ginger, brandy and opium …'[34] Eight days after finally reaching the Russian border, Mark reached Akstapha, where he boarded the Trans-Caucassian railway bound for Tiflis and Batoum, port of call for the steamer to Constantinople. 'Isá, Jacob and Michael came to the station and bade me a tearful farewell; and I feel sure that the sorrow they expressed was sincere … we had seen much together and a mutual feeling of respect had grown. Certainly I must confess to a lump in my throat when Isá quavered through the window of the parting train "*Masalaam*. I pray our God He help you always." I can only add *Inshallah*.'[35]

During the time that he had been travelling, Edith may well have been on Mark's mind, but, he later told her, he 'neither wrote nor spoke of you to any man'.[36] On his return, he began to write to her, his first letters, posted in May 1899, being quite formal, addressing her as 'Dear Miss Gorst' and signing off 'Yours sincerely, Mark Sykes'. By August, she was still 'Miss Gorst', while he had given himself a nickname, 'The Terrible Turk', that was accompanied by a drawing, and was an allusion to a phrase originally used by Gladstone when condemning the slaughter by the Turks of thousands of Bulgarians in 1876.

A month later, he was beginning his letters with the words 'Honourable and Well-Beloved Co-Religionist' shortly to be abbreviated to 'H. and W.B. Co-Relig'. As soon as he returned to Cambridge he invited her to dinner. 'You may remember,' he said, 'how ... little I spoke at dinner, and then only did I know that I had a real affection for you', adding, 'I tell you, if ... you had a hump in the middle of your back, a beard like a Jew, eyes that squinted both ways, were bald as a highroad, and had only three black teeth in a mouth like a cauldron, still my affection for you would be the same.'[37]

However much his thoughts may have been on Edith, he was also fired by a desire to return to the East. 'I am preparing already for my next journey,' he wrote to Henry Cholmondeley in August. 'Entering Turkey by Russia on the Van Side, my rough scheme so far is to buy a complete Equipment gradually & send it to Erivan in small quantities, and then to arrange with Maunsell to send me mules to the frontier, & a certain dragoman I know of there. Then to use those mules & my own equipment for about 5 months, thoroughly visiting Koordistan [*sic*], presently working down to Baghdad where another dragoman & fresh mules would await, from Baghdad I should work across to Jebel Hauran and thence southward.'[38]

Such a journey, which was to take up the better part of a year, was expensive, in spite of his attempt to save money by buying his mules outright rather than renting them by the day. He calculated the expenses as follows: 'Jacob, his servant, £40; Dragoman, £50; Cook, £30; Soldiers, £60; Fodder, £60; Mules, £54; Outfit, including carriage, £200; Muleteers, £30; Cash, £200; and Journey to Turkey and back to London, £35.' By his very poor mathematics, he reckoned this as adding up to £819, the actual sum being £759, or approximately £82,000 at today's values. 'I include, as you see,' he explained to Cholmondeley, '£200 cash for accidents etc, but I count on selling my mules and equipment for at least £150 at the end.' His intention was to leave England on 15 June 1900, towards the end of the summer term, and end up in Cairo on 10 May 1901, and, with this trip in mind, he intended to devote his next year at Cambridge to the study of the Middle East and its political aspects. 'I think if I am able to do as I propose,' he told Cholmondeley, 'I shall be as well informed on Eastern subjects as many M.P.s who pose as Orientalists.'[39]

Chapter 4

South Africa

In spite of Professor Browne's reservations about Mark's capacity for 'not learning', he found him a delightful companion, and he was the perfect choice to tutor him in the history and politics of the Middle East. Though Browne had paid only one visit there, to Persia between 1887 and 1888, he had made good use of his time, travelling through the whole country, and mixing with the company of Persians, mystics and Sufi dervishes. It was a trip that eventually resulted in the publication of his book *A year amongst the Persians*, as well as numerous articles on subjects such as the rise of the Babi movement. Together he and Mark spent many a happy hour exchanging anecdotes about their travels, while he also did his best to instil a little history into his pupil, as well as attempting to increase his Arabic vocabulary. Their political views, however, were poles apart, with the Professor adopting a Nationalist view, while those of the undergraduate Mark veered towards the Imperialist.

Browne could only do so much tutoring with Mark, whose mind was almost permanently elsewhere. Firstly he was writing up an account of his recent travels with a view to having it published under the title *Through Five Turkish Provinces*, an ambition that was to be realized the following year. At the same time he was involved in numerous journalistic activities, contributing several pieces, for example, to the Cambridge student magazine *The Granta*, edited by his old friend George Bowles. In No. 266, for instance, he not only provided the leader, an article on the Militia titled 'A Sangrado Policy', but also a skit called 'The Granta War Trolley', a cartoon entitled 'Taste', the dramatic criticism, and an illustrated limerick. In addition he drew a series of sketches caricaturing various aspects of some of the British newspapers. These included 'The Pillory of *Truth*', '*The Times*' Sphinx', and 'The Imperial Ecstasy of the *Daily Mail*'.

In October he wrote to Henry Cholmondeley, 'I am starting a newspaper named 'The Snarl.' I calculate the loss on three copies about £10. I think the venture is worth trying … it may possibly pay its expenses. I calculate on a certain sale, but at the same time I am paying somewhat for the contributions and also on the necessary advertisement, so please send me a cheque book. I shall not tell my mother I have one, or use it for any other purpose but that of paying contributors … If you think my father will write to stop me, do not tell him as the production is well worth trying & may make me a certain kind of reputation.'[1] *The Snarl*, was co-edited by a Cambridge friend, Edmund Sandars, but appears to have been entirely written by Mark, who also designed and drew the cover. The magazine was sub-titled *An Occasional Journal for Splenetics*, and was a vehicle for him to let off steam on a variety of subjects.

Say what you please – say 'D—n!' say 'H-ll!'
Say 'botheration!' Say 'You Tease!'
Say 'Don't!' Say 'Dreary me!' Say 'Well!'
Say what you please!
Say that the Transvaal's made of cheese!
Call Chamberlain Ahitophel!
Say women ought to have degrees! –
Say printers might know how to spell!-
Say *petits* pois means little peas! –
So long as this line ends in *l*,
Say what you please.[2]

In the only two issues that were published, he railed against compulsory chapel, attacked the Cambridge Union for degenerating 'hopelessly and finally into the recognized organ of the great conformist conscience', described the degree of Master of Arts as being nothing more than 'the triumph of mediocrity', and criticized the dons for their 'narrow-minded ignorance of the world'. In the barely concealed anger and snappish tone of its articles, *The Snarl* anticipated the modern-day journalism of writers like Will Self and Charlie Booker.

The Cambridge life that Mark was now thoroughly enjoying was rudely interrupted by a conflict which erupted at the outer reaches of the British Empire. At the end of the Napoleonic Wars, the British had acquired the colony of South Africa to which the government had then actively encouraged British settlers to emigrate. This was the cause of conflict with the original, Afrikaans-speaking, Dutch population, who were known as 'Boers', many of whom migrated northwards, on 'The Great Trek', where they established two independent Boer republics, the Transvaal and the Orange Free State, both of which were eventually recognized by the British. However, the discovery in the second half of the century of, first of all, diamonds at Kimberley, on the borders of the Orange Free State, and then of vast gold deposits in the Transvaal brought a massive influx of foreigners, 'uitlanders', mainly from Britain, who were needed to develop these resources. This caused increasing tensions with the Boers, who began to fear that they would soon become a minority in their own country. In 1899 their worst fears were realized when the British Colonial Secretary, Joseph Chamberlain, demanded full voting rights and representation for all uitlanders living in the Transvaal. It was over this that Paul Kruger, the President of the South African Republic, declared war on Britain in October 1899.

Having spent much of his childhood playing war games in the park at Sledmere, reading books on the great generals, and studying Vauban's theories of fortification in the Library, it is not surprising that Mark had an affinity with the military. His heroes were Marshal Saxe, Marshal of France in the reign of Louis XV, and the Emperor Napoleon, as whom he had a penchant for occasionally dressing up.

In his first year at Cambridge, he had decided to apply for a commission in the army, filling in the required E536 form 'Questionnaire for a candidate for first appointment to a Commission in the Militia, Yeomanry, Cavalry or Volunteers'. Citing his height to be 5 ft 11¾ inches, he had applied to and been accepted for a volunteer militia battalion, the Princess of Wales's Own Yorkshire Regiment. In this he was following in the footsteps of his ancestor, Sir Christopher Sykes, who in 1798 had raised his own volunteer militia, the Yorkshire Wolds Gentlemen and Yeomanry Cavalry, to help defend the neighbourhood in case of an invasion by Napoleon. Though Mark had done some training with the Regiment in 1898 and 1899, it must still have come as a shock to hear, in the middle of his Michaelmas Term, that they were to be mobilized to serve in South Africa.

'I now have to go to South Africa', he wrote to Henry Cholmondeley, 'which is the most infernal nuisance.'[3] It was a nuisance compounded by the fact that his mother's debtors were once again clamouring for payment and Mark, fearful that his father was immovable in his refusal to pay up, felt himself bound to step in to prevent the whole estate going 'to the thieves' shelter'.[4] Such a disaster was not inconceivable, since the sums involved were huge, the entire debt being calculated at £120,000.[5] '[I]f I make myself liable for all these immense sums,' he wrote to Edith, 'and no arrangement can be made with my father, with the Estate duty added to all, I shall stand in a somewhat precarious position'. What he found most humiliating, however, was 'to be constantly arguing on a hypothesis of my father's death which is to me the most loathsome feature of my repulsive affairs'.[6]

Over the next two months Mark fought hard to reach a settlement that would be agreeable to all parties, while simultaneously having to be prepared for his leave to be cancelled, and his subsequent departure for South Africa. The number of false starts was marked by the numerous letters of farewell he received from Edith.

In return he kept her entertained with tales of his daily life. He was at Sledmere at the end of March for his coming of age, a very muted affair owing to the war.

These last days have seen me amusing myself by reading old books and arranging a room for me to sit in … I have been receiving piles of congratulatory telegrams and letters concerning my coming of age, mostly of this description …

'13 Queer St.
Dear Sir,
I hasten to congratulate you on your majority, should you Sir require any small temporary loan from 5 to 20,000 pounds etc, etc …'

I received a silver inkstand from the labourers, a very pretty thing, where at I was very pleased.[7]

He also amused her with some of the nonsense written about him in the local papers.

By the way, it never rains but it pours … an extract from the Yorkshire Evening Post. 'Mr Mark Sykes who has just come of age … is a <u>fine</u> singer and can tell a yarn with anyone.' Fine Singer!! I'faith a fine singer, that should amuse you. See me sing

or tell a yarn with anyone.[8]

Back in London, on April Fool's Day, he took a friend to dinner and a play. 'I had great fun before the play,' he told Edith.

> I have a little friend not a bad fellow, but an esthete [*sic*], who is very decadent in fact. Likes Burne-Jones pictures, Aubrey-Beardsley [*sic*], Ibsen plays, Revolting French Novels, and only likes dining at the Trocadero Restaurant where the food ... consists of Truffles and hot pâté de foie gras ... I said dine with me at the Marlboro ... after a little arguing he agreed, and came expecting rich filth, now for a punishment I ordered

> Scotch Broth (with vast lumps of meat floating in it)
> Boiled Turbot (fresh and enormous)
> Beefsteak Pudding (Suety, wholesome, succulent, heavy, hot, crammed with Oysters, Lark's Kidneys)
> Boiled Oranges and Rice Pudding (a nursery dish)
> Welsh Rarebit (in a dish the size of Lake Windermere)
> Hard English Cheese and Brown Bread
> Wines. Still Hock 1876.

Poor little thing, I believe you would have pitied him, he
gasped at the Scotch Broth, gaped at the Turbot and the
Beefsteak Pudding, words cannot describe appearance, his poor
little decadent stomach fairly rose,

the effect of the huge dish of Welsh Rarebit I must leave to
your imagination suffice that he staggered from the table
almost speechless and the best of it is he cannot be revenged on
me because I can eat anything.[9]

All the while the negotiations between Mark's parents were becoming increasingly frustrating: 'things do not look so well as before,' he wrote in early April, 'as my father now says he won't do anything before I return from the War because says he "I might be killed and then of course he wouldn't have to pay anything at all." This hardly strikes me as a very noble thought.'[10] The stress began to take its toll. 'I have very little to tell you,' he added, 'but you'll be glad to hear I am steadily losing flesh. I am now reduced to 12st. Have lost 6lbs.'[11] The greater the indecision, the more angry he became. 'My father arrives tonight,' he wrote a week later, 'another struggle with him, tomorrow lawyers, another talk, the day after if all goes well an unsatisfactory settlement … a surly misanthropy begins to pervade my nature … I have never lacked bodily comfort and never experienced mental rest, for this reason am I misanthropic yet how can one help it the world is bad, vile, corrupt, and there is no remedy, socialism is ridiculous, Anarchy is futile, reforms bring no good, only stamp old evils to raise new. There is no Utopia, evil triumphs, religion is dead, honesty never existed … The whole world is a mass of individuals struggling for their own ends … here you have a party, some ends are gained and they break asunder and fall on one another, fighting, struggling, and the most noble calling of this vile race of mortals is the military, for it is for their mutual destruction.'[12]

Three days later, on the evening of 20 April, a solution was finally thrashed out at a meeting in the Metropole Hotel in London. 'Oh my dearest co-religionist,' wrote Mark, 'At last it is finished. I'm sitting here writing to you, your photograph is in front of me – well it is all over. I must tell you me dear co-relig what happened … After arguing, fighting, changing, erasing, quarrelling, cursing, to-ing and fro-ing, the following arrangements were made.' It was agreed that a mortgage of £100,000 should be raised to pay off the debts. From then on Jessie would receive an annual allowance of £5,000, from which a third would be deducted to help pay off the interest on the loan, while Mark would receive £2,000 per annum, out of which he would give his mother £500 annually. 'At last it is done,' he wrote, 'and I start for S.A.

tomorrow, thank God! Alhamdollilah! ... Now I must say goodnight and goodbye, God willing I'll see you at Cambridge in September, goodbye <u>puella honesta et rara</u> ... Masalaam.'[13]

Mark boarded the RMS *Norman* on 21 April, his spirits high at having finally got away from his squabbling parents, but his heart tinged with sorrow at leaving Edith. 'I felt a considerable sensation of misery when I recalled my last visit,' he told her, 'and thought how long it would be before I should see you again, and how long it will be before I even hear from you alas! ... By the way I don't think it I likely I am going to meet "the someone else" you are always so full of, at any rate on this steamer, here are all the female passengers.'

He went on to describe the majority of passengers as being 'Jews of the most repulsive type, in fact it is for these beasts that we are fighting. They jabber about the mines all day long, I hope they will be made to pay. I would extort the last farthing from the most jingo loyal Jew in the British Empire before I'd fine a traitorous gentile.'[14] Such a shocking and sudden outburst of anti-Semitism needs to be seen in the context of the times when the need to blame someone for the war was sparked off by a series of early and disastrous defeats. These took place in the space of one so-called 'Black Week', at Stormberg, Magersfontein and Colenso, the latter being particularly crushing with the British suffering 1,137 casualties to the Boers' 37. Sent to report on the war for the *Manchester Guardian*, the highly influential economist J. A. Hobson identified a small group of wealthy Jews, with influence in the British press and the British Cabinet, among them Alfred Beit and Julius Wernher, who, for the sole purpose of their controlling South Africa's diamond and gold industries, had encouraged the Governor of the Cape Colony, Sir Alfred Milner, to take the belligerent stand that had led to war. It was the cause of a wave of anti-Jewish feeling.

Another figure with a vested interest in the war also happened to be on board, the multi-millionaire mining magnate and founder of Rhodesia, Cecil Rhodes, to whom Mark had been given a letter of introduction, 'He is a large, ill-made, somewhat muscular man,' he recorded, 'there is nothing whatever striking about him except a certain nervous twitching and folding of the hands and arms which was I believe a characteristic of the great Napoleon. The annoyance which I felt when I looked upon this man was considerable when I thought of the misery and desolation brought about by his machinations. I could hardly restrain myself.' His secretary expounded Rhodes's views on how he saw the future of the Transvaal and the Free State as their becoming Crown Colonies. 'Why could they not have a constitutional government?' asked Mark. 'Oh no,' he replied, 'because our enemies would be in the majority.' 'No comment is necessary on these words,' wrote Mark, 'it comes, to speak plainly, to the uncontestable fact that we are fighting to take away the liberty and independence of two Republics which are not even our colonies, this is the most monstrous admission ever made by any country in the last 100 years.' In the course of a short conversation, however, Mark did find himself agreeing with Rhodes on one subject, 'his unrestrained and open contempt for the stupidity of our generals'.[15]

Mark finally touched dry land at the beginning of May, when *Norman* docked at Port Elizabeth, which, along with East London, was one of the ports in the Eastern Cape used for the landing of troops, horses and equipment, for transport by train to the front in the Northern Cape/Free State region. The tide of the war had begun to turn since 'Black Week' owing to heavy reinforcements having been sent out from home under the command of Field Marshal Lord Roberts, with Lord Kitchener as his Chief of Staff. The besieged towns of Ladysmith and Kimberley had been relieved, and in mid-March Roberts had occupied Bloemfontein, the capital of the Orange Free State. The week Mark arrived, the siege of another town, Mafeking, was almost over. It was to be a long time, however, before Mark saw any action. His first few weeks were spent guarding the harbour. 'I look like this', he wrote to Edith. 'We are doing nothing and neither shall. Our Colonel is as foolish and incompetent as ever …'[16]

After a few days the regiment were sent to guard an important railway bridge, Barkly Bridge, an isolated spot right in the middle of the bush. Here Mark received a letter from his old tutor Alfred Dowling – 'Doolis' – fantasizing that he was in the thick of the action. 'It is rather provoking', he replied, 'reading your inspiriting [*sic*] account of what I may be doing

and what I am doing …

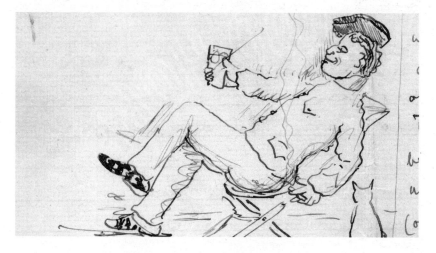

My business is to guard a bridge with 50 men, sleep 10 hours, read 8 hours and eat drink and smoke the rest of the twenty-four. This at least is what I might be doing, but a sudden fit of unwonted energy has seized me and I keep my men well employed and the bridge well guarded. I really in the last fortnight have achieved a good deal, made a rifle range, constructed a mud fort capable of holding all my men, practised the alarm twice by night and three times by day, and produced a very efficient guard.'[17]

With his boundless enthusiasm, he appears to have knocked his fifty men into an extremely effective fighting unit. 'I can now man the trenches and have all ammunition served out in 6 min at night, and

4½ by day, which is creditable as the men have to cross a bridge 290 yds long on a narrow footplate with 2000 rounds of ammunition.'[18] The men of the militia impressed him enormously, and he described to Doolis their spirit and temper as being 'marvellous and interesting … these men are not soldiers, they are not educated bank clerks … they have no sense of glory, but an immense sense of humour, an inordinate love of liquor, and a vast conceit of themselves'. Even the few troublemakers among them came in for praise. 'I would trust these same men anywhere, all they want is handling and tact, with that you can accomplish wonders, I have only had two drunks the whole time, and they are as keen as mustard, they take everything as an excellent joke, and laugh, whistle and sing all day.'[19] Of the officers he did not hold such a high opinion, referring to most of them as being 'wretched and contemptible creatures not worth talking to or about'.[20]

Mark also gave Doolis his opinions on the war:

1. Boers are beasts.
2. British colonists are liars or Jews.
3. British soldiers are splendid.
4. African farmers who wanted to rise but didn't dare are skunks.
5. South Africa is a desert.
6. The war was necessary to maintain prestige in other quarters.

People may blame Generals and Heads of Departments
however much they choose, but as far as mortal men could
work, everyone in the Army from highest to lowest has worked
splendidly and successfully. Against a European force in
England of half the size again, the S.A. Field Force would have
proved the most splendid and unconquerable army ever beheld.

He ended the letter by telling Doolis, 'I do not suppose I shall see any fighting, and have hopes of returning in October, if all goes on as it is doing now.'[21]

Unfortunately for Mark, just as he was beginning to feel that he was actually doing something useful in the war effort, he was sent back to Port Elizabeth, where he found himself guarding the harbour, 'a most unpleasant duty which recurs every four days,' he wrote to Edith. 'It lasts 24 hours in which time one does not go to bed. I am surrounded with putrefying meat and dead horses.'[22] He also saw his hopes of an October homecoming receding. 'Oh when shall I get out of this wretched country, the idea of another year here is too awful to contemplate … the war will go on for months and months, hopelessly, aimlessly, ignominiously, there is no end to it and I cannot see one, as long as one Boer lives, and we have killed very few.'[23]

His fears about the war were justified, for the Boer Generals, Louis Botha, Christiaan de Wet, Jan Smuts and Koos de la Rey, having come to realize that fighting a British style of warfare against far superior numbers was never going to result in victory, had begun to adopt guerrilla tactics, using small and mobile military units. This was perfectly exemplified in a skirmish that took place on 23 July at Retief's Nek in the Orange Free State when two battalions, the Black Watch and the Seaforth Highlanders, under the command of General Archie Hunter, had a column of Boers holed up in a dangerous hollow high up in the mountains. After a day and a half of fighting, and in spite of their overwhelming superiority in artillery, they had lost eighty-six men, while the Boers simply melted away into the mist.

'Goodness knows what will be the end,' he wrote to Edith. 'I myself prophesy 2 more disasters, 6 months guerrilla warfare and then a compromise. What that will be I cannot pretend to forecast, but I should hope for an offer to the Boers of equal taxation, votes and a popular government after six months Martial law. I think that in that way they might be enticed into peace. We could always break our word afterwards. No one could object, we have broken our word so often before. This is political. In politics there is no right or wrong, strength and guile are the only standards.'[24]

Boredom set in again, which he blamed for a bout of illness, which laid him low. 'I am here on the sick list, sore throat from having nothing to do, and loafing and grousing,'[25] he complained to Doolis. After a few days in hospital, he was sent to recuperate at the Humewood Beach Hotel, 'THE HOTEL OF THE EASTERN PROVINCE'. 'You will wonder what I am doing here,' he wrote to Edith. 'Well I am recruiting my shattered health. I have had swollen glands and a sore throat, and a very nice doctor was kind enough to strike me off all duty for 10 days. You seem to imagine me reading like this

as you ask me if I read as you do … It is very pleasant here as one has a very good roof over ones head and plenty of food.'[26]

His reading was in preparation for another trip to the Middle East. 'I have a grand scheme for a journey thro Turkey, Persia and Russia,' he told Doolis.

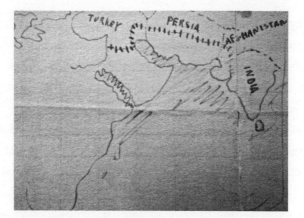

'I am reading it all up to be prepared to start the moment I can. O for the East, and real feelings. Allah Ho Akbar,[27] Din we el Mohamad! There fighting is real fighting, blind healthy rage & fury! Here its [*sic*] stealth and dodging, nothing else! And also unending.'[28]

There was an additional reason for his desire to make another journey to the East. Having received the proofs of his first book, *Through Five Turkish Provinces*, though not unsatisfied with it, he regretted that he had so little time in which to write it, having completed it in three weeks. He felt that if he could now write a really good book, from a more detailed journal and with better photographs, that was published and widely reviewed, it would help him to realize a new ambition. 'If I could do so successfully,' he told Henry Cholmondeley, 'I might then have some hopes of standing for Parliament, a thing I shall never do until I am known to a certain extent. I can see that it is absolutely necessary to prove that I am an individual of fairly balanced mind, owing to all the rows and scandals which have taken place in the last few years. Otherwise the impression would be that I may be a hopeless fool, or a worthless scoundrel ... I wish to prove that I am neither. To be successful one must be known ... I wish to be known as a person fairly versed in Eastern affairs, which I shall try to be, but even if I am not I may contrive to make people think I am which is half the battle.'[29]

Weeks of inactivity eventually sent Mark spinning into a state of depression and self-pity. 'I am sick of the War, sick of my rotten worthless regiment, sick of South Africa,' he moaned to Edith. 'Try as I will I can get no amusement, no interest. I can only long for the end and release.'[30] His mood was not improved when he received a letter from home that he described to Edith as being 'very unsatisfactory', and which revealed that his mother had been lying to him all along about the scale of her debts, and that there were far more than she had acknowledged: 'many years ago,' he told Edith, 'she found that a series of small fibs produced money, and now she is incapable of speaking the truth … Every sort of lie has been told, one of the choicest being that I proposed resigning my commission and enlisting in the army! unless more money was raised. I am absolutely determined to do no more. I have been humbugged long enough & I will not be responsible for a series of follies and extravagances which will continue for ever. For years I said that there would be no peace or rest until my mother had no control of any money. I am more convinced of this than I was then.' The only solution he could see was for her allowance to be tied up so she could not touch it, and her personal expenses – house rent, servant's wages, wine merchant, food supply and milliner – paid out of it by a firm of solicitors. 'I do all I do and have done all I have done from a sense of duty,' he wrote exasperatedly, 'and for no other reason. I have lost all affection.'[31] It was a sad state of affairs.

At the end of August, back at Barkly Bridge, Mark's spirits finally lifted. 'H and W.B.L.C.R.,' he wrote to Edith on the 29th, 'the unexpected always happens, particularly to me. Now can you believe it, in two days I Mark Sykes, alias. T.T. start for Pretoria with the regiment. Alhamdolillah![32] ALHAMDOLILLAH! DIN! DIN!! At last we are going forth to strike the Malignants. At last I shall be able to earn my medal. At last, ALHAMDOLILLAH, at last!' The regiment were to be replaced by the 4th Derbyshires, who had disgraced themselves the previous June by surrendering to General de Wet at Rhenoster Bridge. 'The men are very pleased to get up to the front,' reported Mark, 'and so is everyone else. It was too awful festering in Port Elizabeth … Don't suppose I forget you. You are also coming up to the front in my writing desk …'

Unfortunately for Mark, while the men set off for Pretoria, he was left behind at Barkly Bridge to await the relief. When he went to see them off, the atmosphere on the train station was one of jubilation. 'The men ... were cheering and bellowing like madmen,' he wrote. 'When the train stopped I was on the platform with cigarettes and the officers who seemed quite mad lept [*sic*] out and danced round me in a ring ... I never saw such a sight as the train. Every window framed a purple mass of shouting faces. A kaffir appeared dragging a sack of mealies. One fellow cried "That's 'ow they'll be draggin thee off battle field next week". The other answered "Howld yer noise, them bores ain't got a bullet that'll gou thro' me!"

'"Ow's that Jack?"

'"Why I allus 'as a slice o' bully beef in me coat for a chest pertecter!"

'And they laughed and cackled, but what was so pleasing was that they were all quite sober, so the enthusiasm was real. As the train moved off I shouted all the Bedawi war-cries and urged them in Arabic to slay and spare not, in the name of the Prophet.'[33]

Mark's battalion never reached Pretoria, being detained instead at Springfontein, close to Bloemfontein, which had fallen to Lord

Roberts in March. There they had to wait two weeks for the relief to arrive. In the meantime, back at Barkly Bridge, Mark was in the process going almost out of his mind with boredom. 'I am growing stupid & slow,' he complained to Edith. 'I can think of nothing. Had I some work to do I should not be so bad, but as it is I look like a squeezed lemon;

Here is my expression of mind! As you will perceive bordering on idiocy.'[34] That things must have been slow is borne out by the fact that he had started reading Shakespeare to his men. 'I have been reading aloud to the men,' he wrote. 'I mentioned I think the "merry wives of Windsor". What is very funny is that the men saw all the jokes and enjoyed them ... We had a 21st birthday feast, at which there were 9 guests, and alack the day! 60 empty bottles afterwards.'[35]

When relief finally arrived in the middle of September, Mark boarded a train to find himself in command of 179 Yorkshiremen and seventy Kitchener's Horse, a regiment made up of men who had made their way to South Africa from various parts of the world, and for whom he had little time. 'Kitchener's Horse are a disgrace to the British nation,' he wrote. 'They are Italians, Americans, Spaniards, Germans, Tramps, corner boys, cattlemen, ships cooks, Norwegian sailors or unmitigated blackguard Englishmen. None can ride or drill, they range from 16 to 60, & would you believe it they each receive 5 shillings per diem, more than the S. Major of a line battalion ...'[36] The journey up to Bloemfontein took two days, and the train never travelled faster than 10 mph, and generally 5 mph, so slow that many of the men simply got out and walked. About eleven miles outside Bloemfontein, the train stopped for no apparent reason, and for one and a half hours they made ready for an attack that never came. 'The state of affairs is very curious,' wrote Mark. 'The country is conquered but there are 1500 Boers about 9 miles E of us & 3000 about 15 miles north. 8 miles outside you may be sniped anywhere. Alarms are of constant occurrence, & I have every hope we shall be attacked.'[37]

On outpost duty, a dead-end job at a place called Naval Hill, he thought for a moment that such an attack had finally come. 'Last night I was just dosing [sic] off about 12 o'clock when I heard "I say, turn out, they're all around us. Hurry up!" & I turned accordingly thus

and found everyone on the alert and lights flashing on all the surrounding hills. What was the matter we never made out. The lights were not ours certainly and we spent 2 hours on the "Qui vive" but nothing happened ...'[38]

During the hours of inactivity, Mark entertained his men with tales of his journeys, and on the strength of his descriptions of some of the food he had eaten in the East, they promoted him to cook. 'I give them Arab dishes, Kebabs and Belaff [*sic*] etc,' he told Edith. 'I made a tremendous dish yesterday by stewing a chicken, a tin of unsweetened milk, three onions, a leek, ¼ of an oz of pepper, ⅓ of an oz of salt, a lb of beef, 6 potatoes, a spoonful of cinnamon & a cabbage for 4 hours. The result was splendid. We receive our Rum twice a week & it generally finds its way into the stew. Here I am ...'[39]

Mark's next posting was in an even more dismal spot, Bloemspruit, 'otherwise known as Paradise Lost'. 'I am now in command of an outpost,' he told Doolis, 'remarkable for its stinks as it is the dumping ground for Dead Horse. I think that you would not be very happy here as your love of "Beasties" and "the Beautiful" would some what clash with the surroundings ... Someone said this was a land of birds without song, Rivers without water, men without honour & women without beauty. It is perfectly true. The whole place is full of rumours & we have to turn out at 4. A.M. to line the trenches. My command are details and of the 50 men 12 are Scots Guards, 12 Grenadiers, 12 Bedfords, and the rest Worcesters. When we sally forth in the morning we present a strange sight …

The men now wear anything they desire … You will be surprised to hear that nearly everyone out here is sick of the War. Of course it will go on for a long time as no one unwillingly gives up all they have to an invader …'[40]

It was while guarding 'Paradise Lost' that Mark put to use knowledge that he had learned in the Sledmere Library when he was a boy. 'I found out something rather interesting about our fortifications,' he described to Edith,

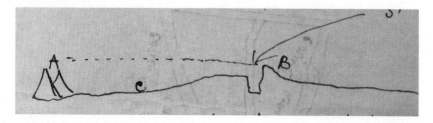

'The trenchs [*sic*] – B – cover the camp – A – in this way, but if an alarm was given I found out that the men would have to expose themselves running over the rise – C. I was told by the Sergeant that many men had been killed in this way during the war. I cudgelled my few brains for a time & remembered what I had read in a book by Marechal Saxe 1715 called "The Art of War". The words were something as follows. "And should your camp be in a hollowe and ye defences upon a rise, that your troops may reach ye ditch in safety, cause to be made a covert way, which is a deep ditch from the camp to the defence, thus introducing your troops to the defence unobserved by the enemy, similarly may they be withdrawn without his knowledge." The following plan easily explains what the wise old Marechal meant.

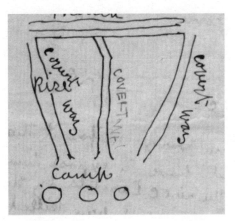

This is an example of how little we progress in the art of war. None of our modern books seem to give this trick …'[41]

It was at the end of December, when he was moved 100 miles up to Rhenoster Bridge, that Mark was really able to make use of his knowledge of creating fortifications, in the course of which he finally came to the notice of the senior army commanders. The success of the Boer Generals' guerrilla tactics, allowing them to capture supplies, disrupt communications and undertake raids on the occupying forces, while all the while evading capture, had put an end to any chances of the war ending before Christmas. The British army had a new commander-in-chief, in the person of Lord Kitchener, of whom Mark strongly approved. 'Kitchener must indeed be a man,' he told Edith. 'He will not for one instant tolerate the idle, useless or stupid. Every mistake is followed by swift retribution. How they fear him! How they hate him! And above all he is not a snob … I can tell you there is a hot time coming for everyone. Boers & Troops will suffer, but I think the war won't last long if he has a free hand. Hunter applied to Lord R. to hang six Boers in the market-place. Lord R. refused, but Lord K. will not. He is no genius, but he is (thank God) a brute & that is what you want in a War when geniuses do not happen to exist.'[42]

On his arrival at Rhenoster Bridge on 18 December, Mark found 'the whole place in the most disgraceful state of weakness'. He hoped, however, that within a week he would be able to make it 'almost impregnable'.[43] For three months it had been in the hands of the Royal Irish Fusiliers, the stupidity and apathy of whose officers shocked him. He gave as an example the fact that the camp, along with its trenches, was in a dip and, having a range of vision of no more than 800 yards, they had built an observation post on ground that was a mile away. 'I found an old water tank support about 20 feet high,' he told Edith. 'So what do you suppose T.T. did? Well 23 hours after my arrival, the support looked like this

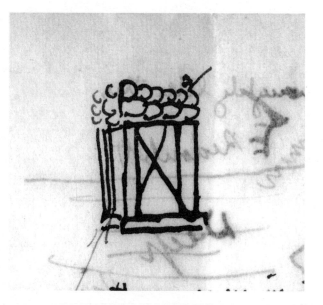

with a look-out man on top who has a range of vision of a 16 mile circle. At night there are three men in the top surrounded by sandbags and able to pick anyone off who chances to come. Now can you conceive that all-tho [*sic*] this place has been occupied for 6 months, tho' two regiments have been cut up here, tho' it has been attacked three times, no-one has taken the trouble to perform this simple little action??? The trenches here are an absolute disgrace, and tho' they had the remains of the wrecked bridge & sufficient metal to make an enormous fortress, we are defended by biscuit tins filled with earth that a bullet goes thro like a knitting needle thro an orange. I asked the officer whom I relieved if it was bullet-proof! "Aw – Er – Of course it is. Do you suppose I'd have put 'em up if they weren't." I was so savage I snatched up my rifle, loaded it, and sent a bullet thro the defences. He looked surprised and said "Bai jove, lucky the boers didn't come!"[44]

Kitchener's orders were that from now on the Boers were to be actively pursued and routed, and a scorched-earth policy was to be implemented on their land, and Mark's first taste of action came between Christmas and New Year 1900. 'I write to you today,' he told Doolis, 'to inform you that I Mark Sykes have been under fire, not a very heavy one, but still I have been actually within sight and touch of the Boeren.' For some weeks they had been constantly pestered by a group of Boers holed up in a wooded hill some seven miles from camp, so it was decided to despatch a column of 200 mounted infantry, 300 footmen and two guns to dislodge these guerrillas. The expedition was a fiasco. 'I joined the little column with 30 men,' wrote Mark. 'We started at 8 o'clock at night and after one hours marching lost our way, and then discovered that we had made a complete circle and were back in camp again!! However at 3 next morning we made a fresh start. Of course by this time the Boeren got wind of what was afoot. When we arrived at the fatal kopje, this is what we saw through our glass

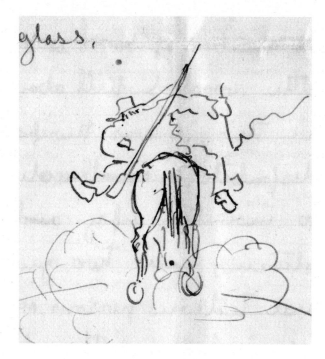

that is the enemy one strong in full flight, the remainder of course having shoved off about two hours before our arrival.'[45]

After setting up camp on the hill and spending the night there, they set off back to base, which is when they were attacked. 'The enemy … sniped us all the way back,' Mark recounted to Edith. 'The bullets fell about pretty thickly, and it was excessively unpleasant … All that nonsense you read in books and papers about the sensations in battle is unutterable twaddle. All you know is you are walking along and there is a spurt of dust and a "fut" on the ground. You say to yourself "here I am under fire 'fut'." There goes another bullet "fut". If that one had been 10 feet nearer it would have hit me "fut". They certainly are firing at me personally "fut". I wish this would stop "fut-fut-fut". Some one will be hit if this goes on much longer! … The bullets that came near us were fired at a long range. As I passed the artillery who were shelling the Boers, I said to the Subaltern "Rather an extreme range for rifle fire." "Yes", he said, "wasting his ammunition". The next time I saw him was in the ambulance with his skull fractured and half his cheek torn off. It is a filthy business, and there is neither honour or glory in it. Exterminating a pestilential race of peasants ... reflects little credit on anyone.'[46]

With the Boers operating in small groups and virtually impossible to engage in large numbers, Mark saw Kitchener's policy of burning down their farms one by one as the best chance of bringing to an end a war that could drag on for years. 'A Boer farm is a supply depot,' he explained to Doolis, 'for the evening it is a comfort to him. If we could garrison every Boer farm we wouldn't burn them, but as that would require about a million men it is out of the question. Therefore with every kindness and gentility you must bring in the women and children, and such men as you can and burn the farm, and what's more important such commodities as you cannot bring away. When this is done, the party of 10 boers who are in the neighbourhood must shift elsewhere. This has been proved again and again ... if Kitchener goes on as he does for another 3 months, the war [will] be drawing to a close ...'[47]

The problem was that though large numbers of women and children were captured during these raids, there were relatively few fighting men taken prisoner, a fact which led Kitchener to the realization that hustling the enemy might not be enough, and that other weapons were required. He devised a system of blockhouses, already used to defend the railway lines, that would be within rifle distance of each other, and be connected with a grid-mesh of barbed wire, thus creating a huge steel net into which the militia columns could drive their quarry. The creation of fortifications such as this was grist to the mill to Mark, who had already shown himself to have an ingenuity that was not always possessed by the Royal Engineers.

'The R.E.'s built a watch tower but omitted to put a roof on it. I brought my renowned genius on to it at once. I discovered an old Kaffir cooking pot, or cauldron, which I placed on top upside down, result

The three legs look rather funny sticking up in the air. It is quite bullet-proof, and affords good shelter however, and shields the observer from the foe!'[48] His men soon gave him the nickname the 'Real Engineer' as opposed to the Royal Engineer, and early in 1901 he was writing to Edith, 'Here I am at the end of another week having been working with my boys 12 hours a day and Sat & Sun included ... this place up to a week ago was absolutely untenable having 554 loopholes & 36 men to man them with ... I got permission to do what I liked. In 6 days I built 7 blockhouses, one of them 20 feet high. My only reward has been that I am told I ought to have done it quicker! But all the same I score because the place is tenable in spite of generals and staff and red tape.'[49] To Doolis he boasted of his 'grand fortifications', telling him, 'I think the post is now impregnable against anything under 600 Burghers',[50] while the Chief Engineer told him his defences were the best on the line, and they were going to take one of his plans as a model for several other places. He was later to be congratulated by Kitchener himself for his good fortifications and told that he was the only officer in the regiment to have shown originality. 'So you see,' he wrote to Henry Cholmondeley, referring to his childhood war games at Sledmere, 'my experiences in York Dale and the Park have been of some use to me.'[51]

Though it was against army regulations, Mark used black native labour to help him build his fortifications. 'They are really rather nice people,' he wrote to Doolis, '(I like them better than Englishmen) but Hush-sh-sh-sh-sh, what dreadful blasphemy have I whispered. They cheer me every morning, and volunteer to work for me. I give them a good pinch of snuff every other evening and watch them while they work. They are different to Arabs as they continually roar with laughter.' He was interested by the fact that they knew how to play Tria, an ancient game using pebbles that he had only seen played in the Middle East. 'Another game they play is as follows. They all fall on one man whom they dance on, kick, stone, beat, punch and roll in the dust, the victim laughing loudly all the time.'[52] Mark considered himself strict but fair with his black workmen. 'I said "If you work well I give you rum. If you work ill I give you whips!" They all worked splendidly. The rum I gave them was

'1 tablespoon of Rum
1 tablespoon of Worcester Sauce
3 tablespoons of water.'[53]

Seeing the success he was having with them, Mark's superiors asked him to train up a number to act as night watchers along the line. 'I like them and I think they like me. They are all Basutos ... & a splendid set of fellows, and really detest brother Boer who has undoubtedly treated them abominably.'[54]

Mark was unusual in his relationship with his black workers, who were treated little better by the British army than they were by the Boers. Though they were supposed to volunteer, they were invariably pressed into service, and were not expected to surrender, even though it was well known that if they were caught they would be either flogged or shot. 'Therefore our noble government,' he wrote, 'puts them out in groups of three alone on the line with old Martini rifles & 20 rounds of ammunition. They have to be out <u>every</u> night to watch for boers. No English soldier is allowed out of camp in daytime without 150 rounds … Besides the Martinis jam very easily, and are really bad rifles, but what matter. Blacks are cheap & and if they are taken no more will be heard about it …'[55]

He enjoyed drilling these men, who were willing and eager to learn, and he disobeyed orders by giving them as much ammunition as he thought necessary. He got little reward for his efforts and had to fight for everything he required. 'I am so weary of stupid … obstinate, mulish senior officers,' he wrote to Edith, 'that I could almost cry.'[56] He extracted a revenge, however, which he described as having been 'grotesque and glorious'. 'You know that the General Staff all wear a peculiar kind of cap like this

What do you think I have done? At my own expense I have put all my blacks into Staff caps. No one can object. How I wait for the day when that vile old general comes round to inspect them. Thank God he has no sense of humour or it would only amuse him. The blacks of course are as proud as can be of their head-dress and I shriek with laughter when I see them …

Anything more incongruous than a smart general's cap and their appalling rags cannot be conceived.'[57]

Up till now, Mark's letters had been peppered with references as to when he might be home. 'I think the war will last another 3 months,' he wrote to Edith in early March, though he added, 'if it does not end then, it will never end',[58] while he told Henry Cholmondeley, 'The war continues continuing as usual. The boers draw more and more into their shell, and now never seem to fight at all. They occasionally blow up the line, and now and then they fire at a sentry, but for that you would not know of their existence.'[59] Though after days of inactivity, there was the occasional burst of action, often of a chaotic nature. 'About 3 nights ago,' he reported, 'the big gun on the hill opened fire on a place where some boers were supposed to be. I turned out with my merry men, and fired volley after volley at the place where the shells were bursting. Now comes the comic portion of the story. The gunners on the hill were wrongly informed, but, but between the place where the shells burst and my men there were 200 boers crawling up to the bridge, and by a chance, 1 in 2,000,000, my bullets fell just on top of them and <u>slew</u> eight … You see the gunners were shooting at the wrong place and hit it, while we shot at the wrong place and hit the right one.'[60] Such incidents were few and far between, however, and the general atmosphere was of complete apathy.

'Oh when will this war end?' Mark moaned. 'The last piece of intelligence is the time expired Militiamen are to be asked to volunteer for – another year! Oh good heavens! … There are certain things that will tax anyone and a year in this infernal country is one of those things. Flesh and blood will not stand it. I do not speak of myself but the rank and file … The men under me are slack and stale. They are sick of waiting for Boers who never come and watching thro' the night and living the lives of pigs. They do their work like men asleep and only pause to grumble … many is the man who now asks me what the devil we are fighting for or about, and I'm hanged if I can give a reasonable answer … People talk of the war lasting three months longer. You might just as well talk of three years for all the hope of an end that one can see.'[61]

In one of the nearly 150 letters he wrote to his fiancée from the front, in itself an indication of the amount of time he had on his hands, Mark recounted an incident which to him went some way to explaining the long duration of the war: 'our new commandant is one Col Pengré, a hopeless old woman. There are no other words for him. He has all the ways of an elderly female invalid. Well one day he said "Do you know I-I think I-I saw some buck over the-ah the other day. We'll go and shoot some eh? What? Eh? Yes we-we-we'll go and shoot some." So 250 Mounted Infantry, a gun and 50 infantry in a wagon proceeded to sally forth to shoot buck. As you may know the formation for shooting buck is not the same as that for shooting boers. Result, 8 boers who had been looking on very gravely crept quietly up and took two Mounted Infantry prisoners. I make no comments, but I wonder what people in England would think if they knew their money was being wasted in that insensate kind of way.'[62]

The weather did little to raise anyone's spirits. After weeks of it being unbearably hot and dry, made worse by dust storms and clouds of ash that blew over from the burning farms, the rains came to create a new kind of misery. 'We have had now six days,' he wrote to Edith, 'of solid, drizzling, pouring, pattering, drenching rain. My camp is a swamp, the river is a torrent, the veldt a marsh. I am dressed in anything I can get hold of, and, as now at night it is bitterly cold, I present a curious spectacle, going round and glaring into the darkness for Boers.'[63]

The situation was made worse by an outbreak of typhoid fever, a disease that was endemic in South Africa. Thirteen of the regiment fell sick, though the only casualty was Mark's subaltern, Darman, who died just as the fever was abating. 'It really is a sad thing,' he wrote. 'His parents dote upon him, so do his many sisters. He was very popular amongst the men and even the Kaffirs[64] who worked for us, usually so laconic and indifferent, expressed regret. I ... feel sorry for his family. He was a fellow of great promise and humorous as well – but in truth we are lucky so far and if (Inshallah) no others die it will be a marvel.'[65] The following month, Mark himself was struck down with malaria. 'I really thought I was in for it,' he reported, 'but the destroying angel took Howard and Mockton instead of me. I am very fatalistic, and think that it is your fate and nothing can alter it by a minute.'[66]

That Mark received no promotion for his achievements was probably down both to his unwillingness to socialize and play Bridge with his superiors, and to the fact that in his letters home he was openly critical of them: of their stupidity, their laziness, their drunkenness, and their lack of understanding of 'the Art of War', the implication, though never stated, always being that the war would have ended long ago had he been running the show. They acknowledged that they needed him, however, and in November 1901 he was attached to the Royal Corps of Engineers and sent to Honigspruit in the Orange Free State, where he found himself in charge of sixty-nine black workers 'of all ages and sizes' with the brief to dig ditches and erect fortifications. 'I wish you could see me,' he wrote to Edith, 'because in consequence of my being attached to the R.E.'s, I am entitled to a cape-cart, a servant and two horses (?). Here I am'

He had hoped to go home, and wrote rather miserably to Edith, 'Do you know that today is the second anniversary of our parting. I can remember every detail and it only seems yesterday. Indeed my life since then has been so dull and colourless it is the last thing I can remember of any importance.'[67]

The place he was assigned to build defences for was called Amerika Siding. 'It is a large walled camp,' he described. 'It has 570 yds of circumference and a garrison of 50 men, that is 1 man to every 12 loopholes. They will not encrease [*sic*] the garrison. They will not reduce the fortifications, and the result is that it is indefensible, not for want of money, not for want of labour, not for want of knowledge, but from pure … stupidity and apathy. If Botha[68] came down here I dread to think of the results.'[69] The situation was not helped by the fact that the men were exhausted, many of them getting only one night in bed per week, and enteric was rife, as was drunkenness. 'Most people seem to take to drink out here,' he told Edith. 'I have not come to that yet … No regiment can perform any function without at least 3 officers getting drunk.'[70]

Mark was up against it from the start. First of all he was struck by lightning, which put him out of action for two days. Then, when he tried to order all the materials that were required for the building of his fortifications, he was told that 'the Colonel wants them all for his stable, which is naturally far more important'. The more he pestered for them, the more he was met with 'jeers and jokes for my pains'.[71] In the meantime 'the boers here are very busy and snipe and fire every night', while the prospect of the war dragging on loomed large. 'We are cast-a-ways, wrecked and forgotten in this desolate land. This war will last another 18 months if it lasts a day, that is if everything goes well.'[72]

He soldiered on and was soon able to report that he and his workers had dug a trench five miles long, which he thought a remarkable feat for eighty men, considering 'some of them are so old they cannot walk, others so ill they cannot stand'. He found that changing their rations had improved their work rate. 'How like our nincompoops to feed them on salt beef, 1lb per day, & biscuit, men who never touch meat, and whose fare from their infancy has been mealie pap[73] & sugar. However, I have put that piece of folly straight.'[74]

'I wish you could see me at work with the blacks', he wrote to Edith, 'as you know with coloured people there is always a tremendous din and dust and howling and laughing and roaring and swearing, which combined with the heat makes an exhausting atmosphere. I personally you will observe am directing operations while my fat dog

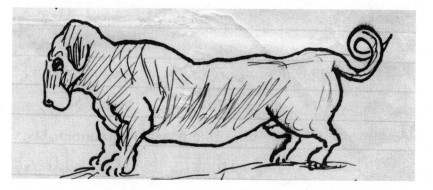

assists and at the same time discusses a bone … he is a cross between a mastiff and a dachs, weighs 4 stone, measures 4in in the waist, stands 6in from the ground and is 4 feet long, has solemn pathetic faithful brown eyes, tusks like a walrus, and a sleek chestnut coat which he inherits from his dachs relations. He is called Bella on account of his melodious voice. He is the only person I care for out here …'[75]

Mark's final few months in South Africa were blighted by illness, beginning after he had been ordered to move himself and his men up to the Cape Colony, orders that led them all to believe that they might finally be going home. Instead they were dispersed to different posts, Mark himself ending up at Knapdaar, where he ate some poisoned meat and ended up in hospital, 'of which I am not really sorry,' he wrote to Edith at the end of January 1902. 'The utter futility of the Army, the hopeless bungling, the senseless folly, quite break one down.' He also told her, however, that being sick might have saved his life, since otherwise he would have been with his company on board a train that was involved in a serious accident. They had been sent to guard a certain part of the line: 'on the way back about 10 o'clock at night some boers fired at the train hitting two men. Our men replied. The Armoured train, hearing the firing, dashed up and smashed into the 3/Yorks train killing 9 men and injuring 28 … My company lost 3 killed and 8 injured … So you will be glad I expect that I was not one of those. I am getting better but am not cured yet. Poisoned tinned meat is a bad thing to get inside you, but a piece of railway carriage is worse. The whole accident is typical of the army and its leaders and serves to disgust one a little …'[76]

Scarcely had he recovered from the food poisoning than he was struck down by another, far worse ailment. 'I woke in agony with an abscess of the left ear,' he wrote from Frere Hospital in East London, 'which presently burst leaving me as deaf as a post. I saw two doctors … one flourished a watch round my head and bawled "can you hear that?" I said "NO". He remarked that I was deaf.

The other doctor said "Your [*sic*] deaf I think". The next day ... I could hear very little, and the doctors sent me here ... The truth is that doctors are very much in the dark about ears and deafness ... and confine their own efforts to looking preternaturally wise, holding ticking watches, tuning forks and saying "Hum!" and "Ha!" which pleases the deaf man and does no harm at all.'[77] Contemplating what being deaf might mean to him, he wrote, 'I have often thought if I went blind I should live in the Queen's Hall, and if I become deaf I should live at the Louvre or British Museum. It is a most pestilent nuisance to be deaf.'[78] It was a disability from which he was to suffer for the rest of his life.

By the end of March 1902, there were signs that the war was drawing to a close. Though it had been a long-drawn-out affair, Kitchener's relentless policy of scorched earth and driving the enemy into fewer and fewer corners had finally got the better of them. The men were worn out, and their families had become refugees, numbering tens of thousands, housed in camps where disease was rife and they were dying like flies. The Boers were finally ready for the negotiating table. On 25 March, Mark told Edith, 'I really think this correspondence will soon be drawing to a close as the state of affairs evidently points to the Militias returning home to England.'[79] He was well again and had been granted a fortnight's leave, allowing him to turn his attention to thoughts of writing a one-act play about Swift that was to be 'a comedy with a sinister climax'. He also gave consideration to what the future might hold for him back home, deciding that a career in politics was not going to be part of it. 'I have just written a snorter to some individuals who want to know whether I will stand at the next election for the Buckrose division as a conservative. I have told them that I am neither A BUFFOON, AN OFFICE SEEKER OR A HYPOCRITE … that I have neither a large stomach nor a white waistcoat, and am in fact in no way fitted for a local magnate, that I have no sympathy with the opposition, but I consider the present government the most hopelessly incompetent jelly that has ever quivered in a british cabinet with which I left them and bade adieu to the conservatives of East Yorkshire!'[80]

'The end of our servitude is at last at hand,' Mark wrote to Doolis, 'and we shall be soon on the high seas for home … What a hideous nightmare it has been.'[81] Though he still had one to face back in England, in the form of his mother, whose troubles were by no means over, his homecoming promised to be a joyous affair, with his coronation as heir to Sledmere to look forward to and, first and foremost, his reunion with Edith. 'Oh my well-beloved co-relig. if you only knew what a solace you have been to me, can you imagine what my life would have been without you? In the midst of all the miseries, doubts, fears, and speculations of which I have been the victim, you have helped and comforted me.'[82] And when they finally met, Edith was to find that the over-sensitive, rather arrogant Cambridge student she had last known had matured into someone more serious and thoughtful, who now sported a moustache, and who was filled with a sense of righteous anger tempered with ideas of how to put the world to rights.

Chapter 5

Coming of Age

On 15 May 1902, Mark wrote to Edith, 'The 3/Batt. Yorks Regt, 19 Regtl. District is Dis-em-bowled. The men went away yesterday. I have to go to Sledmere tomorrow to be received in state.'[1] This was no exaggeration. As heir to an estate that covered over 40,000 acres of land, on which the family were looked up to with a reverence almost akin to idolatry, his homecoming might just as well have been that of a prince. It was reported not just in all the local newspapers but the nationals as well, with the readers being spared no detail of its lavishness. The only thing that marred the occasion, which all the tenants had spent days preparing for, was the weather. It poured with rain.

The decorations were elaborate. Between the gates of the parish church and the big house, three triumphal arches had been erected, the first bearing the words 'Good Luck', surmounted and flanked by horseshoes, with the letters 'M' and 'S' on each side. In the village, another large arch bore the words 'Honour the Brave' in large white letters, while at the entrance to the house a third arch, made of evergreens, proclaimed 'Welcome Home'. Lining the village street were brightly coloured Venetian masts decked with strings of flags, while at the local station of Fimber a final triumphal arch bore the words 'Welcome, Welcome'. Here Mark was expected to arrive by train, to be met by 150, mostly mounted, tenants and friends, a plan that was scuppered owing to the derailment of a horse-box further up the line. Eventually he turned up by car at 6.30 p.m., a half-hour late.

'The assembled tenantry,' wrote the columnist for the *Yorkshire Post*, 'who had patiently sat on their horses in the pouring rain, set up a glad shout of welcome. A carriage and four, with two outriders, was in waiting, and in this Captain Sykes took his seat, along with his cousin, Mr Cholmondeley. A procession was then formed, headed by the band of the 2nd V.B. East Yorkshire Regiment, the carriage following, then 75 of the mounted tenantry and the rest in carriages. At a foot pace it travelled the three miles between Fimber Station and Sledmere. At the entrance to the village … a body of the labourers and employees of the estate gave Captain Sykes another hearty cheer, and then proceeded to take the horses out of the carriage and draw it through the gaily bedecked village … The school children of the village took part in the welcome, cheering and waving tiny flags as the procession approached … Captain Sykes offered his warm thanks for the hearty reception given to him, but the dripping rain and the approaching darkness forbade any lengthened outdoor proceedings …'[2]

Three weeks later, his coming-of-age celebrations, which had been previously postponed owing to his departure for South Africa, finally took place when several hundred local dignitaries, tenants and villagers were invited to a grand supper-ball. Two huge marquees had been erected in the park and no expense had been spared on their decoration. A multitude of pennons and flags decked the roof of the supper-tent, in which the guests first assembled, the walls of which were hung with crimson drapery, while every pole was adorned with a combination of laburnum, lilac, laurel and spruce. Each table was covered with flowers and behind the high table there hung a blue banner with 'M.S. 1879–1900' embroidered upon it in gold. When supper was over, the speeches and toasts, to Mark's relief, were kept mercifully short. The company then moved into the equally splendid dancing-tent, whose green-and-white-striped walls were hung with hundreds of ornamental oil lamps, their glittering lights reflected in a profusion of mirrored panels. Huge Japanese umbrellas, twenty foot in diameter, and baskets of flowers were suspended from the ceiling, while four enormous gilded Tritons stood in the middle of the floor. Mark declined any offers to dance, a pastime he had little time for. 'The more I think of dancing,' he had written to Edith earlier in the year, 'the more wildly unreasonable does it seem. It is not even a game.'[3] Instead he returned to the supper tent, where he could smoke and talk to old friends. Just as on the occasion of his homecoming, the weather was unpropitious and the rain poured down all day.

The Sledmere celebrations were a welcome diversion from the other dark clouds on the horizon. After his homecoming, Mark had gone to spend two days with Edith, days that he told her had been the happiest of his life.[4] He had then gone on to visit his mother in her new London residence, no. 2 Chesterfield Street, a house she had inherited from her recently deceased brother-in-law, Christopher Sykes. He had found Jessie 'in a terrible state', by which he almost certainly meant she was drunk. This upset him terribly, and the self-pity returned. He wrote to Edith feeling 'very wretched and depressed'. 'Pray, O dearest co-relig, forgive me if I trouble you with private griefs, but you are my only friend ... I must admit that things are worse in every way than they were two years ago. And I can see nothing before me but wretchedness ... I was only talking to you the other day about being without a home. I wonder if you can realize what it is to be in my position, but you are so sympathetic and large-hearted that I expect you do. But if ever I seem to you undemonstrative, remember my past and present life, and remembering that forgive my shortcomings.' He added, 'I feel a beast to write you this letter, but it is a relief which I sadly need.'[5]

Over the next few weeks, living with her in Chesterfield Street, Mark's relationship with his mother deteriorated, and on 19 June he wrote to Edith, 'this accursed place stifles me ... the last two days seem like two years. I can't go out for half an hour without finding some awful horror on my return. Nothing has gone wrong, but one never knows the future, and alas one does the past ... The hopeless misery of it all for me is that I have no natural affection for my mother, alas that it is I who say it, it is a hideous confession to make.'[6] He was still protective of her, however, for wherever she went she was the subject of speculation and gossip. 'Yesterday I put three society Beldams [*sic*] to flight in a picture gallery,' he told Edith on 27 June. 'Those three Beldams (painted old harlots) saw my mother but did not see me. My mother's back was turned. They began making comments, winking, nudging and so on. I looked at them, they then stopt [*sic*]. I continued looking at them. They shuffled. I continued looking at them (now smiling). They retreated to another room, where I followed them and stared them so completely out of countenance that they fled from the building, which gave me great satisfaction.'[7]

Edith's wise advice was that he should be patient, assuring him that Jessie's condition was sure to improve. She was, after all, carving out a new career for herself in the literary world. On her return from South Africa in 1900, she had written and had published a small book entitled *Side Lights on the War in South Africa*, and since then had contributed regularly to *Review of the Week*, and to Frank Harris's illustrated magazine, *The Candid Friend*, writing articles on politics, profiles of personalities, the occasional travel piece, and book and theatre reviews. The latter periodical, which was published weekly with the purpose of 'drawing attention to the virtues and failings of public men and public institutions',[8] was unfortunately filled with just the kind of gossipy articles that Mark detested. 'My mother's journalistic craze is getting very annoying to me,' he told Edith. 'She now writes for a most low and abominable paper called The Candid Friend ... It is that sort of journalism that makes me foam with rage, and the twaddle that is written in the thing ...'[9] She had also founded her very own weekly, *The Sunrise*, a mish-mash of gossip and politics, which was also much disapproved of by Mark, particularly as she had, without his permission, chosen to publish in it extracts from some of the letters he had written to her from South Africa, under the banner 'An Officer at the Front'. Thus despite the fact that these journalistic enterprises kept his mother busy, and out of his hair, he gave her no support, and when in the summer of 1902 she amalgamated *Sunrise* with a revival of Samuel Johnson's magazine, *The Rambler*, he wrote to Edith, 'I am more than annoyed Re "Rambler". The Sunrise was bad enough but + Rambler, it will be fearful.'[10]

Jessie paid no attention, and attempted to win him over by plugging his book, *Through Five Turkish Provinces*, which had been published in the autumn of 1900. An account of his journey to the

Haurân, it had received favourable reviews, though Mark considered them 'one series of ignorant, meaningless praise'. He was convinced that the book had only attracted attention because of who he was, and wrote to Doolis, 'I can perfectly imagine how it is done; Editor "O look here, here's a book by that young fellow Sykes! – cut it up – O no, he's a son of Tatton Sykes, you remember those trials, he'll be deuced rich!" Result: "Mr Sykes's brilliant little production on his trip to Siberia shows energy, valour, and literary talent of no small order."'[11]

His modesty was quite unfounded, for he had real talent as a writer, which he now put to use on a new project, undertaken with his old Cambridge friend Edmund Sandars. Together they had spent some time at Sledmere reading all the latest books on military science, such as the *Infantry Drill Book* of 1896, which had been given to all soldiers heading out to fight the Boers, and *A Handbook on Field Artillery* by a Lt.-Col. Pratt. They then wrote a parody of these very serious works under the pseudonym of Major-General George D'Ordel, using the binding and format of the *Infantry Drill Book* as a blueprint. They called their great work *Tactics and Military Training*, and they dedicated it to General Sir John Barbecue KCB, an old warhorse who had learned 'modern warfare' in the Crimea, had ignored the Boer War on the grounds of its 'irregular conduct', and strongly disapproved of 'the new craze for learning and innovation'. 'I will send you a copy of the Saunders [*sic*] Sykes Drill book as soon as I can,' Mark promised Edith. 'There are some funny parts to it. Mostly I fear Saunders ... Here is a definition (Tactical) ...

'WOODS Woods are places often so covered with trees as to be invisible to the soldier etc etc.'[12]

Tactics purported to be published posthumously, as D'Ordel himself had died in his chair at the United Military and Naval Club, after reading the new drill book by Lord Roberts, a serious army reformer. The book was open at the preface, and a deep nail mark underscored the following passage: 'Nor are the men allowed to degenerate into mere machines. The efficiency of the individual as a fighting man is the test of a good battalion.'[13]

Though strictly fictional, the characters of Barbecue and D'Ordel were rooted in reality, Mark having come across many such figures in South Africa. Moreover, he had only recently been exasperated by the short-sightedness of the military authorities over one of his experiments. Though the British army had used camouflage since the mid-nineteenth century, it had only been for uniforms, and had proved particularly effective in Afghanistan and India, where the drab colour blended so perfectly into the dusty landscape. Soon the 'khaki drill' uniform was used throughout the British army. Mark had a new idea. While passing the time at Sledmere on his return from South Africa, he had carried out various tests as to the best method of camouflaging a field gun, and after many trials had come up with the idea that the most effective way was to daub the gun in streaks of colours taken from gamebirds, having noticed that the colours of a partridge made it hard to see in the landscape. He considered the results so successful that he managed to persuade some of the top brass to come and see them for themselves at the training camp at Aldershot, along with members of the Press.

'You take a gun, daub it over with blotches of red, blue and yellow, and immediately it becomes, for all practical purposes, invisible,' wrote the correspondent of the *Daily Express*. 'This is the discovery which is said to have been recently pointed out to the military authorities by Captain Sykes of the Yorkshire Militia, and experiments which have taken place at Aldershot prove it to be true in a remarkable degree. Six guns and their limbers were so daubed and streaked ... and placed on the Fox hills. The Artillery officers in Aldershot were invited to locate them with field glasses at a distance of about 3,000 yards. So admirably did the combination of colours harmonise with the background, that none of the officers, although knowing the direction in which the guns lay, were able to pick them all out.'[14] The correspondent for the *Daily News*, showing a remarkable ability to see into the future, asked, 'Is it possible that our huge battleships and monster cruisers will come out in stripes of red and blue and yellow?'[15] The officers, however, appear to have missed the point. 'The gun is a great success as far as I can see,' Mark reported. 'One of the scornful today came up and said, "Haw-whe-ahs this blessed invisible jim-jam of yor-ahs, eh?" I said, "Within four hundred yards of you in the open, look for it!" (My temper was getting rather short.)

The fool glared and screwed his eyes up, but couldn't see it, until I told a man to show him where it was. The fool then said, "It's an awfully clever trick, don't you know, but of course it's quite impractical. How could they march past if no one could see the guns? Haw, haw, haw!"'[16]

So the army missed a trick, and history now credits the French with having invented camouflage as a mean's of disguising field guns, twelve years later during the First World War.

Mark's various enterprises did not go unnoticed and he was beginning to be seen in political circles as a young man to watch. Among those who saw his future potential was George Wyndham, a dashingly handsome Tory romantic, and one of the leading members of the 'Souls', the aristocratic clique promoting intellectual dexterity and physical beauty that was formed in the late 1880s as an antidote to the philistinism of the Marlborough House set. A man who once described himself as 'an artist who has allowed himself to drift into politics',[17] Wyndham had risen fast in his political career, acting first as Under-Secretary at the War Office during the South African war, then, at the age of thirty-seven, being made Chief Secretary to Ireland, one of the most difficult offices in British politics. He saw Mark as having just the kind of mind that would make him the perfect Private Secretary, and, in September, invited him over to Phoenix Park to have a look around.

'I am going to Ireland,' he informed Edith, 'and Gatty* has told them I am a very amusing person – well I expect Gatty will get his head broken.'[18] He arrived on 18 September, reporting about the fellow guests he was supposed to amuse, 'they are very nice people, – only there is a Prince Francis of Teck who patronises, and talks rot. If he gives me much more of his princeliness there will be a rumpus. There is also old Lord Rowton, who I always admired, also Lady de Lisle who used to be a dowd, and now ever since old de Lisle has kicked, is very smart and wears few & scanty evening garments. Also there is a fat good-natured French girl with nice manners who … tells one one talks French Beautifully which is one of the most forgiveable of lies …'[19] He was particularly fascinated by Lord and Lady Lytton, who looked to him as if they could live comfortably on a diet of two raspberries and a violet, once a year. 'In my opinion,' he said, 'if a man is built on the lines of a very beautiful cup of eggshell china, he most certainly should not marry a "Dresden Shepherdess" marked "Fragile". The results will be too delicate.'[20]

Wyndham himself had not yet arrived, the man in charge of the party being a secretary 'with a doughy face and a big brain'. 'The CHIEF, as they all call Wyndham, arrives tomorrow,' Mark reported, adding, 'The people hold angry meetings on his lawn and everybody laughs. People once laughed in 1791 when another nation held angry meetings, but what is that …'[21] What these angry gatherings were about, he did not allude to, but Ireland was riven with discontent, largely over a lack of good education, insecurity over land ownership, and the ever-present and thorny question of Home Rule. Mark took all this in, and took note also of the people who might be of use to him, such as another of the secretaries, Philip Hanson. 'I have discovered a man in the shape of one Hanson,' he wrote, 'on whom I shall keep my eye fixed. I think I perceive in him one who will make a considerable mark. Remember the name and the man, it may be useful in the future. He is only 30 and secretary to Wyndham. He is a North country man and very hard'.[22]

* Charles Gatty was a writer and academic who had been at Cambridge with Mark, and who had also once stood as Home Rule candidate for Dorset.

Encouraged by Edith, Mark told Wyndham that he would accept the post, but not before he had tied up two important loose ends. In September 1900, he had spelled out his intentions towards Edith in a letter from South Africa. 'My dear person, I must show you definitely what my intentions are,' he had told her, 'and this must be kept secret … It was and is my intention, provided you agree, to marry you. But for anyone to marry before he is prepared to achieve something is to my mind absurd. Now in this you agree with me, when I have made my "grand tour" & worked at my books, I shall be in that position.'[23] Thus, at the beginning of November, he set out on his great journey, the purpose of which was to write a book that would put his name on the map. It was a trip that would take him across the Ottoman Empire from Damascus to Tiflis, then one of the Governorates of the Russian Empire, and better known today as Tbilisi, the capital of Georgia. He took with him a companion from his Cambridge days, John Hugh Smith, an Old Etonian banker's son who he thought would benefit from a taste of some rough travel. He threw him in at the deep end.

'It will be 12 days before I am off this boat,' Mark wrote to Edith from Naples, on board the mailboat *Le Saghalieu*, 'which is the foulest Messagerie in the Service. Even the Captain laughs at it … I wonder how little Master John will like this business. I shall frighten him with tales of disease and pestilence. One glimpse at the deck passengers will settle his decadent stomach I expect.'[24]

Mark's valet, McEwen, had put him in a foul mood by packing 'as only a doting drunkard could', leaving half his things behind while sending a lot of things that were not wanted, including a pile of the wrong books. In spite of this he still saw the funny side of things. 'This morning as the ship was pitching a little,' he wrote, five days into the voyage, 'I jammed my back against the wall to shave, and was getting on pretty well, when behold the wall opened and set me sitting, with a shaving brush in one hand and a razor in the other, in the middle of two Greek ladies in light attire.

The wall was a door leading into the next cabin.'[25] His ill humour was short-lived, however, and he was soon telling Edith, 'the knowledge that all is settled and that ones life is in ones <u>own</u> hands makes me so happy that I am very, very amiable to everyone. Nothing could annoy me now nothing!'[26]

It was a situation that did not last long, for when, on 13 November, they finally arrived in Beirut, it was to find that the supplies required for the expedition had not arrived. 'Oh Woe is me!' he wrote exasperatedly to Henry Cholmondeley. 'What evil have I done that I should be so accursed? The whole of my camp is still stuck at Marseilles! – and owing to the strike has been stopped there ... meanwhile I am wasting time and money in the greatest discomfort.' He expected to be stuck for about five weeks, which would throw out all his calculations of time, space and money: 'but what annoys me most,' he told Cholmondeley, 'is I fear you may think me extravagant, and after all these years of hearing a certain person explaining how easy it is with the greatest economy to waste 2 or 3 hundred thousand, you may think me the same, but to prove to you I am not, I have been living on the ground without a tent for the last 15 days and eating the veriest garbage'.[27]

At least he was happy to be back on familiar ground, telling Edith, 'Alhamdolillah! How nice it is to be back in the East again, even in this land of Cookites. It is glorious. I will show it to you some day, my dearest.' He regaled her with the progress being made with John Hugh Smith. 'John Hugh has improved beyond compare. He hardly mentions Wagner or Molière or rubbish, and is bewildered beyond words. In a few weeks his mind will be completely cleansed of all that is bad and there is a tremendous deal of good in him. The only thing I fear now is his stomach which I shall look after with the greatest care.'[28] A few days later he was writing about him to Professor Browne in Cambridge. 'He wants to try Hasheesh and says it will be a new emotion. I think I shall let him, particularly as the soda water is not of the excellent and hot-copper-cooling brand at Cambridge. It will cure him of any other dangerous investigations he may wish to perpetrate. O ye hammering anvils! O ye clanging Smithies!! O ye piercing broad-awls!!! O ye throbbing tom-toms! What a headache he will get!'[29]

Smith really was the innocent abroad and to begin with this was the cause of much amusement to Mark. 'He went into the Khan es Zeit the other day at Damascus,' he told Browne, 'and was shown round by an old fool called Haji Ali

It was only when Haji Ali proposed breaking by force into the women's quarters that it dawned on John that the revered Haji was as drunk as the Metaphorical Lord. I laughed till I cried watching the two going round the Khan followed by about twenty blackguard boys.'[30] To Edith he reflected: 'I wonder what would become of him alone. It is extraordinary how simple the most learned young gentlemen are if they have never knocked about at all.'[31]

Underneath his ability to see the humorous side of things, however, a note of irritability was beginning to appear. 'I don't know what is the matter with John Hugh Smith,' he was soon complaining, 'he sleeps the whole day. Directly he gets in he snores on his bed, till there is a meal, sleeps in the carriage out driving, slumbers in the train, and yawns on horseback. He won't get up till 10 o'clock and complains that the food touches up his liver cruelly … The Mosquitoes also puncture him fiercely he has broken out in spots. I had his decadent hair cut yesterday

which apparently grieved him as he has done nothing but look at himself in the glass ever since.'[32] And when they reached their first stop, at Damascus, he wrote to Henry Cholmondeley from the Hotel Victoria, 'John Hugh Smith is getting rather shaken by the purple East and has just come to me with a face of horror saying "Do you know that three people sleep in the kitchen!" as if it was surprising. He has much to learn yet!'[33] It really was beginning to look as if the decision to bring along Smith as a companion had been a colossal mistake.

The expedition was led by a new dragoman, called Yussuf Haddad, Isá Kubrusli having recently died, and Mark had also hired a personal servant, Jacob el-Arab, an Arab who had converted to Roman Catholicism. Before leaving, the whole party posed for a photograph, which comprised, in addition to Mark and Smith, one dragoman, one servant, one cook, seven muleteers, Chello the dog and a child, inserted into the photograph by the muleteers to bring them good luck.

From Damascus they travelled to Palmyra, the ancient ruined city that lies south-west of Tadmur. Here Mark noticed change in the air, the eagle eye of Cook's having fixed on the business possibilities of the place. He accurately predicted the future of such destinations. 'In a few months,' he surmised, 'most probably an advertisement will blossom in Ludgate Circus, informing the world that –

'TO PALMYRA AND BACK IN FIVE DAYS £10
RUINS AND TOMBS!
RELIABLE GUIDES Etc!

'and Tadmor will have fallen once more; her colonnades will be strewn with beer bottles and orange peel; the elderly virgins of England will be hustled with aching backs and tired eyes through her courts; the dyspeptic colonels and "Poppas" of America will be driven by chattering servants from Zenobia's bath to Zenobia's bed, from Zenobia's bed to Zenobia's temple; the young Oxford don will write poetry in the Temple of the Sun during the vacation; the English Clergy will write to the *Times* concerning the disgraceful charges of the hotel; and Tadmor in the wilderness will be peopled as Jerusalem, Nazareth, and Luxor are peopled, by trippers and tourists ... and Palmyra's glory will have departed.'[34]

They reached Aleppo, via Homs and Hama, on 17 January, Mark having travelled the last nine miles at a gallop in order to get as soon as possible any letters that might be awaiting him from Edith. He found five, which gave him 'much information and much good cheer'. Replying to them, he told her that he had so far written eighty pages of his book, most of which he considered readable. Smith, he told her, though much improved since the journey began, 'cannot get the confidence of the servants ... I will tell you one fault he has which is breathing & eating with his mouth open, a habit that the Arabs look on with the greatest horror ... He has also been put to the last extremity. On the way back from Palmyra, Ain el-Beda to Feruqlus, 17 hrs ride, half way he lay down in the road and said he would faint, but didn't of course. The end of it was he rode on but had to be given biscuits to keep him going.' The result was that they split up for the next section of the expedition, from Aleppo to Urfa, with Mark taking the rugged route through the Taurus mountains, while Smith took an easier route through the Euphrates Valley.

When they met up again in Urfa, Mark wrote to Edith that he found 'Little John' entirely changed. He had, worryingly, become 'very bold, unconscious and manly' and was 'beating natives in the most unphilosophic manner'.[35] They did not stay long together, parting again at Diarbekr, where Smith embarked on a raft down the Tigris to collect stores at Baghdad. They were finally reunited at Kerkúk, where Mark noted, 'My only trouble is about John with whom I have never had the slightest approach to a quarrel, but why do all the natives hate him so? He will not understand things and I have given up telling him. For instance, a Pasha[36] came to dinner last night, who knew Chamberlain, Dufferin etc, etc, and J.H.S appeared at dinner in one old Khaki coat, 4 days beard and his chest bear [*sic*]. Result Pasha servant says in an audible voice to Jacob "why does this Jew dishonour the table of the Bey Effendi[37] etc, etc."[38] On another day, near the Kurdish town of Keui Sanjak, there was a fearful row when he hit the dragoman and cursed his religion, using 'the filthiest Arab oaths', the result being that Jacob el-Arab, the other servant, had to be restrained from knifing him, while the muleteers were ready to cut up the saddles. 'It has been a fearful drag,' wrote Mark, 'he does not know half of what goes on and I think it better not to tell him … the poor little innocent has no more idea than the man in the moon.' The Arabs, he went on to tell Edith, had given him a nickname, 'El Yahudi Ingliz',[39] which to them was the greatest insult possible.

To avoid further trouble. Mark decided to send Jacob on to Mosul with the luggage, while he and Little John made a detour through the Kurdish mountains, a cooler journey that would take them through steep and rocky terrain that was often hard for the horses. At Rowandiz 'we passed the opening of a deep and gruesome gorge, winding in and out of the mountains on the right of the path. It would make a famous background for any artist illustrating Dante's meeting with Virgil, and even at midday has a shuddering effect on the observer, with its dark abysmal depths and craggy perpendicular sides … Riding and musing through these lonely valleys one's mind cannot but wander into the past and assay to pry into the future. Wild, grey, craggy rocks, and green wooded villages, what have they not seen? The early races fighting, clinging, slipping, staggering and swaying …'[40]

Two days later, at the dauntingly steep Gallé Polunja pass, disaster struck. 'It was here,' recalled Mark, 'that my horse, Osman Shawish, who had carried me for nineteen hundred miles, died of sunstroke and colic – poor beast, he was well enough in the morning, but suddenly dropped after noon, and expired in an hour. With all the pluck of an Arab, he stood up until, within five minutes of his end, struggling to keep up with the caravan he had followed so long: his attempts were pitiful to see, and it was a sad relief to all when he gave the final shudder. The last breath whistled back through his distended nostrils, and his bloodstained eyes glazed from agony to peaceful death. We left him where he fell.'[41]

From Amadia, two days' distance, they followed for the remainder of their journey, up to Lake Van and thereafter Tiflis, the same route that Mark had taken on his previous trip, suffering one major disappointment when they reached the town of Zahko. Here they were entertained by the local Agha,[42] who fired their imaginations with descriptions of a castle of great antiquity that lay on his estate and was hitherto unvisited by travellers. Even though 'Little John' had dubbed this man 'a vulgar cad', a description Mark considered 'not a very unsound criticism', he had fired their imaginations. 'We decided to make an expedition to the place,' wrote Mark, 'and discover it. The nearest village was something of a detour, but considering that the object might repay, we deserted our heavy luggage which we dispatched to Sairt, and, turning southwards, rode across the valley to Bahuna ... At Bahuna we were met by the Agha, whom we immediately questioned about the famous castle; he too gave a stirring account of it and minutely described the bazaars, inscriptions, towers, and gates it contained ... The Agha and some friends announced they would show us the way, and we started full of expectancy, dreaming of our names going down to posterity as the greatest antiquarian explorers of the century. One hour's hard walking brought us to two large stones. "This is the gate," said the Agha ... a few more paces brought us to some oubliette-shaped cisterns ... "those are the stores." A little further on we found a valley containing a number of stunted oak trees. "There is the castle." We stared aghast – there was the castle, a few traces of the foundations of a village of any age and any period. "Where – where are the inscriptions?" "There," said the Agha, pointing to a water-worn rock. Our rage knew no bounds.'[43]

At Lake Van, in spite of his previous experience there, Mark made the serious mistake of allowing Little John to persuade him to hire a boat to cross the lake. 'We were of course wrecked,' he wrote, 'and that within four hours of starting, through the senseless cowardice of the Armenian crew.'[44] This did little to curb his annoyance with his friend and may have been the final straw that made him vow to himself never to travel with him again. North of Igdir, they caught the train at Kars that eventually took them across the Russian border to their final destination of Tiflis, now Tbilisi, the modern capital of Georgia. 'It was delightful to hear the civilized Russians on board talking so beautifully of progress and light,' Mark commented; 'they are marvellous Orientals! A Russian engineer who shared our compartment discoursed on Dickens, Thackeray and Shakespeare; he also pointed out to us how gloriously noble was the mission of Russia in civilising the barbarous, backward East – not brutally as England does, but gently and paternally. My eyes filled with sympathetic tears, and Smith's voice broke with a catch in it as he murmured to himself, "Dear, dear old Russia!"'[45]

After months in the East, the two travellers got a sharp reminder in Tiflis of one difference between East and West. 'We stayed a day in Tiflis and saw poor people for the first time since we left Europe. By poor I do not mean Dervishes, or beggars, or cripples, or blind, for in Turkey there are many of these, but they are not poor. They have but to ask for bread, and a Zaptieh, a Pasha, a Haykh, an Imam, a street boy, a merchant, a soldier, a robber, a peasant, or a baker will give it to them without comment; for in Turkey, unless there is absolute famine, no one need starve. But in Tiflis we saw the poor of Europe – the poor who live in foul, narrow alleys, the poor who stare with gaunt grey faces of hopeless misery, the poor who work for a miserable wage, the poor who build railways and manufacture "civilisation" … Tiflis is in fact a European town; the East has been rolled back for a time, and the happy, swashbucklering, open-handed people, who fought and loved and lived their lives are now ground into the mill of progress …'[46]

Mark returned to England in late August bringing with him his Arab servant, Jacob, and was immediately tied up in manoeuvres with the 1st Yorkshires, which kept him from a reunion with Edith. His priority was to get his father's final approval for the wedding, so the ceremony could take place before he had to join Wyndham's staff in

Ireland, and on top of that he needed to complete his book so he could get the manuscript off to the publisher. 'I am going on,' he told Edith on 21 September, 'and have found a female typewriter and shorthand writer to whom I shall have to dictate my book! From rereading it I think I might as well dictate Joseph Andrews.

However she is neither young nor beautiful and there is nothing harmful in the book, so I presume it may not be so difficult.'[47]

The following day he had 'the best of all possible news' to impart to his future bride. 'My father is in no way inclined to make any kind of difficulty and appears very pleased. He came down to see me today and I drove with him & visited no less than 8 churches. Between the visits he arranged to come to London on the 15th where he says you are to dine with him ... As he is going away from England on the 31st of next month, we had better fix on the 28th October ... He stipulates for 8 o'clock in the morning – but I will be in London on the 9th and we can discuss it all then – I say 8 o'clock you idle creature ...'[48] A sign of his father's approval was that he immediately raised his son's allowance from £2,000 p.a. to £4,000. Edith was delighted at the news and immediately set about making the arrangements for the ceremony.

It was a plan that was rudely cut short by the contrary nature of Sir Tatton Sykes, who had suddenly panicked at the thought of a grand London wedding which would only revive memories of his own disastrous union. 'I have been obliged to alter all the arrangements,' Mark wrote to her on 27 September. 'We have to be married at York, owing to my father who insists … I am awfully sorry to have had to act without consulting you, but the matter was of such vital importance that I did so. You had better come up with your "people" the day before; you will have to stay at a hotel I will name later. I hope you will not be annoyed or inconvenienced. I dread and fear putting you out, but my dearest what else could I do …'[49]

The wedding took place on 28 October at St Wilfrid's Church, York. True to form, in the weeks leading up to the ceremony, Tatton changed his mind on a daily basis as to whether or not he would attend, but when the day came he was in his pew, sharp at eight. It was a quiet affair, with no more than fifty guests, and a ceremony conducted by the Bishop of Middlesbrough. Henry Cholmondeley acted as best man, and Jessie, dressed in green velvet with a hat to match, behaved impeccably. Edith, described by the local paper as being 'a bright, pretty girl' whose 'gentle, gracious manners have already secured her many friends', wore 'a white cloth dress, trimmed with ecru lace, and had a Spanish mantilla of white lace'.[50] After the wedding breakfast, which took place at the Station Hotel, the bride and groom departed for London, and the following day set out on their honeymoon, which took them first to Paris and Rome, and then to Constantinople and Jerusalem. Both parties were rapturous in their happiness. 'Neither was luckier than the other,' Mark's biographer, Shane Leslie, was later to write. 'It proved one of those few marriages made in Heaven.'[51]

Looking at the marriage from the point of view of Edith's parents, Sir John and Lady Gorst, Mark was quite a catch. Clever, good-looking and charming, he was not only heir to a great fortune, but, with a growing reputation as a soldier, a traveller and a man of letters, there was the likelihood of a glittering career ahead of him. Indeed, with his appointment as George Wyndham's Private Secretary, he was already on the first rung of the ladder. Moreover, he had returned from his recent journey to find that D'Ordel's *Tactics* had been a bestseller, going through six editions in its first few weeks. It had been widely and excellently reviewed in all the daily newspapers and weeklies, including *The Army and Navy Illustrated*, whose reviewer had recommended it to 'every soldier interested in the Service'.[52] The *Spectator* called it 'exceptionally amusing and perhaps exceptionally instructive', adding, 'It is laughter-compelling on every page.'[53] Now he was ready to start work on his next travel book, and had ideas for further D'Ordel publications, but first of all he had his Irish post to take up.

He got off to a bad start in Dublin, having arrived to find that 'The Chief' was not expected for another few days, a fact that irked him as he could have spent some more time at Sledmere with Edith. He also sensed an atmosphere of slackness and disorganization in the Chief Secretary's Lodge, and was annoyed that there was no one to show him the ropes. 'I have been here twenty-four hours,' he complained to Edith, 'and know a little less than when I arrived … I have to pick up what they have been doing for four years with the end of a stick out of a dustbin.' One of the first jobs he was given was to précis an eighty-four-page report, only to find that one already existed at the back of it. He had so little to do that, to kill time, he found himself making trips to Dublin Zoo with one of Wyndham's close friends, Charles Gatty, a literary figure who had also once stood as Home Rule candidate for Dorset. 'I went with Gatty to the Zoo … The keeper at the monkey-house is so like a monkey that one cannot help turning aside to smile …

Poor Gatty was quite out of Drawing after seeing the wild beasts fed. He said he felt he wished he had never been born into such a cruel world.'

So bored was he that he was almost ready to quit before he had started. 'Politics fill me with disgust,' he fumed, 'but I will go through with this infernal job as long as you can stand it … I don't know if I can possibly hold out in the office work. I want air and real work. Give me a native regiment to organise, a rebellion to raise, a map to make, a block-house line to construct, a Vilayet to govern and I will do it; give me an independent command, anything you choose but this, this life of a cat …'[54] Nor did things improve even when 'The Chief' finally showed up, for Wyndham gave him little to do, tending to rely on his other long-standing private secretaries for most of the work. Mark wasted no time, however, taking the opportunity of having time on his hands to correspond with Edith on the subject of where they were going to live during the months when Wyndham was based at Westminster. Having spent much of his childhood being dragged round hotels, he knew exactly what he wanted. 'Now about rooms,' he instructed her, 'we want our <u>own Kitchen and Cook</u>, you know how I and you Hate, Loathe, detest, Abhor, Condemn, Spit Upon, and Utterly Damn Restaurants where The Vegetables are green, the waiters are greasy, the service disgusting, the company bestial, the surroundings vulgar, the IDEA LOATHSOME. Therefore find a roomy spot with a kitchen and a low rent even at Mile End!'[55]

Christmas was at least cheered up by a visit from Edith, though she complained to him that Charles Gatty was over-familiar. 'Did a nasty Gatty call it by its Christian name', Mark teased her, 'and was it most enraged. But really you have married me, and … you will find that anyone who holds you in any respect and has any ear for music, will naturally call you Edith, and not MISSIZ SIKES, or MISSIZ MAHRK (I spell phonetically). If you had been Christened Jemima, there might be some hope as it is worse. Unluckily no one knows your other name is Vi'lit. If you choose to sink the Edith and assume the former, no one will call you by it & you may sweep over the earth in all your Matronly Dignity …'

Edith eventually found a suitable flat in south-west London, 7 Lennox Gardens, which was conveniently close to the Irish Office, and they settled there in January 1904. Mark dealt with his frustration at the little required of him by Wyndham by immersing himself in completing his new book, *Dar-ul-Islam: A Journey through Ten of the Asiatic Provinces of Turkey*. Illustrated throughout with seventy of his own photographs and twenty pages of hand-drawn maps, it was an account of his travels with John Hugh Smith. Its success lay in its blending of history and descriptions of place with amusing anecdotes and sharp flashes of humour. One of the themes running through the book was his hatred of the way the West was beginning to spoil the traditions of the East. He gave as an example of this an inedible dinner served to him by the Sheik of a village outside Palmyra, for whom it would have been easy to serve his guests traditional Arab food eaten with the fingers, which, as Mark noted, 'is excellent for anyone with a good appetite and digestion'. Instead he insisted on them partaking of a 'Dinny Vranzay' (*dîner français*), described as follows:

'We were ushered into a dining-room, where we found a table covered with a fringed table-cloth ; upon it were flaps of bread and European crockery. The soup was brought in by a retainer, and the Shaykh, with the air of a man proud of his table, ladled it out bravely. The first spoonful did not disclose the full nastiness of the mixture; rank weeds and vermicelli certainly were some of its components. Presently this steaming mess was removed and replaced by a dish of fat – fat of the ancient camel, a portion often reserved by the Arab as lamp-oil! Here, however, the Shaykh used petroleum and fed his guests on this monstrous grease. This was flanked by more grease! The Pasha, unmanned, spat out his second helping, the partially chewed portion was deftly removed by an attendant and returned to the dish before the Shaykh, who had the grossness to devour it himself. Naturally we ate no more of the garbage, but the very sight and smell of the six other dishes were enough to shake the strongest stomach ... we will spare the reader further details, suffice it to say here was a typical instance of smearing the East with the Gosmobaleet slime of the West.'[56]

The word 'Gosmobaleet', Mark's own rendering of the Levantine English for 'cosmopolitan', he described in a footnote as being 'descriptive of that peculiar and horrible sickness which attacks a certain percentage of the inhabitants of interesting and delightful lands. The outward symptoms in the East are usually American springside boots (Jemimas) and ugly European clothes ... The final stage is that in which the victim, hating his teacher and ashamed of his parentage and nationality, is intensely miserable.'[57] When the book came out in the spring of 1904, it was well received and widely reviewed, not only by the dailies and weeklies, but by distinguished writers like Rudyard Kipling, who wrote to Mark, 'I sat down to read it and stayed there for the rest of the evening ... I don't know Turkey, but I can see the dust and the delay and the confusion at the wayside *serails* as I can smell the smell (much like ours in India, I take it) of the towns. What you said about the cold in "warm" countries went to my bones, Nothing is colder than the East when she chooses.'[58] H. G. Wells also commented, 'I've just been leafing through Dar ul Islam and I perceive it's going to be a great lark to read and that I'm going to learn things. I like your "down" on civilization and suchlike.'[59]

As if it were not enough to have written a 300-page account of his journey through the Ottoman Empire, Mark also embarked on a new D'Ordel project with Edmund Sandars, this time a satire on another of his *bêtes noires*, cheap journalism. *D'Ordel's Pantechnicon: An Universal Directory of the Mechanical Art of Manufacturing Illustrated Magazines* was the work of Prometheus D'Ordel, Gent., brother of the late Major-General, and introduced the reader to a 'Model Magazine' entitled *Scragford's Farthing*. Based on popular publications like *The Strand Magazine*, it suggested that magazines had gone downhill since the great days of the *Spectator* in the eighteenth century, and the quality of journalism with them. Conan Doyle was parodied as 'Doothey Boyle', author of *In Grypula's Grip*, *Grypula's Adventures*, *Ay Revoir Grypula*, *The Strange Episode of the Brazen Face*, and *More Grypula's Adventures*, while his latest novel, *The Search for the Iron Toe*, provided the obligatory serial. Though it did not achieve the success of *Tactics*, *Pantechnicon* was warmly praised, one reviewer describing it as 'probably some of the most brilliant nonsense ever written'.[60]

Though literary success was undoubtedly within Mark's grasp, his ambition was not fulfilled by writing. He continued to involve himself in military affairs, an area in which he felt confident in his talents, and his light workload with Wyndham allowed him to indulge in a week of training with the East Yorkshire Regiment in the summer of 1904, which he threw himself into with all his usual zeal and energy. Since the Colonel was constantly being called away, he often found himself in charge of training 250 volunteers. 'We had fearfully hard work, at least I had, to knock the men and officers, particularly the latter into shape,' he told Edith. The officers were a problem, he said, because they mostly consisted of small tradesmen who, though they were well off and keen to learn, had no instinct of command. 'The leading of men is not their gift,' he wrote. 'That rotten feudal system, splendid in its day, has left us a rare legacy of unchangeable things. It has left us the gentleman who is often a bounder and it has left us the poor snob, and good worthy cad whom nothing will ever make capable of leading his fellows to kill, rob or plunder the rest. In the East, where there are neither gentlemen or cads, it is otherwise.'

It was all worthwhile, however, when they got out into the field, and he could demonstrate his powers of leadership. 'The field days were great fun,' he enthused. 'I took the Battalion over a river three feet deep. I rode in on Noura and on they all came roaring with laughter. If it had been one of their own officers they would have laughed but they would not have crossed … I damned and cursed and swore at the volunteers and led them and drove them and coaxed and upbraided them and made life a Hell for them – but when I left them at Fimber, do you know the whole crowd cheered like madmen and sang "He's a jolly good etc" till the train was out of sight.'[61]

Of one thing Mark was still certain, he was not yet ready for politics, and he turned down without hesitation a request from the constituency of East Hull that he should stand for them. Instead, he told Edith, 'I am thinking of asking Wyndham for a job either in India under G. Nathaniel[62] or on the reorganisation of the Militia – I prefer the first if you do.' But whatever it was to be, he added, 'I must have an employment which I am capable of working in – that is to say one requiring energy, thought, and originality.'[63] Doubtless his ruminations about his career were now even more focused owing to the imminent birth of his first child.

Chapter 6

Return to the East

While training with the East Yorks, Mark had received some surprising news regarding his father, who was travelling in Australia with his new companion, Louise de Lichtevelde, a French widow who had originally come to Sledmere to teach him French, but whose standing in the household had risen on the departure of Jessie. From then on she had taken on the task of running the house, where she was addressed by the servants as 'Madame', and would also accompany Tatton on his journeys abroad. 'Our Papa,' Mark relayed to Edith, 'has distinguished himself in Australia by calling a man called Colonel Lyster a Thief, and stating that he had robbed him of £2,000 in 1896 – This was untrue and result is a fearful row and the Colonel bellowing for my father's blood …'[1]

Evidently no blood was shed, for on 24 July 1904 Tatton returned home in apparently rude health to receive some welcome news. 'I went to Selby to meet him,' Mark recounted. 'He arrived with Madame & Sievers, the valet, who looked both like the Corsican brothers, my father like a rejuvenated Budha [sic], (calm, smiling and oblivious of the world) in shirt sleeves as the day was rather warm. I took him into the gentlemen's-er-lavatory and explained to him what was going to happen. He said-yes-ay-yes-yes-yes-to be sure-of course-yes-ay-yes-yes – and looked intensely relieved. As he made no comment I guess he is very pleased, but of course he would never say so, but … by his evident satisfaction at seeing me I think he really is more rejoiced than an onlooker might think. He kept constantly saying "Where's Ethel?" which is of course your name henceforward …'[2]

The good news that Mark imparted to his father was of Edith's pregnancy, and on 31 August she gave birth to a healthy, fat baby girl they named Freya, an event which temporarily took Mark's mind off his problems. In the final weeks of her pregnancy, Edith had been with her family, while Mark remained at Sledmere working with Edmund Sandars on another D'Ordel book, a treatise on 'spin' to be called 'An Introduction to the Culinary Art of Preparing and Using Statistics'. He eagerly awaited her arrival: 'I have been fearfully busy,' he told her; 'we worked from 9.30 in the morning till Midnight yesterday, but we are getting on well ... I suppose Freya is as fractious as ever – you are expected here on Wednesday.'[3] When they finally arrived, Mark's indecision about his future was temporarily put to one side as he learned a few lessons about fatherhood with a hyperactive baby. In October, he travelled to Dublin, and after pestering 'The Chief' one more time for a change of job, and prevailing on Edith to bend the ear of her brother Jack, then an Under-Secretary in the Foreign Office, Mark was offered a post as an honorary attaché at the British Embassy in Constantinople, a city in which he would be able to put to good use the knowledge he had acquired during his travels through the Middle East. His wife and daughter were to accompany him there, but before taking up the posting in the spring of 1905, he decided to take Edith on a holiday to Palestine, partly as recuperation from a bout of pneumonia she had suffered over the winter. Tatton also accompanied them, this time without 'Madame', but with his own private cook so that he did not have to endure the spicy Oriental food that might upset his delicate stomach.

While staying in Jerusalem in February, they were introduced to another inveterate traveller who also happened to come from the north of England. Gertrude Bell was the 37-year-old daughter of Sir Hugh Bell, an industrialist from County Durham. Educated at Lady Margaret Hall, Oxford, from where she had graduated with first-class honours, she had established a reputation as a traveller and adventurer, publishing her first book, *Persian Pictures*, in 1894, a description of a journey through Persia, where her uncle, Sir Frank Lascelles, was the British Minister. Fluent in Arabic and Persian, she had also travelled extensively throughout the Middle East and, like Mark, was acquainted with the Druse living in Jabal-al-Druse. She was passing through Jerusalem at the beginning of a trip to study the archaeology and the tribes of Syria with the object of combining all the material she collected, together with the numerous photographs she planned to take, into a book. Like Mark, she was wilful, headstrong and usually right, so it was not unlikely that when they met, sparks might fly.

It was the British Consul, John Dickson, who suggested to Bell that she might like to meet Mark, and who arranged for them to have dinner. It turned out to be a fruitful evening for Bell, who was in dire need of a cook. Mark and his father both recommended an Arab called Mikhâil, whom they described as being 'trustworthy and extremely brave', qualifications which decided her on hiring him, even though Mark admitted that his cooking skills left much to be desired. Though Bell described the Sykeses in her diary as being 'darlings', and Mark as being 'most amusing', there was obviously competition between them from the outset. 'He is going up over much the same route that I intend to take,' she wrote, before gleefully criticizing his extravagance. 'He has an immense camp, and what he must spend over it I tremble to think. He told me with pride that he had bought eight mules, four donkeys and four horses for £360. Now the very outside price of the best mules is £20, by which reckoning he must have spent £200 on four horses and four donkeys. You will realize how preposterous that is, when I tell you that no travelling horse ought to cost more than about £18. However, he is pleased, and I make no doubt his dragoman is pleased too … The main point is to arrange my journey so as not to fall in with him, bless him, for if I know the East, prices will double all along his route.'[4] In spite of Bell describing the dinner as having been 'the merriest of evenings',[5] it seems Mark must have taken umbrage at her insinuations that he had been grossly overcharged, for he bore a grudge against her that was to spill over the following year.

This was the last trip for some while on which Edith was able to accompany Mark, since she was now pregnant with their second child, a circumstance that concentrated his attention on getting them housed in Constantinople, where he was to take up his post as honorary attaché to the British Ambassador, Sir Nicholas O'Connor. O'Connor, who had a tall, frail figure, and deep-blue eyes with a hypnotic quality, was described by Mark as being someone who 'always seemed to me to have stepped out of the pages of one of Thackeray's eighteenth century novels or the memoirs of Horace Walpole'.[6] A distinguished diplomatist who, amongst other posts, had served as envoy to the Emperor of China in Peking, and as British Ambassador to Russia, he had a good understanding of the undercurrents in Eastern politics, and had a particular liking for the Turks, with whom he had a great influence. In particular this was owing to his close personal relationship with Abdul Hamid, the 34th Sultan of the Ottoman Empire, a man of both great political expertise and personal charm, who exerted autocratic control over an Empire that was in decline, critically weakened by a combination of war, rebellion and crippling debt. 'Though the whole of Sir Nicholas's term of office,' wrote Mark, 'was one long series of inevitable conflicts between the Palace of Yildiz and the British Foreign Office – if there was one person whom Abdul Hamid cared about, whose word he trusted, and whose conversation he enjoyed, it was the British Ambassador's.'[7]

Apart from being one of the nerve-centres of diplomacy in the Middle East, Constantinople was also a wonderful place to live, particularly the neighbourhood of Tarabya, or Therapia, located on the shoreline of the Bosphorus Strait. It was where all the foreign embassies had their summer residences and commanded beautiful views across the water to the old City with its glittering domes and minarets, and it was here that Mark rented a house before returning to England to collect Freya and Edith. He also went to Sledmere to visit his father, who had recently suffered from a minor stroke. He found him in good spirits. 'I have seen my father,' he wrote to Edith. 'He is incredibly better, drives and walks round the mares etc, etc, eats well but sleeps badly – The only result of the illness is a slight clouding of his brain. It cannot be said that he suffers from hallucinations but something very like them.' He gave as an example of this the fact that Tatton had asked the Clerk at the bank, a Mr Pearson, if he could lend him £5,000. He was also 'stricken with terror before and after every undertaking of the day'. Mark told Edith that he accepted what he had been told by his father's physician, Dr Tinsley, which was that 'as long as he lives you will always have trouble with him'.[8]

While Mark felt relieved by the now constant presence of 'Madame', allowing him to leave for Turkey knowing that his father was in good hands, his mother, needless to say, could not stand her, always referring to her as 'that woman'. When news had reached her of Tatton's illness, for example, she wrote to Mark to tell him that she was disgusted that the opportunity had not been taken 'to get rid of the woman'.[9] Though the relationship between Tatton and Madame was almost certainly platonic, Jessie was always suspicious that there was more to it. These suspicions came to a head in 1908, when she discovered that on a trip back from Australia on board the steamship *Mongolian*, Madame was referred to in the Ship's Book as Lady Sykes. Through his solicitors, Tatton made it clear that there was nothing to read into this, admitting that he had heard of her being dubbed 'Lady Sykes' at Colombo, but it did not bother him. Jessie chose not to pursue this, but the incident only served to make her hate Madame even more.

Mark's usual boyish enthusiasm bubbled over when he started his new job in Constantinople. He was back in the Ottoman Empire, the part of the world he understood and loved most, and he had his heavily pregnant wife and child with him. Settled in Therapia, awaiting the imminent birth, he wrote to Henry Cholmondeley, 'I am now very satisfied with my work, which is more "real" than the Irish Office.'[10] Four days later, on 24 August, Edith gave birth to a son and heir for Sledmere. 'I hope the boy will not be called Tatton,' wrote Jessie from a villa she had taken in Bavaria. 'Richard is certainly a better name and has a fine Anglo-Norman sound about it – also the founder of the

Sykes family was really that Mr Richard Sykes whose letters you have read and who built the main body of the house.'[11] Richard he was named, though with the names Mark and Tatton to follow.

There was not a word of congratulation from his father. The only communication from Sledmere was a letter from Aunt Kate, Henry Cholmondeley's mother, which included a hastily scribbled postscript from Henry. 'I see no reason why the birth of my son should be kept a deadly secret,' Mark wrote indignantly to his cousin. 'Personally I should have expected a telegram from Sledmere, from at least the people in the place, a thing not much in itself but still showing a little human feeling, and which if they had been told they would have done if I know them at all. As it is, it is nine days since I telegraphed I have not heard a single word … as you know I am far from senti-mental but there is a degree of stoical frigidity which is beyond my philosophy.'[12]

As things turned out, Mark was to be as frustrated in Constantinople as he had been in Ireland. Having travelled so extensively in the East, he considered himself an expert on the area and was certain that he would have the ear of the Ambassador. He had powerful convictions of the vital importance of Britain keeping up and consolidating the good relationship with Turkey, which had been forged in the nineteenth century when Russia was a common enemy to them both. It was paramount, he felt, that she should guard against British predominance in the region being undermined by the Germans, who were building railways and helping to train the Turkish army. They were also seeking to gain oil concessions, the strategic importance of which was only just beginning to be realized. On this subject Mark managed to persuade O'Connor to allow him to do some intelligence-gathering.

At some point in late September/early October 1905, he made contact with a German engineer who was working for the company that was surveying the territory of Northern Iraq for a planned Berlin-to-Baghdad railway. From information garnered from this employee, he prepared a detailed account, illustrated by his own maps, which was eventually sent by O'Connor to the Foreign Office in Whitehall. It was titled *Report on the Petroliferous Districts of the Vilayets of Baghdad, Mosul and Bitlis*, and began: 'The following accounts of the various Petroleum springs and asphalt deposits have been compiled from a report made to the Imperial Ottoman Government by an Engineer dispatched to the above mentioned Vilayets in 1901.' It then went on to list, for example, 'No VI Baba Gurgur ... The Petroleum Springs of Baba Gurgur are among the richest and most workable in the Vilayet of Mosul. They cover an area of about half a hectare and owing to the great heat are constantly burning. The petroleum in this zone seems limited to an area of 25 hectares, but still the deposits are of great promise.'[13] Much to Mark's despair, the Foreign Office showed extraordinary complacency in the way it dealt with his report, remarking that it was not worth printing, and appearing to show a complete lack of interest in the subject. It was frustrating for him to realize that in the matter of oil concessions the Germans were going to steal a march on Britain.

For all the trouble he took on reports such as this, and others he wrote for the Ambassador from various journeys round the province, each one illustrated with his own maps and photographs, the views of his own which he expressed in them fell on deaf ears. He was, after all, no more than an honorary attaché, and any ideas he might have had about influencing policy were soon quashed when he found himself landed with mundane tasks such as reading newspapers for press cuttings, cutting them out and pasting them into albums. In order to avoid succumbing to terminal boredom, he decided to concentrate his attentions on writing a new book, an idea he had mentioned to Henry Cholmondeley. 'I am sketching in my mind's eye', he told him, 'the construction of a really big work on the Ottoman Empire, of which so far I have not written a single line.'[14]

With the blessing of the Ambassador, before returning to England he was to make one last great journey to research the proposed book, a trip that would take him from Constantinople to the borders of Persia and back to Aleppo. Edith and the two babies were to return to England, the plan being that once they were well settled, she should return to join him for the last leg of his adventure. Before they left, Mark wrote to her from Damascus, where he was busy making arrangements for the trip and had run into Gertrude Bell, about whom he had little good to say. '10,000 of my worst bad words on the head of that damned fool Miss Bell,' he fumed to Edith, 'confound the silly chattering windbag of a conceited gushing flat-chested man-woman globetrotting rump-wagging blethering ass! Now what do you suppose the fool did? She went to the Kaimakam of Salkhad and told him … that I was the brother-in-law of the Prime Minister in Egypt etc, etc, all of which the worthy official wired off to Nazim Pasha who nearly had a fit.' This was not, as it happened, mischief-making on the part of Bell, but a mistranslation of what she had actually said, which was that Mark's brother-in-law, Jack Gorst, was the Financial Minister of Egypt, but, as a result of this misinformation,

Nazim, who was the Wâli of Damascus, denied Mark permission to go into the desert, thereby allowing Bell to steal a march on him. 'I told you that woman was an ass and now I hope you will perceive she is. She leaves every place she visits in an uproar – she knows possibly of Persians – but of this crush she knows nothing … and has just missed getting me into very hot water. If you see the loon before I do, give her neither encouragement nor entertainment as she is just a damned mischief-making woman, let loose out of a London Drawing room into the Syrian desert … Poor Richards the Consul has aged ten years in two – poor wretch, I needn't tell you Miss Bell has not lessened his worries, he could kill her.' His irritation was further compounded by his belief that she had misled him. 'Of course she is doing the very route I told her I hoped to do, after she said that she was going elsewhere – an Infernal liar.'[15]

When Edith left towards the end of February, he was sad to see them go. 'It was indeed a dismal day when you left me alone in that repulsive crowd of Attachés and things at the Station,' he wrote to her from the SS *Urano*, en route to Alexandretta, going on to describe the drunken state of his servant on his return home. 'The house was desolate, and Finch who had (as he now says) been to James's Silver Wedding (where a tumbler of Claret proved to be Port) reminded me more of McEon [*sic*] at his worst than anything else. He was smoking one of my cigars, and sitting in the pantry with Ismail, Dimitri, Fosca and the carpenter looking at him. He had on the most inane expression and refused to go to bed …'[16]

Joseph Finch, Mark's English valet, appears to have been a liability, for a couple of days later Mark was cursing him. 'Yesterday Finch appeared on deck with a face of ashy paleness, his voice shook and was husky with fear. "I beg your pardon, Sir" he whispered. "I beg your pardon Sir, but them five sun 'elmits as got left behind." "Damn" says I, "We must buy some in Smyrna."'[17] He then went on to admit that he had also mislaid the rolls of map-making papers, Mark's walking boots, the camera tripod and all the film. Since Finch had previously also left behind the tables, the mosquito nets, wine, whisky, brandy, the baths, the table, coffee, tea, rice, sugar and the comfortable pillows, this was the last straw. 'With a piercing cry,' wrote Mark, 'I fell upon the deck in a swoon.'[18]

On 20 March 1906, Mark disembarked 'Finch-less' in Alexandretta, which lies at the foot of the Nur Mountains on the southern Turkish coast. Here he met up with his team, consisting of his loyal servant Jacob, acting as dragoman, a Greek cook, Dimitri, and five Syrian muleteers. He found them in excellent spirits and everything was got ashore without difficulty. There was extra good news when it was revealed that 'Finch the distinguished has found all the lost luggage and will be at Aleppo in time to cross the Euphrates.' But he desperately missed Edith. 'It is very lonely here without you and the babies,' he wrote to her from Aleppo, 'and I feel my best work will be done when you join me.' Jacob was presented with new photographs of her, with which he was delighted, agreeing, as Mark wrote, that 'you now look really beautiful, very different from the thin creature they saw at Jerusalem. Jacob said quite unthinkingly "Jamais je ne crede que notre Madame devient si beau que cela [*sic*].'[19]

One of his intentions was to do a study of all the different Kurdish tribes, but for the first time he found loneliness made work hard for him. 'I do miss you so', he wrote, 'but indeed I hope the sacrifices we are both making will be repaid by the work done, but it is hard to do it all the same – I have got 48 brand new tribes – but my very dearest it is difficult plodding along alone. No babies and no Edith make this tour emptier than the desert …' He calculated that they would be together again at the end of June, when he would come to meet her in Constantinople, and he asked her to bring with her a supply of 'Lazenby's Soup Squares' ('1 6d Square will make a Pint and a Half of Strong Nutritious Soup') and 'Compressed Dried Vegetables'. In the meantime a distraction was provided by attempts to sell his horse, which had become completely wild. 'Frantic efforts are being made to sell that swine of a red horse. I think he must have something wrong with his brain for he is becoming almost quite unmanageable, and just as he was on the point of being sold for £25, he yesterday broke out of the stable and tried to savage the purchaser ... it beats anything I ever heard.

On account of this contretemps, Jacob has retired to bed ... to brood over this disaster ...'[20]

The journey began in earnest on 1 April when they left Meskene, to the south-east of Aleppo, to cross the Euphrates into the Jazirah, the plains that lie between the Euphrates and the Tigris that were home to Kurdish and Arab tribes of shepherds. 'When you go into the Jazirah,' wrote Mark, 'it is essential to divest yourself of all preconceived notions. Wipe John Stuart Mill, Omar Khayyam, Burke,

Ruskin, Carlyle and Bernard Shaw out of your mind; learn the book of Job by heart for philosophy, the Book of Judges for Politics, the Arabian Nights (Burton's translation) for ethics; ride by balance, not by grip, keep your girths loose, look out for rat-holes, be polite and dignified in your conversation, *don't* talk about the superiority of the European civilization, and you will learn a good deal. If you adopt any other line of conduct you will very likely get into serious trouble.'[21]

In Roman times the Jazirah was an area of important shrines, vast agricultural cities, flourishing trade, an efficient system of irrigation and wealthy shepherds. By the turn of the twentieth century only the shepherds remained, nomad Kurds from the highlands and Bedouin from the Arabian deserts. 'Between them, these Kurds and Bedawin,' Mark noted, 'have made the Jazirah the merriest and most entertaining little kingdom of disorder ... In March and April, north, south, east and west, all Jazirah is at war, not because the people are bloodily minded, not because they are rapacious, not because they are savage, but because it is such fun. In the spring of the year, when the grass is rich, the camels sleek, the sheep fat, the horses swift, what better sport is there than a foray into your neighbour's pastures? – a twenty hours ride, a wild swoop on some unguarded herds of camels, and a vainglorious homeward flight or perhaps a thirty-mile battle over hill and dale, with 500 young bloods aside, yelling, whooping, brandishing lances, firing from the saddle, tumbling over neck and crop in the dust when a horse misses its footing, surrendering or fleeing when the action becomes too close? Now and again a man is killed it is true: but that is a rare event which adds the necessary spice of danger to the glorious pastime of desert battle.'[22]

Mark's first opportunity to send a letter to Edith came on the fifth day of travel when they reached the town of Raqqa, which boasted a weekly post and a telegraph clerk. The only mishap he had suffered, he told her, was his horse rolling on his saddle, which broke and had to be tied up with a piece of string and was thus not very comfortable. 'I do wish you had been able to do this part of the journey,' he said. 'The weather is quite cold and the people most amusing. The whole place is bubbling over with local wars, but no one has been killed or likely to be … It is lonely without you and I wonder what you are all doing. Dimitri and Finch are both getting a wild look of the desert …

Now I have maps to make, diaries to write, medicine to give to the sick, and the ruins of Ragga [*sic*] to photograph.'[23]

En route to Mosul, Mark described visiting the camp of Ibrahim Pasha, an important Kurdish ruler who held jurisdiction over much of the land through which he was travelling. A tall slimly built man with a large nose, piercing inquisitive eyes, a large mouth, and small and delicately formed hands and feet, he had spies in every town in the district and his camp was known to be a refuge for robbers and evil-doers on condition that they behaved themselves while in his district. 'On our arrival the Pasha came out to greet us and embraced me after the Bedawin fashion – that is by kissing my right shoulder. I was immediately led into the great tent which was supported on over a hundred poles and measured 1,500 square yards of cloth. Coming from the glare of the mid-day sun it was at first difficult to distinguish anything clearly in the recesses of this vast tabernacle, but at the farther end about 150 men were standing around the low divan on which Ibrahim sits. He led me to the divan which was placed before a camel-dung fire, on which stood the usual number of coffee pots. In the course of conversation he showed a wonderfully accurate knowledge of the affairs of Europe, England's relation with Ireland and many matters which pointed of other sources of information than Turkish newspapers, of which of course he had a plentiful supply.'[24]

On the following day the Pasha gave orders to strike camp and move. 'The whole of the baggage train,' described Mark, 'which numbered no fewer than 2,000 animals, was on the march in an hour and a half from the issuing of the order ... On the march the Pasha rode a young white *dalul* (trotting camel) at the head of the caravan, accompanied by 50 horsemen of his private staff and a pack of about 15 couple of gazelle dogs – the whole forming a sufficiently striking picture.'[25] Mark spent five days travelling with the Pasha, whom he described as 'a type of man who passed away in England with Warwick ... In him we see the feudal baron, and the eastern despot and the nomadic chief; amid his tents we may guess some idea of the life in the camps of Timur and Attila ... in his weakness and strength some of the faults and qualities of Mithridates.'[26]

After leaving the Pasha and reaching the Sinjar Mountains, said to be the place where Noah's Ark finally came to a rest, Mark encountered his only spot of trouble. This was the home of the Ezidi Kurds, known as the Yazidis, who for centuries have been dubbed by Moslems 'devil-worshippers' because a spirit they worship, Malak Taus, is known in Arabic as 'Shaytan', which is the word for devil. 'I always understood,' Mark wrote, 'that the Yezidis, who inhabit the mountains were a much maligned people, groaning under a cruel oppression, and so on, brave, courteous, industrious, with an ingrained love of freedom ... My experience, however, does not encourage me to put much faith in the theory …'[27] Entering the pass, his party were suddenly surrounded by men dressed in white robes, brandishing rifles in a threatening manner. 'The men were wild-looking ruffians,' he continued, 'with a lowering look of animal ferocity in their eyes that might well give one pause to think whether one had been wise to visit this nest of Satan's brood. After an hour's anxious ride, we reached a small encampment. Not a word of welcome was vouchsafed us. As I ate my lunch a savage-looking man snatched the food out of my plate and wolfed it without a word. On every hill, white figures flitted about crying shrilly, and pointing to my party. My escort looked doubtful and anxious. Presently a tall somber [*sic*] man came up and spoke to us in Arabic. He was a Shaykh. "Go," he said. "I will go with you. Go quickly, you will bring trouble to us if you stay and trouble to yourself. Mount and be off!"[28] He later told Edith, 'In Jebel Singar … I tumbled into a rebellion and just got through by the skin of my teeth.'[29]

Amongst the very few letters written by Edith to Mark that have survived are a number sent to him during this period of separation. They are particularly poignant not just because they were missing each other so much, but because she was suffering terrible anxiety over an illness that baby Richard had been suffering from. Though he was on the mend, 'he must be kept on his back for six weeks'.[30] Little Freya, however, was thriving. 'I show her your photograph every day and she says "bonjour Papa" to it. There is a picture of Our Lord that she insists on calling "Papa" or "Garcon." I tried to impress the name Jesus on her but she paid little attention to my religious instructions.'[31]

Replying to her from Mosul, where he was staying with some Dominican friars, he told her, 'My heart bled for you when I thought of the agonies you must have suffered alone. Poor Freya with her red sausage hands has been deserted. How she will punch baby's head when she gets hold of him … How I miss you. I had intended trying to meet you 1 June but as I see you ought to stay a little longer in England I will keep to my old plans. We must both make sacrifices for the baby mustn't we?'

He asked her to bring a new camera for him and a good tripod. 'Re. Camera, damn the expense, and please take 40 or 50 photographs in England with the engine before you bring it out. I must make sure of good photographs, and at present my makeshift tripod is rather like a prehistoric pup ...'[32]

Mosul was stiflingly hot, the only cool time of day being at 4 a.m. when he was asleep. It made him feel like 'a lump of dough' and this, together with the prospect of the delay in seeing her again, cast him into gloom. 'I don't know how I shall pass the next 8 weeks without you,' he told her, 'but it will be like heaven when you come.'[33]

Heaven, after the hell of Mosul, which he considered 'an evil city', a hotbed of drunkenness and debauchery, where there lingered 'that dead Paganism which the Cross and Mohammed have slain, but have as yet been unable to annihilate'.[34] He couldn't wait to leave and his last view of the town, he wrote, 'was typical of the whole place. Well within the city, a cluster of some three hundred houses stands by the river. This quarter is the abattoir and tannery and dyery for the whole town. Its streets are ankle-deep in decaying guts and offal; the kennels run with congealing blood and stinking dye in sluggish and iridescent streams, nauseous to behold and abominable in odour. A fume of decaying flesh hangs in the air, piles of dung, horns and hoofs stand in the filthy alleys, while here and there the puffed carcasses of beasts, diseased and cast aside by the butchers, lie an offence against the sun.

The houses are daubed with clotted filth, while naked men flit to and fro upon their noxious business.'[35]

Owing to a war that had broken out in the Jazirah, the route that Mark had planned to take on leaving Mosul was unsafe, and since there were rumours of something 'wrapt [*sic*] in mystery' taking place on the Persian frontier, he decided to go and 'take a peep'. When he got there, he heard reports of Turkish troops moving to the front and local tribesmen having been told to hold themselves in readiness to advance on Persia, but of actual hostilities there was no sign, and he was unable to discover exactly what the situation was. 'What is going on there I really haven't the least notion,' he wrote to Francis Maunsell, the military attaché in Constantinople. 'There are 31 Battalions and 4 mountain Batteries and Shaykh Sadiq and a Ferik[36] and a Yavar[37] and Pashas, but what they are doing they do not know, nor do I. I went to ask, but before I could put any questions, they all said "Why are we here? Have you any English newspapers?"'[38]

In the rocky mountainous district around the frontier, their horses and mules began to cast their shoes, while Jacob's German brown top boots also fell foul of the rough terrain.

'3 hours walking brought him to this state,' recounted Mark, 'so he had to be put on a donkey. Then it began to rain and rain and rain and rain so we had to stop in a filthy village and live on eggs. Then we started off again, what with the rocky mountains, the swamps and sore feet 10 miles a day was our normal march. At last we reached a village called Deyra where to our horror we learned that the floods had carried away the ferry and that there was no blacksmith within 20 miles and he was at Erbil. So grimly we had to trudge back to Erbil which we reached last night.' He was cheered up, however, by the thought that he and Edith would soon be reunited. 'O ... my dearest dear, within six weeks we shall be together again never to part – it is terribly lovely – and reminds me of the dismal life I led before I was married – still I have done some work, but nothing to what I shall do when I have you to talk to ...'[39]

En route to Zahko, an ancient Jewish community known as 'the Jerusalem of Assyria', they ran into trouble crossing the river Zab, a tributary of the Tigris. 'Oh such a job getting here,' he wrote to Edith. 'The floods were simply frightful and our poor animals had to swim over the Great Zab just as in the Assyrian inscriptions ...'[40]

The problem was that the ferry was doubly overloaded and soon began to take on water in the fast-flowing river. The muleteers panicked and began to throw the mules overboard. 'In the confusion an oar was lost,' Mark later wrote, 'and the danger became very serious. A horse jumped into the river, nearly sinking the boat which drifted helplessly downstream. Never did I hear such heart-rending prayers and imprecations as came across the river. The dread of death pushes the Arab mind to horrible limits ... In a few moments the boat was driven ashore, whereupon the men who had been shrieking for mercy fell to fighting among themselves with obscene words and ill-directed blows, hysteric tears of half-quenched fear and an omnipotent and bestial fury fixed in one strange passion ... By us the passions are attempted to be suppressed; with Syrians they are cultivated.'[41]

Shaken, they then rode another 100 miles in the boiling sun. 'At last we got here quite worn out,' he told Edith. 'I had not even tasted rice for 11 days having had to eat boiled wheat instead. My stomach was like a football from it ... Finch has had sore feet, but they are nearly well and I am for the moment quite done up. However we shall soon be in the cool mountains and by the time you get this letter you will be packing up your trunks to join me ...'[42] By now their long separation was beginning to take its toll. 'Oh how lonely I am without you,' he wrote. 'All the Muleteers are praying for your advent as they say I am getting so ferocious.'[43]

That Edith also missed Mark acutely is clear from the fact that she was prepared to leave her children for what was to be weeks, in order to be with him. 'Please dear little fellow do meet me at Constantinople,' she pleaded, 'then I shall not have to go so far to see you and have to wait such a long time ... and I shall be so miserable at leaving the babies that I shall want you to console me directly. Nothing but you my dearest could make me leave them for such a dreadfully long time.' She declared herself unafraid of any dangers involved in the journey, except 'there is only one risk I don't want to run and that is being carried off to a Pasha's harem!'[44]

A rendezvous in Constantinople proved impossible, however, as it would have lost them too much time, and he instructed her, 'I shall meet you at Sinope, my dearest, at Sinope ... We will spend 4 or 5 days ... waiting for the caravan and then travel. Now enclosed, you will find a list of things wanted ...

  1 Mosquito nets.   21/3/24

  1 Camera
  2. Tripod
  3. Films, Premo pack.
  4. Luncheon Basket
  5. Cakes
  6. 1 doz ½ pairs Jaeger socks
  7. 2 pair linen spats
  8. ditto for yourself
  9. Do not bring any
      Ham.
 10 Cartridges as mentioned
      before
 11 Compressed vegetables
 12 2 flannel shirts
 13 2 silk ties

Edith left London on 27 June on board the Orient Express, and after spending a few days with the O'Connors in Therapia boarded the SS *Imogen* for Sinope. 'We had a very disagreeable tossing for 27 hours,' she recorded in her journal, 'but Captain Benson was so kind and so concerned at my sufferings that he made every effort to make the time pass as easily as possible. At last, at 3.a.m. on July 5 we anchored off Sinope and M. who had been sitting on a hill with a telescope looking for us came on board.' He later wrote that he never forgot 'that glorious day' when he 'heard the whistle announcing' her arrival. Together they rode a thousand miles, from Sinope east across to the Persian border, then west via Aleppo to the Mediterranean, where they embarked for London. An account of this journey was included by Mark in his final major work, *The Caliphs' Last Heritage*, a study of Islam and the Ottoman Empire, work on which he had

started while at the Embassy in Constantinople, but which was not to
be published till 1915, when the war in Europe had spread to Turkey
and interest in the subject was suddenly revived.

Chapter 7

Family Life

When first approached in 1901 by the Conservatives of Buckrose, the seat held by his Uncle Christopher from 1885 to 1892, as to whether he would stand as their MP, Mark's views on Parliament were still coloured by the healthy cynicism of youth. 'I cannot talk sonorous twaddle for endless hours,'[1] he had told his then fiancée Edith, while railing in a letter to his cousin Henry Cholmondeley, 'as regards POLITIX [sic] you can tell the Worshipful Conservatives that I am *not* A LITTLE ENGLANDER, AN ANARCHIST, A SOCIALIST, A CHRISTIAN SCIENTIST, A PECULIAR PERSON … AND FURTHER … That it is impossible to be a Conservative when there is nothing left to Conserve. That it would be foolish to abolish the House of Peers lest something worse comes in its place. That education requires more attention than it receives. That the Poor Laws require considerable revision. That the Game laws require attention both Destructively and Constructively. That Home Rule is absurd. That the Army requires an entirely new remodelling. That if we are not able to produce an efficient army of mercenaries, we must resort to conscription. That if matters come to the continental status of Labour Socialists and Cranks and the rest, I would gladly stand for Parliament on the side of "the rest." But as that is not yet the case and as I hope I am neither A professional Buffoon, An Office-Seeker or A Hypocrite that they will for the present let my political existence be relegated to the future.'[2]

Six years on, with the experience gained from working for both Wyndham in Ireland and O'Connor in Constantinople, together with his first-hand knowledge of the Middle East, a subject on which he was becoming something of an authority, he finally felt he had views that might be best aired in Parliament, writing to Edith from Diyarbekir in south-eastern Turkey, 'Politics will really be great fun in a years time. O don't you never fear, I'm going into them. We will give battle to cant and incompetence, and we will fight or buy those Labour members.'[3] No sooner had he returned from his travels at the end of 1906 than the rumour-mill was at work and the gossip had it that he might stand as an MP. It soon reached the ears of the *Hull Daily Mail*, which, on a bitterly cold January morning, dispatched a reporter up to Sledmere who, on meeting the young heir to the Estate, described him as 'slim, tall, alert, wire and whipcord and nerves, [with] a clear Anglo-Saxon countenance and a fair moustache'.[4]

'I have seen the young Captain before,' he reported, 'spick and span in his regimentals reciting to citizen soldiery "Barrack tragedies" that befell "Paddy O'Hagan" and "Sandy McNab" and the likes, and I saw him now as Mark Sykes, the studious scholar, the cultured gentleman. What he does, he does thoroughly, and when I found him he was putting the finishing touches to the lecture he was to deliver tomorrow.

'He has the versatility of the Sykeses for generations past. He will quote you Plato, "pulverize" a proposition from Euclid, and crown it all in sixty seconds with an anecdote that will give you "laughter pains". He is a raconteur born. Broad-minded from world travelling, and patriotic to the backbone, he debates with a calm assurance that spells faculty. One day we shall see him twitting Winston Churchill in mellow tones, and chiding Lloyd George with stinging martial emphasis ...'

On this occasion Mark was giving nothing away. 'You know, Captain,' continued the reporter, 'that the opinion is solid throughout Buckrose that you are the very man to win back Buckrose to Conservatism? The gallant Captain never turned a hair. He applied a match to his cigarette and through the smoke he smiled amiably towards me and said – absolutely nothing ...'[5] Three months later, however, the newspaper was able to report, 'At the AGM of the Buckrose Conservative Association on April 11 Captain Mark Sykes will be formally adopted as the prospective Unionist candidate for Buckrose.' His agreement to be adopted delighted the Conservatives, whose fortunes had changed since their original approach, the constituency having fallen to the Liberals in 1892, with whom it had remained, the current MP, Luke White, holding a majority of 1,600. To have adopted such an energetic and ambitious young man who was also well-known in the locality was a boon to them.

The priority for Mark on his return home, however, was to find a house for his wife and family. Since his father was firmly ensconced at Sledmere with 'Madame', and showed no willingness to move out in favour of his son, he instructed Henry Cholmondeley to find them somewhere suitable. He came up with a 400-acre farm on the estate called Eddlethorpe, a surprising choice as Mark had already expressed his distaste for the house, which he considered to be a 'masterpiece' of the 'hideous and revolting' school, 'a vulgar, heavy, clumsy, toneless, soulless image' of the builder's 'beastly mind'.[6] Rather than simply dismiss it, Mark saw it as a challenge in which he could experiment with his ideas about architecture, which were as strong as all the ideas he held. 'Half the effects in architecture of the Domestic kind,' he told Cholmondeley, 'are gained by colour, and height and shade, just as much as by shape, only the colours must be laid on thick and not too carefully … because you happen to have a dark grey climate, there is no reason that I can see why houses should be disgusting in colour. It's a sheer waste of ugliness.'[7]

Using the estate architect, Mr Collett, a man whose experience up to date had been limited to the erection of cottages and farm buildings, he transformed the simple Victorian farmhouse into a flamboyant fantasy the like of which had never been seen on the Yorkshire Wolds. It was a hotchpotch of designs, in a vaguely Arts and Crafts style, which might have been described as 'The Wolds meets the Orient'. He told his friend Edmund Sandars, 'I will excite your curiosity by saying there is a dash of Kastamuni in it.'[8] Two new wings were added, giving the house fifteen bedrooms. Attached to one of them was a three-storey tower, topped by a cupola, which was named 'Mark's Tower', and contained his study, library and dressing-room. There were also a chapel, a nursery, and a kitchen which was approached by four archways surmounted by Cufic inscriptions and covered with Anatolian tiles brought back from his travels. 'I have ventured to spend £190[9] on tiles,' he had told Cholmondeley, adding proudly, 'When you realise that I have got 2,700, nearly as good as the best … you will understand. The colours are wonderful and the designs I am not ashamed of. I had to go to a horrible hole in the middle of Asia Minor and bargain with the maker from 9.00 A.M. to 11 P.M. – starting at £300 & working down to £190. Here is the maker …'[10]

The exterior was bold enough to draw astonished gasps from passers-by. The ground floor was entirely of red brick, the upper storeys were in grey stucco, the hipped roof tiles were red, the chimneys white, while the cupola, the balconies and the surrounding fence were all in black and white. A shield bearing the Sykes coat of arms was placed above the neo-Georgian entrance, topped by a large brass Triton. It was, to say the least, a highly eccentric building, but it suited Mark's extrovert nature. The children loved it. It reminded them of a house out of a fairytale.

While work on Eddlethorpe progressed, the family lived in another estate farmhouse, called Menethorpe, and it was here, on 17 November 1907, that Edith gave birth to twins, a boy, Christopher, and a girl, Everilda, named after the patron saint of Kirkham Priory, a nearby ruined abbey. The name, which Monty James had originally suggested to Mark, was soon found to be a bit of a mouthful, and she was nick-named Petsy. When the new house was finally ready, at the beginning of 1908, it easily absorbed the fast-growing family and the large staff they had accumulated – a governess for Freya, nurses for Richard and the twins, a cook, butler, footman, chauffeur, coachman, groom, gardener and under-gardener.

Considering the unhappy nature of his own childhood, it is not surprising that Mark took to family life. He was able to do with his own children all the things he had missed out on when he was growing up. 'He was a delightful father,' wrote Edith; 'in his leisure moments he invented wonderful games, and when we lived at Eddlethorpe, the whole lawn would be covered with a miniature railway system, each child being responsible for a point or signal.'[11] In the winter months, the railway, made by the firm of Basset Lowke, was brought inside and laid out along the top-floor corridor, the track winding in and out of the various bedrooms. The locomotives were clockwork and were wound up with a key. Mark took it very seriously, and had the children and their friends manning the points to guard against any accidents. 'We had to keep our heads to avoid collisions,' remembered Nino Hunter, a nephew of Edith's, 'watched closely by Uncle Mark who was terribly happy when all went well. But I do remember an occasion when poor Freya got it wrong, and there was a nasty mishap. That time Uncle Mark got quite cross with her.'[12]

He devised elaborate war games, played on the lawn, with coloured blocks and sticks representing cavalry, infantry, guns, wagons, trains and houses, while artillery and shrapnel rounds were signified by the throwing of different-sized bags. Since it was the children's job to move the sticks and blocks, while the adults had all the fun of throwing the bags, this was not their favourite game. They much preferred the Yorkshire stories he wrote for them, which he would recite in a broad East Riding accent, and the tales of his travels in far-off lands, often woven into *Arabian Nights* fantasies, with which he held them spellbound. There were also 'passionate family excursions led by him to York and Beverley and to little-known churches in the East Riding, where there was a Norman arch or a Saxon font, or to some place where there was a ruin – it hardly mattered what – provided it dated from far beyond living memory'.[13]

His great skill as an illustrator was put to good use for 'the babies', as he used to refer to them, and they remembered his entertainments for the rest of their lives. On one occasion, recalled his son Christopher, 'he procured a copy of that most grotesque of English classics, *The Castle of Otranto*, by Horace Walpole, and every evening when he could, he read us a chapter, accompanied by coloured illustrations of the more striking incidents made previously by himself. The pictures were of the kind that can make you laugh aloud, and I remember that he used to laugh aloud as he drew them.'[14]

When Mark and Edith were both away, the children were left in the care of the two nannies, Marie Duntz and Lizzie Nicholson, farmer's daughters whose ideas of what constituted suitable entertainment for their charges were occasionally questionable. One day, Marie told them that she was taking them for a special treat. They were dressed up in their very best outdoor clothes and taken to the farm, which was across the road. There, in the middle of the yard, stood what Freya, a good little Catholic girl, took to be an altar. Beside it stood a man dressed in a long white coat, while on the ground were a number of large basins and bowls and various knives. Then two men dragged a large pink pig, shrieking its head off, into the yard. 'I suddenly realized what we were in for,' remembered Freya, 'and I became absolutely petrified. Richard immediately burst into tears and roared the place down. Lizzie tried to control the twins, who were only two! Before our eyes a sort of hammer and chisel were placed in the middle of the pig's forehead. It was in this way stunned and fell down, and at the same time its throat was cut from ear to ear. I have never seen so much blood in all my life. It was all collected in a basin. By that time I was pea-green in the face.' Luckily at that moment, Lizzie protested and the children were taken away. Later that afternoon they were taken down to have tea with their grandmother, Lady Gorst. 'She was a very sweet old lady,' Freya recollected, 'and she asked, "And what did you do this morning, dears?" and I blurted out, "We saw the pigs killed!" There was the most awful rumpus.'15

On rare occasions, in the absence of their parents, the children were sent to Sledmere to spend a few days with their grandfather. It was an alarming experience. They would arrive with their nannies and take up residence on the top floor of the house, all other floors and passages being strictly out of bounds. Each morning they would be dressed up in their best clothes and led downstairs to the boudoir, to say good morning to Sir Tatton. There he sat in state, with Madame by his side. The routine never varied. They would enter the room, shake his hand and say, 'Good morning, Grandpapa.' Then they would leave, either to go out for a walk, or to return to the confines of the nursery.

Just as he had been by his mother, so Mark treated his own children as equals. While staying at Eddlethorpe one day, his brother-in-law, Harold Gorst, was walking with Mark down a passage, when they were confronted with the sight and sound of Richard, aged two, in the throes of a major tantrum. He was lying on the floor on his back, kicking violently at anybody who dared to approach and screaming his head off that he would not go out for a walk. Marie, his nurse, and Edith were both at the end of their tether. 'Suddenly Mark,' recalled Harold, 'after surveying his son and heir with that queer little contraction of his eyebrows, swooped down, picked him up in his arms, bore him away kicking and struggling into a neighbouring bedroom, and locked the door behind him.' Harold and the two women then stood in the passage expecting any moment to hear the sounds of a hearty spanking being administered to the furious child. Instead, to their astonishment, the shrieks died away to silence. When Mark, three or four minutes later, emerged from the room leading a perfectly serene and normal Richard by the hand, they asked him how he had effected such a miracle. 'I sat him in a dry basin on the washstand,' replied Mark, 'and reasoned with him.'[16]

During the years from 1907 to 1911, Mark spent more time in England with his family than he ever had done and was ever to do again. Winning the seat for Buckrose, however, was to be an uphill struggle, since the Conservatives were now out in the cold, the Liberals, under Henry Campbell-Bannerman, having achieved a landslide victory in the 1906 General Election. 'I am now home for good,' Mark wrote to his old tutor, Egerton Beck, 'and making a political plunge. Tory Democracy is what I am going to try and push, for all it is worth.'[17] This was the philosophy of one of Mark's heroes, Benjamin Disraeli, the great social reformer, who had formulated the policy of progressive Conservatism, declaring that the Conservative party ought to adopt rather than oppose popular reforms, and should challenge the claims of the Liberals to pose as champions of the masses. Under his leadership the Conservatives had thrived. Citing him in his acceptance speech, Mark declared that since then the party had lost its ideals; ideals such as unity 'between employer and employed, class and class, creed and creed, father and son, colony and mother-land, prince and subject, farm and village, village and city, city and kingdom, kingdom and colony, colony and Empire'. These were Mark's ideals too, and he was never to abandon them. The Liberals might be in power now, but in his opinion, and in a remarkable flash of foresight, Radicals being better at demolishing than building, 'twenty years hence there will be only two parties – Socialists and Tories'.

Mark may have distrusted the Labour movement, which he considered too rooted in urban bureaucracy – 'once a State takes over any concern, it proceeds to breed officials like rabbits'[18] – but he never underestimated its power, stating openly, 'If I were a working man, my house insanitary, my wages low, my child sweated, my wife ailing, my employment hazardous, I should vote Labour.'[19] He thus encouraged every member of the Tory party to show himself at heart a true Labour member and to outdo the trade unionists in getting the working man 'a good house, a good wage, a good education', the cost of which could be met by higher taxation on wealth and imports.

Though Mark was undoubtedly extremely conscientious as a candidate, and worked assiduously hard on his campaign, his chances of election were hampered by the fact that he had chosen to stand at a time when local issues were very much overshadowed by more important national ones. In 1908, the then Chancellor of the Exchequer, David Lloyd George, had introduced the Old Age Pensions Act, which promised to pay between 1*s* and 5*s* a week to people over seventy. To pay for this, he introduced a People's Budget to raise revenue of sixteen million pounds, which included increases in taxation for the rich and a Land Tax. When the House of Lords chose to block this, their action precipitated a constitutional crisis, and, in January 1910, the Prime Minister, Herbert Asquith, called an election. Mark's opponent, the standing MP, was Sir Luke White, a self-made man with a broad Yorkshire accent, and, class feeling being aroused as it had been, the Liberals made capital out of the difference between their man and the aristocratic Sykes. 'Follow the Gospel and put Mark before Luke,' cried his supporters, but to no avail. The forces of Liberalism were mobilized, and Mark lost to White by 218 votes.

As it happened there was a second election in 1910, in December, this time precipitated by Asquith's desire to force through a Parliament Act, designed to reduce the powers of the House of Lords. It was a punishment for their having attempted to block the People's Budget. Once again Mark was defeated, but he had not helped himself by, in the heat of the moment at one meeting, referring to his opponent as 'an unpatriotic humbug'. Of this outburst, Sir Luke made suitable capital. He would appear at meetings bearing the meek expression of a martyr and, endeavouring to speak, would find himself overcome with emotion, only able to repeat, as the tears streamed down his cheeks, the words, 'E ca'd me a Oomboog!'[20] Mark was philosophical about his second defeat. 'If you choose to give me a political career,' he wrote, 'I will take it up, but if not, I have my books and can go back to my plough.'[21]

He did not in fact go back to the plough. He returned to the East, hopefully to raise his spirits enough to fight a third election. This time he chose to pay his first visit to French North Africa, sailing to Tunis on a ship with fifty First Class passengers and one bath, for which, he wrote, 'there is no competition. I have not heard the bathroom door clank once since I left it.' In addition the on-board rules stated that each cabin had to be filled with a minimum of three people. 'Behold my cabin,' he noted ...[22]

His discomfort was a prelude to a trip on which any enjoyment he might have experienced from the country was marred by what he saw of French Imperial rule. 'This country is not like anything I've seen,' he wrote to Edith from the Roman site of Maktar, 'with high mountains covered with scrub and yellow ground. The people are really wretched, starving, depressed, aloof, and heavily taxed. The French have at least 15,000 soldiers in the country, and one battalion of Tommies would more than suffice. Conscription is in full swing, and nothing escapes taxation, dogs and cats inclusive. There is no education of natives and considerable extortion ...' Coming across some 'half angry, – half frightened Arabs' they talked of two years of famine with no remission of taxes. 'You cannot believe the real A-brutisment [*sic*] of this country. It's perfectly hellish. It is unjust, hypocritical, unbusiness-like and doesn't pay – huge official palaces, bad roads, red tape. O, it is an eye-opener … There is no hope for these poor Arabs, and the ungodly, useless, lazy French are rotten.'[23]

He was particularly outraged by the behaviour of the French in Algeria, where he saw the natives ruled over by hundreds of petty officials, 'petit fonctionaires [*sic*] who … are the very type of the English Trade Union Official. Algeria and Tunis are hot-beds of jobs for men who want £80 to £100 a year to do nothing but fill in forms … It is a most sickening spectacle to see these odious incompetents muddling (deliberately) a fine people and a fine country.' Though the Arab population outnumbered the whites by three to one, and railways were being built in all directions, mines were being exploited, wines grown and all kinds of profitable businesses started, 'in all these things no native skilled labour is allowed and there is practically no education of the natives, there are no native police to speak of, and hashish eating or smoking, vice of every kind and drunkenness are unrepressed'. It was blatantly obvious to him that the Arabs loathed the French and had no moral fear of them, but that they were bound hand and foot by education, by opportunity and by force. 'I cannot imagine that such a regime can endure,' he mused, 'but per contra I cannot see any chance of a native rising, or any chance of the white proletariat starting or approving any agitation in favour of equal treatment of natives and whites.'[24]

From Tebessa he wrote, 'I can stand this accursed country no longer – It is too vile for words so am off to Spain as quickly as I can get.'[25] His journey was delayed, however, because on reaching the port of Oran he found the ship on which he had taken passage to be a Spanish tramp steamer of 800 tons, loaded below the plimsoll line, with a list to port and only one cabin for himself and Jacob. Even though it meant two days' delay, he decided to forgo his place and went to the opera instead to see a performance of Massenet's *Hérodiade*, 'a very poor thing,' he reported, 'with one tune and a lot of brass and Oriental local colour. The Corps de Ballet were really too awful.

However Herod was very good

and Herodias first rate

In one of his last letters from what he described as 'this abominable country', Mark told Edith, 'I trust to give you better accounts of Spain.'[26] He disembarked in Cartagena on 28 February, but only by the skin of his teeth. 'I have been thro' some dangers but never have I been in such a collection or suite of real hairbreadth escapes as befell us twixt Oran and this place … at 3.15am I was aroused by the fog-horn which sounded every two minutes – I went on deck at five and found the ship in such a fog as I have never seen. It was impenetrable, while the sea seemed alive with ships – and not ships that play the game – ships that didn't know the rules of the road – ships with Captains too drunk to sound their horns … a crazy huddled fleet of ships going from Gib. to Malta, Gib. to Alexandria, Gib. to Genoa, Marseilles to Marbella, Spanish Coasters, Tramps and what not, all running in different directions thro' this dense grey deadly fog … It was the most terrifying business I have ever taken part in.'[27]

Cartagena was in the throes of carnival when he arrived: 'altho' I was half asleep, I went out and saw the most extraordinary sight … the whole of the girls of the town (with their mamas) sat about four deep on each side of a long street illuminated with dimmed lanterns. The whole of the male population walked up and down throwing confetti. Not one rude act or one unpleasant word or one drunken man, soldiers, sailors, officers and anyone else rich and poor patrolled in this way – the girls looked extraordinarily pretty and were wonderfully well bred and natural, the men very jolly …'[28] After a few days, however, his first impressions were cast aside. 'I am getting very sick of Spaniards and their ways,' he complained. 'They are such conceited fools they do not realise that

'A. They have lost South America.
B. Lost North Africa.
C. Lost Cuba.
D. Lost the Phillipines [*sic*].
E. Been thrashed silly by the Moroccans – because they are stupid, proud and lazy.'

He saw the educated class as blaming all misfortune on either the monarchy or the Church, when in fact it was down to their own 'hopeless conceit and hopeless incapacity'.[29]

Nevertheless he was fascinated by Spain and kept Edith entertained with accounts of his adventures, riding on donkeys through beautiful wooded countryside, passing wild gardens and through towns 'more picturesque than I can tell you',[30] where more often than not they had never previously seen an Englishman. In the village of Arroba, reached after a day's ride through wild empty country, he was of particular interest to the younger members of the community. 'The children (Spanish children rule the roost completely) took charge of me and made a song "The Englishman is bigger than an Andalusian Bull" and accompanied me round the town in this manner.'

Above all he was spellbound by the extraordinary variety of architecture in Spain, perhaps best represented in its numerous churches. Citing the Iglesia de San Pedro in Ciudad Real as an example of Spanish Gothic at its most garish, he described to Edith his ideas about how such a church came about. 'Take King's Coll Chapel, block up all the windows in 1620 – put up altars every six years from 1720 to 1845 – paint all the stalls green in 1820, blue in 1850, and yellow & red in 1870 but never scrape off the colours – paint the graining pink and the background pale blue with gold stars, open one of the blocked windows in 1848 and fill with English stained glass, hang pictures of hell and martyrdoms of St Lawrence on the walls beyond reach of a duster, move the choir to the back of the church in 1730, block up the main door, knock a hole in the chancel and make that the door, put a statue in a winding sheet, with half closed glass eyes that roll, laid full length on one of the altars, in the dark it looks like a real corpse, light a little red lamp under a crucifix life sized, with real hair and blood varnished to shine in the flickering of the lamp – put a statue of Our Lady in black crepe and silk with a crinoline, gum tears on cheeks, glass eyes, real hair, cover with gold, silver, brass, tinsel, put in a glass case, and cut a squint in the wall so that the light shines horribly on a white face in a dark cell – fill every spare corner with candlesticks, vases, lecterns, benches, clear away all chairs and put down rush mats and you have an average Spanish Gothic Church ...'[31]

It was typical of Mark that when he finally returned home in April, he was already thinking of going back to Spain. 'I have an idea of a tour in this country which would be amusing and useful to the world at large,' he told what must have by then been an exasperated Edith, 'i.e. to work out the Peninsular War step by step and photograph each battlefield and strategic point travelling always by caravan. It would make a splendid lecture afterwards.'[32] No doubt to her relief, this project was soon forgotten in the maelstrom of events that followed his return, not least of which was the ongoing search to find him a seat in Parliament. In this quest he was championed by his old mentor, George Wyndham, who had been travelling up and down the country promoting his protégé. 'I may tell you,' he assured Mark, 'that I spoke to fifteen meetings in twelve constituencies, and ... I was sent up and down three times and travelled well over 2,600 miles.' By the end of May they had considered seats from Lincolnshire down to Plymouth, all to no avail, at which point Mark's attention was sharply diverted from politics by a family disaster.

He was in London on the afternoon of 23 May, when he received a telegram from Henry Cholmondeley. It was short and to the point. 'SLEDMERE HOUSE ON FIRE. CHOLMONDELEY.'[33] He dropped everything and caught the 3.25 train to York. The fire had started because a roof-beam that protruded into the chimney above the kitchen in the north-east wing had begun to smoulder, and after several days had ignited. The flames, small at first, had inched their way forward until they made contact with other beams supporting the roof. Their slow progress meant that by the time the first suspicious wisps of smoke were seen oozing out of the brickwork of a chimney, the fire had really begun to take hold. The alarm had been raised at about noon, just as his father was sitting down to his lunch. The great bell of the hall was rung, and all the men employed on the estate, farmhands, grooms, coachmen, foresters, bricklayers and carpenters, had been summoned to help. Even the children were called out from the village school. When Henry Cholmondeley entered the Dining-Room to tell the blissful unaware Sir Tatton that the house was on fire and that he must leave at once, his warnings had gone unheeded, for at that moment the eccentric old man was interested in nothing but his food. 'I must finish my pudding', he said, 'finish my pudding.'

There were two fire brigades in the district, the nearest at Driffield, eight miles away, and the other at Malton, twelve miles distant. Both had been summoned, but in the meantime all present had been organized into a human chain and begun a bucket service from the reservoir which supplied the house. Just as this was beginning to prove useless, since it was impossible to get access to the seat of the fire, an advanced guard arrived from Malton, the first being Sidney Yorke, the deputy-head fireman, on his motorbike. 'I never saw such a terrible sight in my life,' he wrote later. 'The roof had got good hold then.'[34] He was followed by his chief, Captain Walker, who brought a quantity of hose, which was attached to fire hydrants near the house, and ultimately unsuccessful attempts were made to play water onto the flames now issuing from the roof at the north-east corner.

Cholmondeley had then taken a vital decision. Seeing that the fire was still burning fairly slowly, he had ordered his human chain to concentrate all efforts on salvaging as much of the contents of the house as possible, many of which were great treasures. Starting on the upper bedroom floors, with the men at the head, then the women and finally, spilling out onto the lawn, the children at the far end, they began by rescuing anything that was easily moveable, such as china, glass, pictures, carpets and smaller pieces of furniture. 'I may as well say,' wrote Yorke, 'a man can go through a lot; I myself have had some very rough and trying experiences in the late South African War; but when one sees female servants in print dresses & caps coming in and out of burning rooms with their aprons full of books etc and all working as cool and collected without the slightest panic, it was enough to make any man's nerves work up to their utmost pitch.'[35] In the vast

Library another group were engaged in throwing the thousands of books out of the windows into sheets and blankets held by those below. Others were unscrewing fine mahogany doors, prising out marble chimneypieces and carefully taking down the collection of family portraits.

'The servants behaved with wonderful pluck and coolness,' observed a reporter from the local paper, 'in removing furniture from the burning rooms, the maidservants acting as coolly and bravely as the men. The fire, however, was now gaining rapid hold and was fanned by a slight breeze, which caused all the upper rooms of the east wing to blaze fiercely.'[36] At half-past two, the Driffield Brigade had finally arrived, but, even though there was no shortage of water, their manual pumps proved quite inadequate to the task, the pressure from the reservoir, used solely for household purposes, being far too low. Shortly after three, the Malton Brigade were on the scene, but even their powerful steam-driven pump, which was able to send streams of water on to the roof and into the blazing upper storeys, did no good, the blaze being now quite out of control. The best they could do was to keep the walls of the rooms sufficiently cool while the salvage work continued.

The roof of the east wing was the first to go, falling in with a 'great crash', but this seemed merely to strengthen the determination of the workers. 'Notwithstanding the menacing nature of their task,' commented the local paper, 'the rescue parties worked most splendidly, and the way in which the rooms were emptied of their principal contents without confusion or disorder was really wonderful.' A new hazard was caused by the large quantities of molten lead from the roof, which poured down the walls and threatened to splash anyone who came too close to it. The men worked on undeterred. As one huge painting was carried precariously down a burning staircase, supervised by the under-gamekeeper, he was heard to mutter, 'Now lads, don't damage t'frame.'[37] There were many narrow escapes, not the least being Sidney Yorke, who was in the Library standing on a pair of steps while he played water onto the blazing bookcases. 'At this time', he recalled, 'the ceiling at the far end of the room fell. This bookcase having now got well ablaze and the ceiling etc falling in upon us, Capt. Walker ordered all out of the room ... but before I could get down the middle part of the ceiling fell in sending the steps right from under me. The plaster fell on my head and shoulders but I scrambled out although partly stunned, being the last one to leave this magnificent library.'[38] He made his escape down a ladder from an open window, and helped to load the huge quantity of books onto wagons which carted them away to be stored in the church and the Coach House.

When Mark's train steamed into York, the station master was there to deliver him another telegram. 'INFORM MARK SYKES EX.3.25 TRAIN FROM LONDON SLEDMERE HOUSE COMPLETELY GUTTED. VALUABLES SAVED. CHOLMONDELEY.'[39] A car was waiting for him, and when he finally arrived in Sledmere, the scene on the lawn was extraordinary, with furniture and fittings, china, bed linen and mattresses, statues, gold and silver plate, paintings and books strewn around as far as the eye could see. In the midst of it all the melancholy figure of his father was pacing up and down, his hands held firmly behind his back.

He had one last request. In the Hall there stood a very fine piece of sculpture, a marble statue of Apollo Belvedere. It had been left till last since it was thought it might escape the flames. However, since the centre of the house was by now blazing and roaring as through a gigantic chimney, it was obvious that the statue had no chance of survival. Sir Tatton asked if it might be saved, a difficult task as it was reckoned to weigh close to a ton, and though the ceiling of the Hall was still intact, the back and east sides were fiercely blazing. 'Scores of hands volunteered to remove the statue,' recorded the correspondent of the *Yorkshire Post*. 'Jets of water were poured on the ceiling, and the hall flooded. Water was also poured on the walls behind the statue, which was itself drenched, to render it cool enough to handle. The front door was removed, and the jambs wrenched down to admit the passage of the large life-size figure. With admirable skill it was lowered from its pedestal into the arms of the stalwart farm labourers and helpers, and finally carried out, with barely a break or scratch to the lawn.' It was the last act of salvage possible.

Throughout the night the Fire Brigades worked to keep down the flames, but it was not until noon of the following day that the fire was finally extinguished. 'It was really a touching sight,' wrote Yorke, 'to see what was once such a magnificent building practically a heap of ruins.'[40] Little was indeed left beyond the four outer walls. 'Although I did not see the fire,' wrote Petsy many years later, 'the shock and horror among the household, and the blackened ruin with the pungent smell, filled me with fear for a long time.'[41] Sir Tatton himself showed stoicism in the face of such disaster: 'all he said when a word of sympathy was offered,' commented the *Yorkshire Post*, 'was, "These things will happen, these things will happen", repeating the words with resigned fortitude and recognising the utter hopelessness of it all.'[42] The reporter, as it happened, could not have been more wrong.

Chapter 8

A Seat in the House

The blow of the loss of Sledmere was softened for Mark a week later when he was finally offered the perfect parliamentary seat. This came about after the Conservative MP for Central Hull, Sir Henry Seymour King, had his election declared null and void after allegations that he had bribed voters by financing treats for children and giving away free coal to certain constituents. In their search for a new candidate, Mark seemed an obvious choice to the local Conservative Association. He was a local man whose reputation had already been established by his conduct in the two Buckrose campaigns, in which he had worked assiduously on behalf of his prospective constituents, travelling the length and breadth of the county to speak at meetings on subjects as diverse as teachers' pay, the problems faced by small farmers, and better conditions in hospitals. He studied the conditions of children in the slums of Hull, sailed out with the fishing fleet, and when severe flooding affected the Wolds in the spring of 1910, he had even written to *The Times* encouraging its readers to donate to the Relief Fund.

He had shown himself to be diligent too in personally answering all correspondence from his would-be constituents, however lowly their background, replies that sometimes ran to several pages. A good example of this is his answer to a Mr William Turner, a 38-year-old shoemaker, who asked him for advice on how he could best educate himself. Mark suggested a course of reading, to be preceded by a three-week abstinence from 'all rubbish, i.e. newspapers, novels, pamphlets (mine included), magazines' while instead contemplating 'big' subjects such as Death, Life, Pain, Eternity, 'but keep off print,' he advised, 'as a tippler must keep off drink'. Then he was to start reading, 'slowly and with great care', and taking notes on, the books that he would send him. They were, in order:

1. The Book of Ecclesiastes.
2. The *Meditations* of Marcus Aurelius.
3. The *Imitation of Christ* by Thomas a'Kempis

These would help him absorb 'some steady and thoughtful philosophy', after which:

4. 'I give you Bacon's Essays, to be read throughout, including even the ones on Mosques, Country Houses, Sports, etc'. These would widen his knowledge of material things.
5. As an introduction to theoretical politics, he commended Thomas More's *Utopia*, to be followed by
6. Swift's last chapter of *Gulliver's Travels*, 'The Voyage to Houyhnhnms', and
7. Act I of *Troilus and Cressida*.

He recommended a study of great men, in the form of:

8. Plutarch's *Lives*, and
9. Rosebery's *Life of Pitt*, before completing the suggested course with two novels by Disraeli
10. *Tancred* and *Sybil*, which, he said, represented a fairly just analysis of the elements which made up the modern world. 'This task will occupy you for some time,' he added, 'but if you carry it through carefully and wholly abstain from current literature during that period, you will find yourself in a more efficient state of mind than at present ... I shall be glad to help you in any way while you go through this period of study, if you wish it, note your essays etc, or criticise them ...'

It also helped Mark that the Sykes family had a strong historical connection with Hull going back to the eighteenth century, when his ancestors had greatly contributed to the growth and prosperity of the city through trade with the Baltic, namely the export of cloth and the import of Swedish iron, a vital element in the manufacture of steel. Add to this the many charitable works of his mother on behalf of the poor Catholics of the city, and his adoption was assured. Delayed by the coronation of George V, on 22 June, the by-election did not take place till 5 July, and three days later, when all votes were counted, Mark was returned as Conservative MP for Central Hull with a respectable majority of 278.

He took his seat in the House on 10 July, finding a warm welcome at the door. 'I found a nice old thing with a top hat,' he recounted to Edith, 'who looks after coats and who said, "I have seen two genera-tions and you are the third, Mr George Cavendish Bentinck, Mr Christopher and yourself."'[1] His entry into the House, he told her, 'was very funny. The first person waiting below the bar was Luke (White) who most heartily congratulated me and wrung me by the hand. I was then marched up, and the Speaker seemed really pleased … George [Wyndham] fussed and fussed and fretted and fumed and worked himself into the most terrible stew. My next exploit was really very funny. There was a division on Friendly Societies. Luke had sworn to help them. Lloyd George divided the House on the question. As I went to the Lobby I found Geoffrey Howard.[2] "Oh do you actually know your way into the Lobby?" "Yes"', said I, "and am showing Luke the way too!" Geoffrey was very sick indeed.'[3]

His first impressions of his Party were not good, describing them as being 'badly managed and stupid', while the Labour members he considered 'barren, shallow rogues' who 'funk, rant and jib, and then fall into line like the underbred brutes they are'. The only person for whom he had huge respect was the Chancellor of the Exchequer, David Lloyd George. 'Lloyd George is really a very great genius. He is the biggest man in the House by lengths. He has charm, fascination, personality, sympathy, agility, and is much more than clever. He may make a very great change in his politics at any moment ... My grounds for saying this are that no man with L.G.'s personality can possibly remain a Radical for very long.'[4]

A week later he was bemoaning that he could have made five speeches since he had been in, had he not held his peace on principle. He was waiting for the right moment, but he was ready to explode. 'Our party are very bad and stupid,' he complained, 'and the speeches are enough to drive one mad with boredom – "while entirely agreeing-er-with the first remarks-er – of my rt. hon.-er – friend, I – er-hem – depreciate-er-deprecate – the further remarks – that is I am in agreement with a part – that is the first, the first part" and so on till I could scream ... These men cannot deliver themselves of their ideas.'[5]

As it happened, during the first month he sat in Parliament, Mark witnessed some of the most dramatic debates of the century. In spite of his having recently won an election, Asquith had conspicuously failed to persuade the House of Lords to agree to his Parliament Act, which would allow the House of Commons to pass legislation without the approval of the Lords. In the end he was obliged to go to the King to ask him to create 250 new Liberal Peers in order to force through the Bill in the form in which it had been drafted. On 24 July, Asquith went to the Commons to state his intentions. 'I have just come from the most disgusting performance I have ever witnessed,' Mark wrote to Edith. 'The House was packed from end to end ... when Asquith came in our people began to howl like madmen and so continued, here are some of their cries, "Who killed the King?" "Have a drink," "Perrier Jouet," "Traitor," "Judas," "Not this man but Barabbas," "Scoundrel," "Dictator," "Tyrant." Asquith was angry, red, frightened, undignified – not a great man in any sense of the word – Balfour, frightened, ashamed, halting ... Lloyd George was intensely amused and laughed all thro' – G.W. bayed like a bloodhound – and our side without exception behaved like weak, hysterical girls, unstrung, leaderless and uncontrolled.' It was, he concluded, 'entirely a revolting spectacle I cannot find the heart to laugh at'.[6]

His opinion of the House of Lords, unsurprisingly considering his patrician background, was somewhat different. On 9 August, he attended their own debate on the Bill and, sensing how close they might be to self-destruction if they refused to toe the line, waxed lyrical on what he saw in the Chamber. 'The scene in the H. of L. was most wonderful,' he wrote, '– a scene perhaps never to be seen again. 400 English gentlemen – independent, honest, determined and at variance – no one knows how the division will go, every speech has its effect – the last deliberative assembly in Europe will have ceased to be as such in another 5 days or perhaps less – Even the hordes of Radicals at the bar among whom I stood were impressed. We shall never see such a scene again. The Lord Chancellor on the Wool Sack and around him Generals, Ambassadors, Lords Lieutenants, Governors, Diplomatists, Gentlemen, and Bishops, – below the bar a knot of greedy adventurers, cranks and lawyers – what a contrast!'[7] In the event, the Lords saw sense and voted through the Bill, an act which Mark held in contempt. 'Tonight the worst has happened,' he told Edith. 'The Royal Footmen & the Bishops have betrayed Toryism finally and forever.'[8]

The long summer recess which followed gave him some time to gather his thoughts and catch up with his family, the numbers of which were about to be swelled by one, since Edith was again heavily pregnant. While she prepared herself for the birth during one of the hottest summers of the century, in which temperatures rose to a record-breaking 98°F and drought ravaged the country right through till the middle of September, much of Mark's time was taken up with the long and difficult decision of what to do about Sledmere House, which his father, having come to a satisfactory settlement with the insurance companies, had decided should be rebuilt. Since Sir Tatton was himself by now too frail and ill to assume practical responsibility for the rebuilding, the task fell on Mark, who, in spite of the huge number of other responsibilities he had, typically relished the challenge. He and his father agreed on one thing. With the outer walls sound, apart from the west front, and the cellars all in good condition, it would be a waste of time and money to pull them down and start anew, when the old house might be successfully re-created.

The work was to be carried out under the direction of W. H. Brierley of York, who was an expert on architectural restoration, and a leading exponent of the neo-classical style, and Mark submitted some sketches to him to prove his point. 'The offices and house I have roughly sketched are what we want carrying out,' he wrote in January 1912. 'The old house was generally regarded by servants as most convenient because of its compactness, and both my wife and I consider that in the enclosed rough draft the old merits of warmth, closeness and convenience are retained.'[9] Brierley had different ideas, however. He believed the way forward was to entirely demolish what remained of the old Sledmere and build a modern house: 'it would be infinitely better,' he wrote 'and only cost about the same'.[10] Mark's reply was to the point. 'I detest modern houses. This is an inartistic and vulgar age. We will build a house that is as little typical of the second decade of the twentieth century as possible.'[11] Brierley had little choice but to go along with his client, but it was an inauspicious beginning.

Edith gave birth to their fifth child on 6 September, a daughter they named Angela. This brightened up what had been a week of mixed blessings; on the good side, the fourteen yearlings sold by the Sledmere Stud at the annual Doncaster sales had fetched a record sum of £20,422, the equivalent of over two million pounds today, but unfortunately the occasion had been marred for Mark by the unscheduled and disastrous appearance at the racecourse of his mother, whose drinking had once again got the better of her. 'Today's sale was quite spoiled for me,' Mark wrote to Edith, 'by the most inopportune arrival of my mother – très très mal – and in a vile temper – Henry and I have decided that next year some steps will have to be taken to prevent a repetition – It was not so bad as it might have been but I couldn't stand it and went away.'[12] Though he was not to know it, Jessie's health was in steep decline.

A considerable part of his time was spent arguing with Brierley about the exact form the new house should take. He didn't like the

initial designs he had submitted, telling him they reminded him of the
Royal Automobile Club in Pall Mall, London. Their most glaring fault
in his opinion was that Sledmere's great library, its pride and joy, had
been re-housed on the ground floor. 'Are you still absolutely fixed to
[the] library on the ground floor in the new building?' he wrote to
Brierley on 18 October, in a letter liberally sprinkled with amusing
caricatures illustrating his worries. 'Consider it will cease to be a
library – there will be gardeners carrying palms,

friends looking in at the window,

people climbing out of the window, people laying tea things, ladies and children arranging flowers, guns coming in at the door.

It will not be a library, it will be a hall – a huge damnable hall. I want a library – it must be on the first floor.'[13]

Mark's strong views were not entirely motivated by practicalities. His sense of the aesthetic told him that a ground-floor setting would deprive the room of one of its most striking features, the beautiful view out across the park: 'it should be in the air,' he told Brierley a few days later; 'the landscape effect from the house is a great part of the room – the windows at the church end do more than light the ceiling. Now if the library goes downstairs it loses six windows and gains four: but it gains shadows after twelve o'clock, so you may say it loses three windows – besides this it loses the light of the sky by having a high horizon.'[14] In the end these worries about the library contributed to Mark entirely rethinking the concept of building a new house and considering the possibility of re-creating the eighteenth-century one.

The problems of Sledmere were thrust to the back of his mind however when Parliament reconvened, his first priority being to make his maiden speech, having had no real chance to do so in the previous sitting, a fact that had caused him immense frustration. 'No opportunity presented itself during the debates,' he had complained to Edith at the beginning of August, 'and one gets practically no assistance of any sort from the Officials – one is entirely alone … There is a debate tomorrow on the payment of members, but I don't know whether I shall take advantage of it or no …'[15] He bided his time until, on 27 November, he was able to do so on a subject close to his heart, namely affairs in the Middle East, in particular Turkey, which was then in the throes of a war with Italy. To lend him moral support, Edith attended with her brother, Harold Gorst, who was working as a parliamentary sketch writer for the *Westminster Gazette*. It is the tradition in the House of Commons that if it is known that a new member is to make his maiden speech, then when MPs rise to catch the Speaker's eye, he will be called first to minimize any nervousness he may be feeling. Unfortunately for Mark he had to wait to speak for several hours, since the Foreign Secretary was making a major statement on Anglo-German relations, which was then followed by a lengthy debate on foreign affairs.

From the Strangers' Gallery, Edith and her brother witnessed the agonies of nerves he was going through as he sat waiting for the interminably long speech of the previous speaker, the leader of the Irish Party, John Dillon. 'I shall never forget the spectacle of the tortures he endured when waiting for his turn to speak,' Gorst recalled. 'Every time that Dillon said something like; "and now, Mr Speaker, to go on to my seventh point," Mark cast an agonising look … and threw himself – quite regardless of appearances – into an attitude of hopeless despair. There was Dillon slogging away at his points without a sign of exhaustion. And there was Mark tossing about on his bench like a ship in a stormy sea. It was one of the most distressing spectacles I have ever witnessed.'[16]

When his moment came, however, he shone, though he took time to get into his stride: 'at the commencement of a speech,' wrote a contemporary, '[he] at first gave the impression of extreme boyishness – a sort of silly, laughing nervousness or shyness, which made one wonder if one were about to listen to the speech of a man or a clownish boy. Doubts were accentuated by his peculiar habit of twisting round his fingers an untidy wisp of hair which invariably persisted in falling across the left side of his forehead. When first I heard him, he gave me a very peculiar quaking feeling for about three minutes, but suddenly the silly shyness, or whatever it was would drop like the discarded cloak of a clown, and thereafter he was the serious statesman. Not for a second longer did he lose the grip of his subject or the attention of his audience.'[17]

'I need not say how hard it is for anyone speaking here for the first time to touch on so difficult, I might almost say so perilous, a subject as foreign affairs,' he began. 'It is with the greatest diffidence that I venture to speak to-day, and I only dare to do so because I have had some personal knowledge of some of the parts of the world which come within the orbit of this particular Debate.' His speech was a passionate one, touching on the dangers of the government's lack of any real policy in the Middle East, and in particular reminding them of the importance to British commerce and strategy of a strong and united Turkish Empire, and calling on them to give more support to the Turks. It was, wrote the diplomat Aubrey Herbert, given 'in the rare complete silence that the House sometimes gives as a recognition to a distinguished contribution to its debates'.[18] Mark's good fortune was that the next speaker happened to be Mr Asquith, the Prime Minister. 'It is my most agreeable duty,' he said, '– if the hon. Gentleman will allow me to do so – to congratulate him very heartily on as promising and successful a maiden speech as almost any I have listened to in my long experience.'[19] Afterwards, Edith teased her Terrible Turk about his display of nervousness. "I thought you always said that they were mostly fools in the House of Commons,' she remarked. 'They are mostly fools,' replied Mark; 'but there are a few who count and of whom one naturally stands in awe.'[20]

Mark's reaction to the great success of his speech, given in a reply to a letter of congratulation the following day, from the *Grande Dame* of the Tories, Lady Londonderry, was uncharacteristically modest. He attributed it to an extraordinary run of luck. '(A),' he wrote, 'Dillon had wearied the House till it was ready to cheer anyone or anything. (B) I knew the subject. (C) It was not controversial. (D) Asquith himself is a Yorkshireman. Take also into consideration that it was a pure fluke that the P.M. spoke directly after me …'[21] Still, it was a brilliant start to a parliamentary career into which he threw himself with gusto, thrilled at having at last found a calling that was worthy of his talents, and perfectly suited his restless and active temperament.

He had soon established for himself a punishing schedule which involved, not only putting in more than the requisite amount of time in the House, but also travelling all over the country to address political meetings and attend fund-raising social functions. Between his election in July, and the Christmas recess of 1911, he attended 31 meetings and 27 social gatherings, spent 50 days in Parliament, taking part in 88 divisions, asking 16 questions, and making one speech. He was always in a frantic hurry. One day, for example, his brother-in-law, Harold, who was staying with him at Eddlethorpe, was just settling down to a delicious breakfast, his favourite meal of the day, when the dining-room door was flung open, and in rushed Mark, shouting at him to look sharp, as they had to be off at once. When Edith protested that her brother had not yet eaten his breakfast, Mark yelled at her, 'Breakfast! Here's his breakfast – I'll take it with me!'

'He rushed to the table,' Harold later wrote, 'and seizing several pieces of bacon on toast, thrust them into his overcoat pocket. A couple of grilled sausages and a slice of ham with plenty of fat on it followed suit. Into another pocket he stuffed the top of a loaf of bread. Then he seized me also, and rushed me out of the room into the hall. I was barely allowed to snatch up my greatcoat and hat before we were in the car and off.'[22] He usually had so many things on his mind that he could not be bothered with what he considered trifles. On another occasion, when he had to attend a very grand political dinner in Carlton House Terrace, and was changing to go out, he was so engaged in a political argument with Harold that he failed to notice his footwear and left for the dinner dressed to the nines, except that he was wearing on his feet a large pair of muddy boots.

A political career meant big changes not only for Mark, but for his family, who were moved to London, into number 9 Buckingham Gate, an imposing four-storey town-house across from Buckingham Palace, and within easy walking distance of Westminster Cathedral. As well as a grand entrance hall and fine staircase, their new home boasted a series of large reception rooms, suitable for entertaining in, a mass of upstairs rooms for the five children and their nannies and governesses, as well as plenty of space to house the large number of servants then required by a family of their size and station. Edith immediately opened an account at Harrods, which supplied her with everything from sardines to shoelaces.

Though Mark adored his family, and spent as much time as possible with them, his new life meant that he was never able again to devote the time to them that he had done since his return to England in 1906. He was, more than ever, a workaholic, and, with the exception of Sundays, when the family would attend Mass together in the morning, and pass the afternoon at a concert either at the Queen's Hall or the Albert Hall, they began to see less and less of him. On weekdays in London he rose every morning at dawn and either went riding in Rotten Row, or walked to Mass at the Cathedral, where he would often act as one of the servers. If the children were lucky, they might catch a glimpse of him at breakfast, though he would have little time to spare since, before heading off to the House at eleven, he had to read all the leading dailies, both from London and from Yorkshire. Then he was off to his office in the Commons to go over his correspondence with his secretary, Walter Wilson, a fellow Yorkshireman.

In the evenings, if he was not out of town addressing a meeting, he would invariably be back in the House, or attending a dinner. Enjoying debate as he did, and being a man of such charm, he found no shortage of invitations to political dinners. He was invited to join an exclusive Conservative dining club known as the 'Tuesday Club'. This club, so called because it met on successive Tuesday evenings, had been founded by Sir Ian Malcolm as a successor to the 'Hughlians', a name given to a group of friends, all supporters of Lord Hugh Cecil, who were bound together by their hatred of Asquith and his Parliament Bill. 'The members,' wrote Malcolm, 'were linked by no engagement to act together politically, but only to observe with free Masonic fidelity the astonishing confidences that were exchanged at our weekly feasts in the Palace of Truth.' Mark shone at these gossipy dinners because of his great talent as a caricaturist, and it became a rite that on each occasion he would draw a cartoon in the club book. 'Mark would grab at the book,' Malcom recalled, 'and, pushing his plate on one side with a sniff and a chuckle, draw forth his fountain pen and bend double over the page until his caricature was completed. We rarely knew what it was that had tickled his fancy so suddenly until the book was passed round, and we were convulsed with laughter at our artist's conception of the passing jest of the moment.'[23]

The caricatures were generally some in-joke connected to a recent exploit of a member of the club, or some piece of political gossip. Sometimes they were rough scribbles, but they could also be quite elaborate. In the latter category falls the series, which he drew in 1917, when Chequers was presented to the nation as a permanent residence for the current Prime Minister. He illustrated a 'Code of Conduct' for the new incumbent, which included such rules as:

'Prime Ministers' eldest sons alone shall have the right to carve the names of their fiancées on the grand staircase.

'In event of the Prime Minister being a woman, the Prime Minister's husband will be regarded by the domestic staff as mistress of the house.

'In event of a Prime Minister being engaged in conference with a member of his Cabinet who is of the opposite sex, members of the domestic staff will knock twice before entering the room.

'Gentlemen guests of the resident Minister will be required to wear evening dress at dinner. In order that the artistic unities may be preserved, they will be inspected by the President of the Royal Academy, who, on behalf of the Trustees, will decide whether their appearance is in harmony with the traditions and surroundings of the Ministerial residence.

SOME OF THE RULES FOR "CHEQUERS."

'An English country gentleman is to be kept on the premises for the entertainment of the resident Minister and to give tone to the establishment.'

Scarcely were Mark and the family settled into Buckingham Gate than they found themselves in mourning. Jessie's drinking, a problem that would not go away, had led to a steady decline in her health as well as her behaviour, the latter having caused an almost complete rift between her and her son in the last few years: 'there seems to be no lengths to which my mother has not been prepared to go,' Mark had written to Edith back in July 1909, 'in the way of telling or inventing stories to show how vilely I have behaved, cowardice, dishonesty, malevolence, treachery, cruelty, are only some of the charges ... it is impossible to remain on any particular or intimate terms with one who will neither listen or pay heed to anything.'[24] Now, aged only fifty-six, she was at death's door after a series of strokes. Though Society may have turned its back on her, and the last years of her life were spent, as *The Times* put it, in the company of 'a small group of intimate friends', she had never ceased to win the love and respect of the less well off, and it was said at her funeral that as she lay in her room, insensible and dying, her servants crept in one by one and kissed her hand.

Her death, on 2 June, did not pass unnoticed by the press, much to the fury of both Mark and his father. In one paper she was referred to as 'the greatest plunger of her time',[25] while the *Daily Mail* called her 'a victim to all the excitements of the racecourse' and drew its readers' attention to the 'notorious litigation' of the 1890s.[26] Lord Northcliffe, the proprietor, received a stinging rebuke from Mark, who asked him 'to prevent the repetition of such vile outrages on the defenceless dead and the stricken living'.[27] When he subsequently apologized and threatened to sack the offending journalist, Mark begged Northcliffe to refrain from doing this, on the grounds that 'of all qualities in my mother, charity and mercy were the greatest'.[28]

On 7 June, a special train took Jessie's body up to Sledmere, from which station it was borne on a cart drawn by four farm horses to a temporary chapel erected close to the ruins of the house. There it was met by the Abbot of Ampleforth and a contingent of Benedictine monks, who sang a Requiem Mass, after which the coffin was carried by tenants of the estate to the family burial plot in St Mary's churchyard. Two thousand people turned out to bid their farewells. The mourners did not include Sir Tatton, who, unfit to travel, remained in London, where he attended a Requiem High Mass that took place simultaneously at the Church of the Immaculate Conception in Farm

Street. The text of the funeral oration was 'Charity covers a multitude of sins', and as he left the church, he was heard to mutter, 'A remarkable woman, Jessie, a remarkable woman, but I rue the day, I rue the day I met her.'

As it happened, he was to outlive her for only a short time. Hit hard by the burning of his home, he had moved with Madame into a house in the village, and here, in the summer of 1912, he became obsessed with the idea that he was going to die at precisely 11.30 a.m. Each morning his groom would bring round his favourite mount, an old cob, for him to ride. On some mornings he would ride out, while on others he would dismiss them with the words, repeated over and over again, 'No, no, can't ride, can't ride, going to die, going to die.' His premonition was not realized. Instead, on a trip to London early in 1913, he caught pneumonia and was laid up, seriously ill, at the Metropole Hotel. At some point, Mark appears to have completely lost patience with his father and all those who surrounded him, including Henry Cholmondeley, whom he despised for being so weak. As for Madame, whom he suspected of trying to take control, he saw this illness as an excuse to finally get rid of her.

The plot failed, because by the time he went to see his father, on 13 March, his eighty-seventh birthday, the status quo had changed. 'My father had made such progress by the time I came back,' he wrote to Edith, 'that nothing could be done as regards Madame – he is now recovering very rapidly but will not move ... so all I have been able to do is arrange the food, and feeding shall be in the hands of the nurses, and that Madame is not to take her meals in the room with him – and that his letters are to go through Henry.' He bitterly regretted not having taken Edith with him, telling her that had she been there, he might have been able to achieve his objective, 'but alone it is impossible,' he complained; 'I feel very defeated and weary and depressed. Never had anyone such people to deal with as Henry, Gardiner, Madame, and my father.'[29]

Feeling that he was on the mend, Tatton told Mark that he was going to remain at the Metropole until he was strong enough to travel back to Sledmere, where it was his intention to 'start on more churches at once'. It was a wish that was never to be fulfilled. Soon after, his condition deteriorated. He remained in London, his health being the subject of weekly reports in the Court Circular of *The Times*. On 3 May, his state was described as 'grave', and he died in the early hours of 4 May. A death in a hotel is never good for business, and the manager, thrown into a temporary panic, had the cheek to ask Mark if he minded his father being smuggled out of the premises in a hollow sofa, which had been specially constructed for such occasions. 'However my father leaves this hotel,' he remarked, outraged by the request, 'he shall leave it like a gentleman.' In the end he accepted a compromise, and the body was removed from the hotel in the middle of the night, and placed on a train up north. On its eventual arrival at Fimber station on the morning of 5 May, it was loaded onto a farm wagon and drawn by a pair of heavy horses the four miles to St Mary's Church. After a simple, brief service, attended mostly by estate servants and villagers and a few tenants, the coffin was placed on a bier in the chancel to lie in state for a few days, while from across the grounds the occasional distant shouts of workmen and the sounds of their tools were blown in on the wind as they finally got to work on the rebuilding of the house, beginning with the erection of an enormous servants' wing on the north elevation, almost as big as the principal block, containing the servants' hall, kitchen, laundry, brewery, gunroom, brushroom, etc., everything that would once have been needed to meet the requirements of a grand Edwardian household.

In the annals of difficult clients, there can have been few more exacting taskmasters than Mark. Nothing escaped his notice, and his patience was stretched to its limits by what he considered to be Brierley's lack of interest in attention to detail, combined with a cavalier attitude to his wishes. He was furious, for example, that his estate carpenter had not been consulted about the mantelpieces and grates for the fireplaces in the servants' wing, which was nearing completion in the summer of 1914: 'as this has not been done,' he commented, 'we have, as I expected, the usual monument of hideousness'.[30] The twelve '929 Glen Eden' fireplaces were what he most disliked – 'Ill-proportioned, Modern, Pretentious, Vulgar, Untruthful' – and he ordered them to be removed. In addition he was unhappy with the dado and skirting rails, the bedroom doors, the windows and the jambs of the shutters. 'So far,' he wrote exasperatedly, 'not one single detail has been correct.'[31]

With work about to begin on the central block, Mark was especially concerned that things should be done exactly the way he wanted them, and he insisted that Brierley was to go ahead with no work until it had been personally initialled by him. 'It is simply a question,' he told him, 'as to whether I am to have the old rooms in spirit or whether I am to have modern vulgarity.'[32] While he professed himself to be 'a lamb', when it came to construction, water, light and planning, 'on ornamental detail,' he said, 'I am and must remain a roaring lion ... I have to live in the house – think how bad for you and me if I live to any age – that I should daily curse your name each time my eye was vexed by a detail my soul could not approve ... it's not a question of leaving the design in your hands, but of not leaving it sticking in my eye. We are on the verge of the old house and we must come to an understanding.' A postscript added to this letter reveals the depths of Mark's irritation. 'I'll break your proud heart yet.'[33]

It is a measure of Mark's extraordinary energy that he was able to spend so much time on the details of the rebuilding, while simultaneously making his name in Parliament. Here he was establishing a reputation as an MP of great adaptability, with a desire to see fair play at all times. 'He had in him a deep-rooted hatred of oppression,' wrote Aubrey Herbert, 'and this passion glowed in his speeches.'[34] His wide knowledge of the East was soon well known, but when he addressed the house in April 1913 on the subject of foreign pilots under the Pilotage Bill, the correspondent for the *Sunday Chronicle* wrote, 'If he should subsequently turn out to be a ship's captain and a doctor of medicine, few will be staggered.'[35] He was certainly a spell-binding speaker. 'When he rose to speak,' wrote his former tutor, Egerton

Beck, 'the House filled, for it was recognized that something worth listening to was a certainty, that even if the speech were apropos of nothing which had gone before, and bore but little relation to the debate as a whole, it would contain points, suggestions and imposing ideas which would be heard from none other'.[36]

He soon gathered around him a group of young MPs who were similarly interested in the East, men like Herbert, George Lloyd and Leo Amery, the latter later recalling 'a cheery dinner at which Mark regaled Gertrude Bell, O'Connor from Tibet, and other Easterners with a brilliant café dialogue, in four or five different kinds of French, between Greeks, Turks, Armenians and Italians. There was also a wonderfully elaborated story of the monk who rode from Bethlehem to Egypt riding a camel, a horse, a mule and a donkey alternately to make sure that for at least part of the way he was doing it exactly like the Holy Family. Mark was a brilliant caricaturist and illustrated our debates as they went along with lightning sketches on the edge of his order paper. For him Arabs, and afterwards Zionists, came first, not as antagonistic but as complementary enthusiasms.'[37]

The speech with which he really made his name, and gained the attention of the whole country, was on the Irish question. Since the 1880s, when Charles Stewart Parnell had turned the Irish Parliamentary Party into a major constitutional political force, there had been a growing demand in Ireland for Home Rule. There were different interpretations to this, the more moderate thinkers of the IPP being happy with a dedicated Irish legislature that would be responsible solely for domestic affairs, while the more extreme elements represented by the Fenians and the Irish Republican Brotherhood wanted nothing less than complete separation from Great Britain, if necessary using physical force. Impressed by Parnell, Gladstone had introduced two Irish Home Rule Bills, in 1886 and 1893 respectively, both of which had failed to pass. Then in 1910, when the IPP found itself holding the balance of power in the House of Commons, its new leader, John Redmond, came to a deal with the Prime Minister, Herbert Asquith, that he would introduce a new

Home Rule Bill in return for Redmond's support of the Parliament Act. There was ferocious opposition to this from Unionists, like the barrister F. E. Smith, who, Mark wrote, spoke 'of a wild anti-Home Rule campaign on a religious basis in Liverpool. I told him frankly that this would not do. He proposes to bring 5000 Belfast Orangemen to Liverpool & to parade the streets with the deliberate object of making a row.'[38] Blood was up, and when the Bill was finally introduced in 1912, and passed with Royal Assent, Sir Edward Carson, the leader of the Unionist Party, who saw Home Rule in terms of Catholic rule and a subsequent decline for them both economically and culturally, organized the Ulster Covenant, signed by half a million Ulster men and women, against 'the coercion of Ulster'.

By the spring of 1914, the Home Rule crisis had brought Ireland to the brink of civil war, with the Unionists insisting that the four counties with a Unionist majority should be left out of any Home Rule scheme, and the Nationalists insisting that Home Rule must include the whole of Ireland. They had each formed their own brand new military-style units, the Ulster Volunteer Force (UVF) and the Irish Volunteer Force (IVF), and were squared up against one another. Threatened with Home Rule being forced upon them, the UVF also made it clear they would rebel against the Bill, forcing the British Cabinet to contemplate some kind of military action against them. The situation was complicated by the fact that a number of British army officers, especially those with Irish Protestant connections, threatened to resign rather than find themselves fighting against the Ulster loyalists. In an article for the *Saturday Review*, published in March, Mark entreated MPs to put themselves above party on this issue. 'The Irish question must be settled,' he wrote; 'the Ulster question must be settled; the constitutional question must be settled; the Army must be saved from destruction … Parliament as a whole has a duty to the people, above all party pledges; no one was elected to help to bring England to ruin; every member's duty now is to save her from revolution and disorder.'[39] In *The Times* he wrote, 'The essential to a settlement is that there should be no victory.'[40]

On 1 April, during a debate on the Irish question, Mark passion-ately reiterated many of these points. 'I have never felt in public affairs,' he told the packed House, 'so great a feeling of personal distress as during the last eight or ten days ... In view of the terrible position in which Ireland and the British Army have been in the eyes of the public for the last few days, that was a very deplorable thought to me. It is impossible to say who is to blame. If one sitting on the back-benches may dare to say so, I feel that the blame must lie upon us all. We have drifted on passions, and both sides have gone from one wild cry to another until we have divided class from class, creed from creed, in order to further our policies, until at the very end of it all one cannot deny that the military forces and the very Throne itself have been involved in our quarrels.'[41]

Calling on Ulster to be temporarily excluded from Home Rule until a federal solution could be achieved, he appealed to both Nationalists and Unionists. 'I believe that somewhere between those two, the solution of this difficulty lies. If it does then the future is much brighter ... I think what I have suggested will do much to lift politics out of the quagmire of personalities, ill-feeling, hate – and pettiness, with which it is affected at the present moment ... but to achieve that it is not so much necessary, I feel, as to appeal to English members of this house, or even to Scottish Members, as to appeal to Irish Members of all political views.'[42] His words struck a chord with many ordinary people, and he was inundated with messages and letters of congratulation. 'I am so pleased you were pleased with my speech,' he wrote to his old Cambridge friend, Professor Browne. 'The Hullabaloo it has caused makes me rather nervous. I feel that Tories look on me with suspicion & the Rads are angling me with flattery.'[43]

Two days later the *Daily Sketch* carried four photographs of him on its front cover, together with his prepared notes and a few extracts from his speech, under the headline: 'THE GENESIS OF A GREAT SPEECH. THE NOTES FROM WHICH SIR MARK SYKES, 'M.P. FOR ENGLAND,' SAID WHAT ALL SANE MEN ARE THINKING'.[44]

The mooting of a federal solution, however, did not go down well with local Unionist parties, and there were demonstrations all over the country. In June, Mark elected to speak at one of the largest when ten long processions of Yorkshiremen marched the four miles from Leeds up to Woodhouse Moor, attracting more and more followers as they went, until they numbered 25,000. 'Unfortunately,' reported the correspondent from *The Times*, 'a small but compact body of Catholic Home Rulers was able by skilful organisation to create a disturbance which at one moment threatened to turn the moor into a Donnybrook Fair ... Secrecy had been observed as to the platforms to which the various speakers would be allotted, but the Home Rulers bursting out in green favours, brandishing blackthorns tied with green streamers, and carrying Irish flags, joined themselves to the procession from East Leeds and thereby got a lodgement in a most favourable position for breaking up the meeting … they began by howling and went on to sing Irish songs. Two of them essayed a jig. When the Union Jack went up at the platform mast some undoubtedly derided it. The Chairman spoke amid howling and Sir Mark Sykes continued to the same accompaniment … A few sticks and stones were thrown … All at once the situation became dangerous. A too zealous steward snatched an Irish flag from the hand of one of the tormentors and broke and tore it. The howling suddenly changed to snarling, and only the tact of Sir Mark, who obtained possession of the flag and handed it back to its owner, prevented a free fight. "I have treated your flag with respect," he said, "because I know how dear it is to you. Won't you hear me now?"[45] The appeal was in vain, however, and when the speaker's platform was stampeded by a mob led by 'a slip of a girl in a green jersey and with long hair' brandishing a shillelagh hung with green ribbons, the speakers were escorted away and truncheons were drawn. This was the pattern of the weeks ahead, a situation, fuelled by prejudice on both sides, that might have spiralled out of control had the outbreak of war not batted it into the sidelines.

Chapter 9

War

In September 1911, the relatively new kingdom of Italy, under King Victor Emmanuel III, decided to widen its territorial ambitions by invading Libya, the last North African state still under the rule of the Ottoman Empire. In spite of the fact that on paper it looked as if it should be an easy conquest, with 34,000 Italian troops lined up against only 4,200 Turkish soldiers, all of whom were posted in garrisons and had virtually no naval support, Young Turk officers under Enver Pasha, supported by many Arab tribesmen, waged a surprisingly successful guerrilla war against the invaders. After months of fighting and a brief realization that they might actually fail in their ambitions, the Italians played a dirty trick.

King Victor Emmanuel was married to the daughter of King Nicholas 1 of Montenegro, one of the Balkan states that, along with Greece, Serbia and Bulgaria, had once been part of the Ottoman Empire. One by one, as nationalism had spread in the nineteenth century, these states had gained independence, and over the years had developed territorial ambitions in the remaining Balkan lands still under Ottoman control, namely in Albania, Thrace and Macedonia. The Italians surmised that if they persuaded Montenegro to declare war on the Ottoman Empire, which it did in October 1912, then it would only be a matter of time before the other Balkan states followed suit and this would drive the Turks to abandon Libya in order to defend the Balkan territory. All this happened exactly as planned, resulting in the First Balkan War, a conflict that, when it ended with the Treaty of London in May 1913, left the Ottomans deprived not only of their last possession in North Africa, but of all their European territory as well. Though they managed to regain some territory in Thrace in the Second Balkan War, fought between June and August 1913, it was merely a brief respite in the Empire's continuing disintegration.

Mark felt strongly that the Ottoman Empire should be protected, a view he propounded in a speech he delivered to Parliament on 12 August 1913. 'If there is one lesson which I think the Balkan events of the past two or three months can teach the world,' he said, 'it is that the exit of the Turk does not always bring an immediate cessation of the troubles which people thought might end with his departure ... I submit that as far as this country is concerned the case for a deter- mined effort to reform and to preserve the Ottoman Empire is abso- lutely overwhelming. The break up of the Ottoman Empire in Asia must bring the powers of Europe directly confronting one another in a country where there are no frontiers, because the mountains run parallel to the littoral, and because there being only three rivers, one moving in a circle, and the others running side by side over a level plain, it is very difficult for any Power to find a frontier. That very awkward geographical situation troubled the mind of Alexander the Great, the mind of Augustus, the mind of Diocletian, and the mind of Constantine ... In fact, even if the Ottoman Empire gave way, and I think there is a serious danger of the Asiatic Empire giving way at the present moment, there would be European frontiers in Asia Minor, and a European war from being an occasional remote possibility would become a probability which people would have constantly to bear in mind ...'[1]

Keen to see the effect that the Balkan wars had had on Turkey, in September 2013 Mark travelled with Edith to Constantinople. Though superficially it was still 'the Constantinople of old' with 'the same cluster of shipping, the same glory of outline and colour, the same perspective of villas, red tiled roofs, ashen-grey wooden houses, and masses of vast yellow barracks ... the old noisiness and bustle',[2] he found it a very different place from when he had last visited, the old Sultanate having been swept away and the Young Turks holding sway. Now, he wrote, 'there is at the root of things a deep change, the change not of life but of death. The fall of Abdul Hamid has been the fall, not of a despot or tyrant, but of a people and an idea … With him fell things good and evil, as they must on a Day of Judgement. In place of theocracy, Imperial prestige and tradition, came atheism, Jacobinism, materialism and licence. In an hour Constantinople changed … Every beastly thought that the exiles of Abdul Hamid had picked up in the gutters of the slums and ghettos of the capitals of Europe burst forth in foul luxuriance. Cinema shows – vile, obscene and blasphemous – brothels filled to overflowing, clubs where vice and politics rubbed elbows, scurrilous prints and indecent pictures flooded the city.'[3]

He couldn't wait to get away. 'It was with small grief that [we] left Constantinople to set out for Brusa.'[4] En route to this ancient capital of the Empire, he wrote to the children. 'We have been up mountains

and thro' rivers

and thro' forests.

This is Papa riding thro a forest. We have 9 men to look after our horses

One was such a nice old man Mama took a fancy to him and wanted to bring him home. One day he said "It's nearly five years since I came out of prison." "Oh poor Man," said Mama, "why did cruel people put you in prison?" "Well, my Lady," said he, "it was a real shame. My brother was a real bad one, so I just stuck this knife into him 5 or 6 times till he was quite dead and they put me in prison." Mama does not like the old man so much now – but he is very polite. This is the old man with his knife …'[5]

At Brusa, Mark was happy to find 'the new regime has done little harm, and, by a freak of fortune, some good … a series of restorations have been undertaken and carried out in the various mosques and tombs which must command the admiration and respect of every lover of Art'.[6] He also 'made a closer acquaintance with the results of the late war. Owing to the fact that all horses were said to have been requisitioned for the troops, the animals brought forth for my inspection as mounts suitable for an English traveller riding over fifteen stone consisted of one blind horse, one farcy horse and one suffering from mange.' Eventually 'horses, mules and other four-legged things were found sufficient to carry us and our belongings'.[7]

One of the very few surviving letters written by Edith was sent to
the children on this trip, describing a most uncomfortable night spent
by herself and Mark after torrential rain had driven them from their
tents to shelter in a Turkish house, whose owner had offered them
refuge. 'We were dreadfully hungry,' she told them, 'so he gave us four
eggs and some milk and then spread out some clean white cotton
quilts for us to sleep on. We were dreadfully tired so we lay down, but
alas! In a few minutes the fleas found us and there were hundreds of
them! So we got up and found two wooden boxes and put them in the
middle of the room and papa sat on one and I on the other and we
leant against each other's backs and Papa took the legs of the photograph machine and made crutches of them to prop himself up. Papa
has drawn a picture but he says I slept all the time! Naughty Papa, it
was much too hard sitting on the box to sleep … I don't think I have
ever been so tired before.'[8]

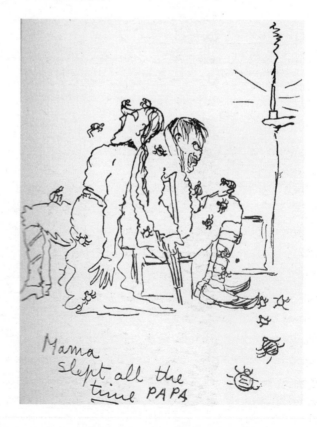

When they reached Eskişehir, a hundred miles south-east of Bursa, Edith felt she'd had enough. 'My wife most cruelly abandoned me,' Mark later wrote, 'and returned home to England.'[9] He continued to Konia, where he witnessed the extraordinary *Zikr* of the Mevlevi dervishes. 'I saw the Dervishes dance,' he wrote, 'really as a beautiful ceremony I have never seen anything to equal it – there were about 50 Dervishes and really for grace of movement you would have to have admitted that Pavlova had met her match. You could not believe that the idea of divine contemplation could be expressed in a dance, yet so it is ...'[10]

At Ermenek he found himself 'back in the Turkey of my youth. Ermenek is rich. There are no railways to take away the grain and send up the prices, and there is abundance of everything that makes glad the heart of man ... The war has carried off the young men; but even in this year of misery, Ermenek is a happy town.' Here he was shown an extraordinary tomb, newly discovered, containing 'three great sarcophagi, each surmounted by a lion of heroic size engaged in holding an ibex in its right paw, while its head was raised in pride ... Having taken flashlight photographs, drawings and measurements, I withdrew, awaiting the judgement of the learned on the monument.'[11] Leaving Ermenek, he passed through 'a wondrous wild country of strange gorges which no photograph can adequately describe ... one seems to see strange herds of petrified monsters, great cathedrals, frowning castles, grinning skulls of giants, huge writhing reptiles, all jumbled together and dissolving and reshaping at every turn of the pass. How pleasant it is to be absolutely ignorant of geology, and to know none of the dull and possibly untruthful reasons why these things are so formed!'[12]

The other highlight of his journey was visiting the great Roman site of Uzunja Burj, where he learned he was the first Westerner to have visited since 'a beautiful German lady', Gertrude Bell, had photographed it six years previously. Accessed via an ancient road 'which threads in an out of the wild and tortuous series of chasms by which the place is surrounded',[13] he noted that 'The Great Gateway, the Tower of Tenar, the Tower Temple, the vestige of the colonnade, are remarkable enough to reward any traveller for his pains.' He prided himself on having rescued a fine artefact from destruction. 'I had the good fortune to be shown a most beautiful, colossal marble statue of a man. The statue erect would have stood some ten feet high. The head was missing, but the tunic, legs, cloak and armour were in perfect preservation. The statue must have been similar to the one of Augustus, as the children and young men had already begun to smash it to pieces. It had only been found about two years ago. So having photographed it, I had it buried at the cost of one *mejidieh*, and warned the village that it had been photographed and that, sooner or later, men of the government would come, and, if it were in the least different from its photographs, taxes would be doubled, houses burned, and general trouble. I await the applause of the civilized world.'[14]

At Damascus, where Mark's journey finally came to an end, his love of dogs brought him within a hair's breadth of an unpleasant death. 'At 7.30am, at Damascus railway station,' he related to Edith, 'there was a delightful old grey bitch who put her paw up and scratched my knee for some food. Osman brought a piece of bread & I held it out to her. She opened an enormous mouth and took my hand in with the whole loaf! But only very slightly breaking the outer skin of my thumb. I washed & sucked & burnt the wound. Devy, the Consul, said Rabies was absolutely unknown in Damascus, and an old Dragoman who had known me from infancy said he knew the old bitch very well & gave me his card.'[15]

Thinking no more about it, he boarded a ship for Constantinople. On arrival in Beirut, he was then approached by the local representative of Cook's, who informed him that there had been a case of rabies in the Lebanon. 'When I got to Smyrna,' he wrote, 'the Doctors English & Armenian insisted that I must take Pasteur treatment unless the dog was known & under observation. So I wired to Devy to see the old Dragoman and get the bitch & send her to C'ople while I went to C'ople & began the treatment.'[16] The Pasteur treatment, named after Louis Pasteur, who developed it in 1885, consisted of a series of painful injections, twenty-one in all, delivered over a period of 18–22 days directly into the stomach with a long needle. Without it the disease was invariably fatal, death occurring within twenty days. Edith rushed out to Constantinople to find him in the best of hands, staying at the British Embassy while being treated by the head of the Pasteur Institute. The long treatment and convalescence, however, delayed their return to England till December.

Soon after Edith's return home to Eddlethorpe, she had to leave for Castle Combe, where her mother had fallen ill with influenza. She died on 29 January 1914, leaving Edith distraught. 'What can I say? What can I do for you? You have given up all hope,' wrote Mark on hearing the news. 'I keep thinking of you all the time – Oh do write and tell me what I can do – and please be careful not to get influenza yourself.'[17] Later in the day he wrote her a second letter expressing his deep love for her. 'I write again because I feel that letters must do something to make less your sorrow … Now my darling isn't it wonderful to think that it is 14 years since I used to write to you … before we were married and how now we love one another even more & more than then – how never a day have we thought or doubted each other … This great blessing should help you to bear this inevitable stroke which in itself is only pain to you and not your mother.'[18]

While Edith remained with her family, Mark threw himself back into the political spectrum, attending meetings up and down the country, with only the occasional mishap. 'Adventures!' he related to her about a trip to speak in Sheffield. 'All went well after I got into the train until Kettering was reached, when the 'strap of the engine, a piece of metal weighting 15cwt suddenly snapped and came off breaking two steel spokes of the driving wheel, smashing the brakes of 3 carriages, smashing 2 gas reservoirs and going thro' the guards van like a round shot just missing the guard's head – we pulled up with a crash amid a cloud of steam & showers of stones. We were then towed by the engine of a luggage train for about 20 miles & then packed onto a platform. Pavlova[19] was on the train and you may imagine the scene of confusion when it was realised she might miss her engagement …

Dressers, Managers, Companions, luggage minders, pet-dog keepers, assistants, etc, etc all sending telegrams in the wildest confusion. Eventually another train was collected & Pavlova, a companion, myself and a Methodist Minister, were sat in a compartment to dine. After Pavlova was dropped at Nottingham, the Minister announced that he would never pay 10/6 to see "any woman caper about a stage!" When I got to Sheffield it was 8.20. I had to take a motor, lost the way & arrived at Elland just in time to see the last man leave the meeting!'[20]

Wherever he spoke, be it at local meetings or in the House, Mark rarely failed to mention his fears regarding the Ottoman situation, telling an audience in Hull, for example, on 16 December 1913, that he had never seen the 'foreign situation more menacing'.[21] By the end of June, 1914, he was warning that the complete break-up of the Ottoman Empire would 'provide us with a German frontier in Mesopotamia', while the break-up of Persia 'would give us a Russian frontier'. Great Britain,' he said, 'will then be like a stranded whale on a mud bank, with a river hippopotamus on one side and a rhinoceros charging down from the hills straight in front.'[22] One solution he touched upon, which came out of his knowledge of the area from long years of travel, and which anticipated policies he was later to promote, was to take advantage of and harness tribal feelings to create 'native states'. 'There are the seeds of native states which exist in the provinces of the Ottoman Empire at the present moment which could be made into independent states. If the worst came to the worst, there are Armenians, Arabs and Kurds who only wish to be left in peace to develop the country.'[23]

Mark's fears of a European conflict were realized at the end of July when, a month after the assassination of Archduke Ferdinand of Austria by a Serb terrorist, Austria-Hungary declared war on Serbia and Russia began to mobilize her army. The news reached him in Wales, where he was training with his regiment, the 5th Yorkshires: 'we have been thinking about Armageddon,' he wrote on 30 July. 'The very latest telegrams seem a bit better, but otherwise ministers & all anticipate war and us involved … I shall try to get the Battn. to volunteer for foreign service … I see the preliminaries to mobilization are proceeding & that the fleet is off … Well God give us good counsel …'[24] On 1 August, Germany declared war on Russia. 'Well things look worse and worse,' he told Edith, 'Germany seems to have taken the plunge … I do not see any way to peace unless Russia cease mobilizing and agree that Austria may chastise Servia [*sic*] but must respect her territorial integrity … I think you may rely on no invasion, but otherwise things are about as bad as can be …'[25] If war did come, he also realized that it would put an entirely new complexion on the Irish question. 'The Nationalists boast that they will not have a united front without Home Rule on the statute book. In this they are very foolish. I believe the Ulster Volunteers will volunteer to serve us – this should smash the Irish because they are avowedly against us now. If it comes to war, the Government have got to face coalition with us, as the extremists intend to vote against them. All this if it comes out will tend to help us towards National solidarity.'[26]

When war was declared on Germany on 4 August, Sledmere was enjoying a bout of fine weather and the harvest was in full swing. They were, however, about to lose some of their workforce, namely the shire horses who pulled the harvesters and the men who looked after them. These men, and their fellow farm-workers who specialized in working with horses, had been recruited by Mark some years previously into a part-time voluntary regiment to which he had given the name 'The Wagoners' Special Reserve'. The idea for this had come to him on his return from the Boer War when he had begun to wonder just how prepared Britain would be should a war break out in Europe. He understood the importance of transport to an army and of getting to the front in as short a time as possible. Knowing that the average time it took to train men to handle an Army pole wagon, where the horses were hitched to either side of a central pole rather than between two shafts, was six months, it occurred to him that, since these were the very same wagons that were used on the Sledmere estate, he had to hand a pool of men, fully trained to handle both horses and wagons, who could be instantly available on the outbreak of a war.

As early as July 1908, he had suggested to the War Office that such a unit of skilled wagoners be formed who, in return for a small annual payment, would undertake to give their services as drivers in time of war, both at home and abroad. Persuading the Army top brass to adopt such a plan had proved an uphill struggle, however. 'For six years,' he later recalled, 'I was steadily repulsed, with all the ingenuity which bureaucracy and red tape can devise. The scheme was new, unprecedented, unheard of, unlikely to succeed, etc, etc, *per omnia saecula saeculorum*.'[27] Undeterred, as was his wont, he cajoled army officials to attend the annual driving competitions which showed off the great skills of the drivers, 'but the official resistance was as solid and impenetrable as ever, every argument that iron skulls could adduce from iron regulations was hurled at my head'.[28]

In spite of this lack of official support, he decided to go ahead anyway, recruiting 200 drivers from around Sledmere, to each of whom he paid, out of his own pocket, the sum of fifteen shillings annually if they agreed to serve in time of war. He even designed an oval badge for them to wear on their uniform, which had a horse's head in the centre and the words 'Wagoners Special Reserve' around the edge. When he became an MP, in 1911, he was finally able, in his own words, to 'harry' Richard Haldane, Secretary of State for War, into finally accepting his scheme, and the Wagoners were admitted into the Special Reserve, a part of the Territorial Army made up of men with specialist skills. By the time war broke out, they numbered 1,000 men and hundreds of horses that came from all over the country, and had pulled everything from coal carts to brewer's drays. They were called up straight away. 'It was the middle of the corn harvest when the postman turned up with the letter,' recalled one of them. 'I went home, got something to eat and got changed and rode straight over to Sledmere.'[29] Within a month they were in Northern France, arriving after a long journey by road and rail to find a chaotic situation, with the British Army in full retreat after their first engagement at Mons against numerically superior German forces.

By the time Mark got out to France to check on the progress of the Wagoners, the British had held the German advance and, after victory in the Battle of the Marne, were pushing them back. Taking a short leave from his battalion, he travelled out early in September, accompanied by his secretary, Walter Wilson. They sailed on the steamer from Southampton to Le Havre, and when he awoke the following morning, it was to find themselves in the middle of a fleet of ships awaiting entrance to the harbour. 'How odd a sight – not, perhaps, seen since the days of Nelson,' he wrote. 'How many Englishmen of fact and fiction have gone to the Gallic Wars this 1,500 years, yet never as a friend: the mythical Dukes of Britain, King John, the Plantagenets, Falstaff, Bardolph, Pistol, Uncle Toby, Peregrine Pickle, Wellington, and a crowd of strange spirits seemed to jostle and hover over the calm sea.'[30]

At Trouville, they picked up an open-topped car with a French driver to transport them to the various places where the Wagoners were at work, and Mark's eyewitness account of what he found provides an interesting insight into conditions in those early days on the Western Front. 'What a drive,' he noted, as they cruised through the French countryside, 'At every turn cheers for me; through lovely lanes, through ancient towns, past Gothic churches and wonderful chateaux. 'Vives [sic] les Anglais. Vives les ... O yes, Hip-ip!' Girls threw roses, men cheered, sentries brandished their arms, farmers yelled over fences ... So on by moonlight. How far from the battlefield the French enjoy the war. In every village after dusk the old and infirm parade the roads. Ancient schoolmasters and doctors solemnly patrol the by-ways and bar the way with chains. Gendarmes look fierce and efficient; village Mairies, with badges, scan our passports and all are really feeling they are doing something.'[31]

Suddenly, out of the dusk, he heard the English voice of one of his Wagoners. 'Give us a lift, Guv'ner. Hi come from Shantilly with Mr Walker's 'orses, Sir. Horl the boys 'an 'orses his abart four kilermeets from 'ere. Fair 'ell in Paris, Sir.' The following morning found them amongst a troop of 256 of the Wagoners Reserve, 'all very popular, efficient and well-liked', and over a period of a few days, they visited eight supply centres where the Wagoners were in service, finding them all in good spirits and morale high.

As they neared Paris, the drive became 'more sinister ... The roads are crowded with refugees – poor homeless folk from east of Paris. The people still cheer and wave, and there is something so trusting, so pathetic, so confident in their faith in our little khaki handful that no one could be unmoved ... Paris itself we found a desert, a tomb: the Hotel Lotti in the charge of a concierge.' Travelling south, they found less cheering and more solemn faces, the roads crowded with 'cavalry, and trains of mechanical transport making clouds of dust in beautiful country lanes. There were many sad sights on the road; poor refugees trudging back in the wake of our advance – an old woman wheeling a dead goat in a barrow, tired children and weary old men. Presently, half-finished trenches, German bisquit [*sic*] tins, cavalry lines, broken stacks; then the whiff of war, the stink of dead things from the woods; here, there, and beyond dead horse of the Uhlans – some shot, some ridden to death; then suddenly a line of waggons: No 6 Reserve Supply Park, with all the men.'

After dinner with the staff, the doctor took Mark down to the local station to see the wounded coming in, nearly 500 of them. What shocked him however was their haphazard treatment. 'Wonderfully cheerful they were for the most part. "Been playing football," said one man with a foot a mass of blood swathed in his putty. An officer at the point of death muttering on a stretcher; a man with a riddled back; another man quite dazed, his arm in a sling "All cut up we was. Reglar trap – all together – no one else left" … Then a man without a face – just a red pad of lint – led by two others. Then a German riding pick-a-back on a Tommy.'[32] He estimated that around 500 wounded men had only one doctor to look after them in the station, which was filthy with dust and oil. There were no hospital trains – just cattle trucks with straw on the bottom.

On his return home, Mark spoke to Edith about doing something to help the wounded soldiers at the front. They contacted the 'Union des Femmes de France', the French Red Cross, and volunteered to equip and administer a hospital of 150 beds, for which purpose a chateau at Compiègne, only twenty-five miles from the trenches, was immediately offered up. They had already paid for the conversion of the Metropole Hotel in Hull into a military hospital, but since it had not yet been used, it was decided to take much of the equipment to France, including valuable X-ray machines. Writing to *The Times*, with the memories of what he had witnessed fresh in his mind, Mark appealed for further donations. 'It has been decided to establish this hospital as near as possible to the scene of operations, where the most urgent cases can receive permanent attention with the least possible delay ... The expenses of administration will amount to £900 a month, and it is hoped with the generous aid of subscriptions to the running expenses to carry on the work for at least six months.'[33]

This hospital, which was fully equipped with a staff of top surgeons, trained nurses and orderlies, medical stores, and three motor ambulances, helped take care of the wounded soldiers who arrived by the trainload from the front, often numbering 700–800 at a time. Working there inspired Edith to open a smaller hospital of only thirty-five beds, L'Hôpital Militaire Lady Sykes, in the Villa Belle Plage near Dunkirk. It coped with the very seriously wounded. 'The majority of the cases,' she told the *Yorkshire Post*, 'are shell wounds, and the wounds are often dirty, and gangrene and tetanus often supervene.'[34] She equipped her hospital from Harrods, which supplied her with everything, beginning with a '16/20 H P Alldays Ambulance complete with 4 Stretchers, Lamps, Horn, Spare Wheel & Tyre', continuing with every kind of foodstuff, from boxes of beef, tins of tongue and gammon, pounds of bacon, gallons of jam and marmalade, tins of peaches, pineapple, apricots and pears, to pots of caviare and foie gras, and including thousands and thousands of cigarettes. She ran it with her sister, Eva, till the summer of 1915, when it and other similar private hospitals were absorbed by the army.

While Mark may have held his wagoners in the greatest affection, his priority when war broke out lay with his regiment, the 5th Yorkshires, also known as the Green Howards, a territorial battalion of the Yorkshire Regiment, of which he was the commander, with the rank of Lieutenant-Colonel. Having persuaded them to volunteer for service on the front, he headed off to Newcastle, where they were then located to train them in preparation for the grim realities of war. 'His training was very thorough', wrote Egerton Beck; 'he would probably not have objected to its being called brutal, but his one and only concern was efficiency combined with the safety of those under his command whom he hoped to lead into action ... One thing Mark would not do: ask those under him to undergo discomfort which he avoided himself. This showed itself in a characteristic fashion; when the battalion had to ford a stream he, the Colonel, dismounted and went through the water with them on foot.'[35]

The regiment was billeted in Council-school buildings in a slum area of the city, and from here almost every day they would undertake a route march of four or five miles into the country. 'This was strenuous but enjoyable,' wrote one of the recruits, Mark's brother-in-law, 2nd Lieutenant Harold Gorst. 'First came a drum and fife band, then a brass band, the two playing "Tipperary" and other popular tunes alternately all the way. Next marched the scouts, headed by myself wearing a golden sword which Mark Sykes had given me out of the collection of his ancestors' weapons at Sledmere ... After the scouts came the Colonel and Major Mortimer, followed by the battalion marching in companies.'[36] On arrival at whatever was the destination on that day, there would be some manoeuvre involving capturing a village or practising trench warfare, or even playing an elaborate 'Umpireless War Game'.

Like everything in which he became involved, Mark gave his battalion his all, though part of him felt he should be doing something more useful. His attention had never left the events that were unfolding in the Ottoman Empire. In the first weeks after the outbreak of war, Britain had sought to guarantee the neutrality of Turkey, with the Foreign Secretary, Sir Edward Grey, making a sustained effort to persuade Russia and France to join him in advising the Turks that the integrity of Turkish possessions would be assured if they remained neutral, but that 'on the other hand, if Turkey sided with Germany and Austria, and they were defeated, of course we could not answer for what might be taken from Turkey in Asia Minor'. Unfortunately, and unknown to him, Turkey had already secretly ratified an alliance with Germany, the Great Power that it believed would give it the best chance of survival.

'We shall rue our delay if we get into a war with Turkey now,' Mark wrote to Aubrey Herbert. 'We have given the devils too long to prepare, and the Germans too long to intrigue.'[37] With the prospect of war in the air, he put his talents to any use he could think of, including writing anti-German propaganda for translation into Arabic. 'I have been preparing pamphlets of a seditious kind for Syria,' he told Herbert. 'There is one confounded fly in the ointment of per-oration. And therefore: O ye Arabs plump for Russia and France whom ye know are sweet even as honey, who never, never say boo to a Moslem goose.'[38] He offered his services to the First Lord of the Admiralty, Winston Churchill, believing that all the experience he had gained from his travels might prove useful. 'I know you won't think me self-seeking,' he wrote, 'if I say all the knowledge I have of local tendencies and possibilities is at your disposal … If operations are to take place in those parts I might be of more use on the spot than anywhere else. My Battn. is practically willing for foreign service, i.e., 85%, and with my personal knowledge of its possible antagonist in the regions I mention, I could make it serve a turn, raise native scally-wag corps, win over notables or any other oddment.'[39]

When Churchill did not take him up on his offer, he wrote to Aubrey Herbert, who had been offered a job in the Intelligence Bureau in Cairo, urging him to go, and giving him advice on how to get the Arabs onside against the Turks, foreshadowing T.E. Lawrence's campaign that was to take place two years later. 'Now the important people whom we should get over on our side are the Beni Sadir – they are desert Bedawin and hate the Turks in their souls. However they must come to us not we go to them. We should establish a base at Akaba and an intelligence officer there with large powers. The various tribal people will come in by degrees. They should first be done up to the nines and given money and food – but no arms. Presently they will begin to talk. The intelligence officer should find out what their idea is – also whether the Beni Sadir will make it up with the Druses. Then premiums might be offered for camels, say an exorbitant price, say £50 or £60, then a price for telegraphic insulators, 2 francs each, then a price for interruption of Hejaz railway line, and a good price for Turkish Mausers and a good price for deserters from the Turkish Army …

'Then try and establish relations with the Druses of the Hauran. Get some of their people down to Akaba (preliminary to this of course peace between the Beni Sadir and the Druses), if possible keep the whole of the Hejaz railway in a ferment and destroy bridges. For this reliable agents would be required who understood demolitions – Armenians for choice.

'Later on a Spring rising of all the Shamiyili desert tribes could be looked for, Anazill, Beni Sadir, Druses, Adwan. If the whole lot moved west along the line, the Turks would be completely paralyzed [sic], and with adequate encouragement, the nomads of the Jaziroli would come on too and make hay round Aleppo. In these raids ... all crops and homesteads should be immune – stock and cattle however should all be lifted as it is on this that the government relies for supplies and taxation.

'With the railway broken and the stock raided and the local government smashed, the Turks will not be able to keep the field and the people will welcome our arrival on the coast say in June or July when Germany should be on her last legs.'[40]

Along with the letter, Mark sent Herbert a roughly drawn map of the Hejaz railway, marked with the various tribes to be found along the route and with suggested points of attack. It is not hard to envisage him sitting at his desk, his leg moving up and down in frustration, as he imagined himself leading the raids, but though he never got to play the Lawrence role, it would not be long before others saw how useful he might prove to be.

Chapter 10

Kitchener and the Middle East

Hussein bin Ali, Sharif of Mecca, and a direct descendant of the Prophet Muhammad, was a charismatic Arab ruler whose title gave him authority over Islam's holiest city and the annual Moslem pilgrimage, the Hajj. In the hierarchy of the Ottoman Empire, he was second only to the Sultan. Born in 1853, he had grown up among the Bedouin in the Hijaz, the province containing Islam's holiest cities, Mecca and Medina, and had been exiled to Istanbul in 1893, where he lived and raised four sons. After the Young Turk Revolution in 1908, he was proclaimed Amir by the Sultan, Abdülhamid II, and showed his strength in surviving the Sultan's overthrow the following year, thus cementing his position in Mecca. He did not endear himself to his political masters, however, bitterly opposing their schemes to centralize Ottoman rule in the Hijaz, which he knew would eventually undermine his autonomy. Rather than wait to be overthrown, and in the light of the looming likelihood of war, he had begun to consider another alternative.

In February 1914, Hussein dispatched his second son, Amir Abdullah, to Cairo with a message for Lord Kitchener, the British Agent in Egypt. They had a brief meeting in the course of which Abdullah gave him an account of the strained relations between his father and the Turkish authorities and of his certainty that they intended to depose him. In the loosest possible terms, he hinted that should such an event take place, there might well be an Arab Revolt, and tried to get Kitchener to advise him what the British Government's position would be under such circumstances. Since Britain was still on friendly terms with Turkey, Kitchener was non-committal, and, being aware that such meetings were frowned upon in Constantinople, on Abdullah's next visit to Cairo, two months later, he passed him on to the British Oriental Secretary in Egypt, Ronald Storrs.

'I visited him in the Abdïn Palace,' Storrs wrote in his memoirs, 'and sat for two hours under the spell of a charm … which long absences have failed to diminish … Travelling by a series of delicately inclined planes, from a warrior past I found myself in the defenceless Arab present being asked categorically whether Great Britain would present the Grand Sharif with a dozen, or even a half-dozen machine guns. When I enquired what could possibly be their purpose, he replied "for defence"; and pressed further added that the defence would be against attack from the Turks. I needed no special instructions to inform him that we could never entertain the idea of supplying arms to be used against a friendly power.'[1] Though Abdullah returned to the Hijaz with no firm commitment, he had at least opened Kitchener's eyes both to the level of animosity between the Arabs and the Turks, and the reality of the Arab desire for independence, knowledge that would soon cause him to take the first steps to bring the Arabs into the war on the side of Great Britain.

Storrs did not forget those spring meetings with Abdullah, in the course of which he had 'unlocked his heart', and he made sure that Kitchener, who was now heading the War Office in London, did not forget them either. 'I therefore submitted a short note,' he recorded, 'suggesting that by timely consultation with Mecca, we might secure not only the neutrality but the alliance of Arabia in the event of Ottoman aggression.'[2] After weeks of waiting, and with the support of the Chief of Intelligence in Cairo, Gilbert Clayton, who had condoned his idea in a private letter to Kitchener, the latter sent the following telegram. 'Tell Storrs to send secret and carefully chosen messenger from me to Sharïf Abdallah [sic] to ascertain whether "should present armed German influence in Constantinople coerce Sultan against his will, and

Sublime Porte, to acts of aggression and war against Great Britain, he and his father and Arabs of the Hejaz would be with us or against us".'3

Hussein's instinct, shared with Abdullah, was that if Turkey were to be drawn into war, then this would give the Arabs a perfect opportunity to make a break for independence. But a revolt was also a dangerous step to take without knowing how prepared they were as a nation. Thus he took the decision to send emissaries to Syria and the principal Arab rulers to sound them out and discover the true state of national feeling and preparedness. In the meantime he composed a letter to Storrs, signed by Abdullah, stating that, while he had to remain neutral for the time being, should Turkey go to war he might be able to lead his immediate followers to revolt so long as Britain promised effective support.

On 31 October, Kitchener cabled in reply: 'Germany has now bought the Turkish Government with gold, notwithstanding that England, France and Russia guaranteed integrity of Ottoman Empire if Turkey remained neutral in war. Turkish Government have against will of Sultan committed acts of aggression by invading the frontiers of Egypt with bands of Turkish soldiers. If Arab nation assist England in this war England will guarantee that no intervention takes place in Arabia and will give Arabs every assistance against external foreign aggression. Till now we have defended and befriended Islam in the person of the Turks; henceforward it shall be in that of the noble Arab.'4 In reply, Abdullah stressed that while his father would have to wait for the right time for a rupture with the Turks, he was committed to a policy of unavowed alliance with Britain. Thus ended the first chapter of the Anglo-Arab conspiracy.

Great Britain declared war on the Ottoman Empire on 5 November 1914. 'Grey has seemingly at last realised we are at war with Turkey,' Mark wrote to Edith from Newcastle, where he was training with his regiment, expressing his frustration at the seeming lack of interest in his experience. 'It maddens me not to be where I could be most useful i.e in the Medn. – is it not ridiculous the haphazard way we do things!'5 Meanwhile he passed the time preparing his 'Terriers', as they were known, for possible deployment to France in January, and keeping the occasional eye on the rebuilding of Sledmere House. 'Sledmere has made a great deal of progress,' he reported to Edith on 11 December, 'drawing room ceiling up & the library ceiling ready for fixing.'[6]

Mark continued his almost daily correspondence with Edith, keeping her up to date with the progress of the battalion, and amused with anecdotes of army life. '[Major] Mortimer invented a tiresome dinner – with dire domestic results – since several wives had come up & the younger & weaker subaltern husbands were, unknown to me, forbidden to dine with their wives – With the result that the Hotel dining room was filled with despondent women including Mrs Wadsworth the bride who repaired to bed in tears – where she was joined next morning say at 12.30am by her spouse, who in the meanwhile had wrestled with other subalterns & got a black eye.

I had hoped that there would not have been too much wine drunk, but I am sorry to say that one or two got more than enough … Englishmen & Russians have the fault that lack of imagination in the first & too much in the second prevents them from being able to amuse themselves without the adventitious aid of alcohol in excessive quantities.'[7]

When there was no sign of the battalion going to France by the middle of February, Mark became increasingly determined to get himself noticed. All the talk in government was now about a proposed expedition to secure the Dardanelles, the strategically important narrow strait in north-western Turkey that connected the Black Sea to the Mediterranean, thereby providing a sea route to the Russian Empire, and he could not resist writing to Winston Churchill to give his opinions on the subject. They agreed that Constantinople and the Dardanelles had become increasingly more important, but he warned him that 'Turks always grow formidable if given time to think'; therefore, 'the blow delivered there should be hard, decisive, and without preamble'. He suggested there were two approaches. '(1) To take the Gallipoli Peninsula and begin negotiating with Bulgaria, or, (2) to play the great stroke and take Constantinople by a combined attack by sea from North and South. This of course depends on Russia's power to produce men, 80,000 troops can take and hold the Gallipoli peninsula, but to hold Constantinople requires a larger force – at least 200,000 since the Turks must have large forces both in Asia and Europe. But whichever way is taken, I am sure it should be done as near as possible in one bound ...'[8]

If Mark's suggestions went unheeded, his persistence at getting noticed paid off in that he was finally offered a job in Cairo on the staff of General Sir John Maxwell, the Commander of the British Troops in Egypt, who had just held off an Ottoman attack on the Suez Canal. His conscience, however, prevented him from accepting it, though much against his better judgement. 'I have made for myself one of the most bitter decisions,' he told Edith. 'I was offered today a position of importance on Maxwell's staff in Egypt ... "You can take this if you like but remember your battn.!" O! If it had only been an order! – What could I do! A Battn. is like one's child. One must on choice choose the thing one is responsible for ... If it had been an order I should have gone without a word and [with] a joyous heart.'[9]

As it happened, Mark did not have to wait long for such an order after receiving an introduction through a friend in the Foreign Office to Captain Oswald Fitzgerald, personal secretary to the Secretary of State for War, Lord Kitchener. They met at the War Office, where Mark impressed him with his views on the Dardanelles and his eagerness to get out there with his battalion. On his return to Newcastle, he also sent him a memorandum he had drawn up titled 'Considerations on the Fall of Constantinople', which Fitzgerald promised to show to Kitchener. As it happened, in spite of Mark's enthusiastic volunteering, there turned out to be no role for the Territorials to play, but he was quite aware that still left him in the frame. Knowing this he wrote to Fitzgerald, 'As regards myself I want to make it quite clear that I could only leave my battalion on a direct order and not as a volunteer. My personal duty is to my regiment, but an order make is different.'[10] That order finally came in March, when he was commanded by the head of the War Office to report to the General Staff in London, where he was given a job under General Sir Charles Calwell, Director of Military Operations and Intelligence, preparing information booklets for troops fighting in the Dardanelles. At one point, he told Sir George Arthur, Kitchener's biographer, 'I was told I was going with the expedition, but at the last moment was ordered to remain in London, and then returned to my battalion for a short time, but was sent for again, and appointed at the personal request of Lord Kitchener as a member of the committee formed to ascertain British desiderata in Asiatic Turkey ...'[11] Declaration of war against the Ottoman Empire had presented Britain's allies with opportunities they had been fostering for some time. Russia saw the immediate possibility of gaining control over the straits leading to the Black Sea, while France viewed the moment as being perfect for securing cultural, religious and commercial pre-eminence in the Levant. Britain's worry was that they might not stop there, but be further encouraged in their regional and global ambitions, concerns that were borne out by the end of the year when, with no quick, decisive victory in sight, Russian demands had grown from merely a claim to the straits to the annexation of Constantinople as well. Simultaneously France stated that it 'would like to annex Syria together with the region of the Gulf of Alexandretta and Cilicia'.[12] When Russia then made it clear that in return for the granting of French wishes, she would view with sympathy the claims of their allies, British policy-makers, in particular Lloyd George and Churchill, pressed that Britain should come up with counter-proposals of her own. In response to this, at the beginning of April 1915, Asquith appointed a committee composed of representatives of the Foreign Office, the India Office, the Admiralty, the War Office and the Board of Trade, under the chairmanship of Maurice de Bunsen, former ambassador to Austria, the purpose of which was 'to consider the nature of British desiderata in Turkey in Asia in the event of a successful conclusion of the war'. Kitchener gave Mark the job of acting as his personal representative. 'Through Fitzgerald,' wrote Mark, 'Lord Kitchener told me that he wished me to keep him in touch with the situation … I used to report to Fitzgerald each night at York House on the various problems that had come up for discussion, and received instructions as to the points Lord Kitchener desired should be considered; this I did as best I could by explaining the views he approved of or suggested.'[13]

Barely thirty-six years old, Mark was by a long chalk the most junior member of the group, his position on such an important committee being entirely due to the fact that he was one of the few people in the War Office who had any first-hand knowledge of the Ottoman Empire. This meant that when there was discussion on subjects such as the terrain that a railway might have to pass though, or the nature and customs of the Kurds, the more senior officials, many of whom were in their sixties and viewed him with some suspicion, often had to defer to him. They also assumed that, as his representative, he spoke with the full authority of Kitchener, which always gave him an edge. With his immense energy and his outspoken and opinionated views, he was soon running the committee. 'He was the most active and concerned of all the participants during the deliberations, submitting memoranda, refuting others, providing detailed maps and interpretive material in little known subjects such as the Kurds and the Caliphate.'[14]

The Bunsen Committee set about considering four possible solutions that Mark proposed to the problem of what to do with the Ottoman Empire, the first of which was partition, in which Turkish sovereignty was limited to a Turkish kingdom in Anatolia, leaving the rest of the empire to be divided up between the Allies, with Russia to receive the northernmost slice of the cake, France the middle, and Great Britain the southern. The second scheme allowed for the Empire to remain as a state, nominally independent but under effective European control in Allied zones of political and commercial interest. The third plan, which reflected doubts the committee may have had about the wisdom of destroying a known entity and thereby creating a dangerous vacuum, was to maintain the Ottoman Empire in Asia as an independent state, while moving the Caliphate from Constantinople to somewhere such as Damascus.

The fourth plan, which the committee eventually recommended trying first, was devolution, in which the Ottoman Empire was preserved but had imposed upon it a decentralized system of administration, whereby it was divided into five historical and ethnographical *ayalets* or provinces – Anatolia, Armenia, Syria, Palestine and Iraq–Jazirah. Each one of these areas had its own characteristics, giving them all an individuality of their own, which made them suitable for the establishment within their borders of a form of local government, thus freeing them 'from the vampire hold of the metropolis' and giving them 'the chance to foster and develop their own resources'.[15]

The report of the de Bunsen Committee was eventually submitted in its final form to the Committee of Imperial Defence early in July. Though it never actually received official approval from the British Government, nor had its suggestions fully implemented, within it lay the seeds of Britain's future policy in the Middle East. It certainly marked the end of Mark's belief that the integrity of the Ottoman Empire should be maintained, a conviction that went out of the window when Turkey sided with Germany, as he wrote in a letter to Aubrey Herbert, marked 'from one genius to another' and posted on 1 April 1915. 'I perceive by your letter that you are pro-Turk still ...

Your policy is wrong. Turkey must cease to be. Smyrna shall be Greek. Adalia Italian, Southern Taurus and North Syria French, Filistin [Palestine] British, Mesopotamia British and everything else Russian, and Noel Buxton and I shall sing a Te Deum in St Sophia and a Nunc Dimittis in the Mosque of Omar. We will sing it in Welsh, Polish, Keltic, and Armenian in honour of all the gallant little nations … stir up mischief in Syria and you will get Germans massacred and the Turks ousted – keep worrying – never leave Orientals alone too long. If you don't feel like fighting them send money and cartridges to the right people – Never give the Turks a moments peace.'[16]

Before the final submission of the de Bunsen report 'Kitchener decided that I ought to go right round the Middle East,' Mark told Sir George Arthur, 'and report on the various situations.'[17] Thus early in June, accompanied by his Private Secretary, Walter Wilson, now a sergeant in the Territorials, and a Syrian interpreter, Antoine Albina, he set off on a tour that was to take him to Italy, the Balkans, the Eastern Mediterranean, Egypt, Aden, India, the Persian Gulf and Mesopotamia, with instructions to report back to General Calwell on whatever he felt might be of interest. Throughout the journey, he kept Edith entertained in his letters, even though 'I could not write to you … anything of any consequence owing to the Censorship.'

In Italy, which had just entered the war, 'it was very interesting that Italians have mobilised most wonderfully and seemed very enthusiastic and keen … At Naples much enthusiasm and I fear want of appreciation of what war means … So to Catania across the Messina Straits where there seemed to me a lamentable want of precautions against submarines.' In Syracuse he found himself 'in odd company at the Hotel. The keeper an Austrian, the constant guest a civilian agent of the German traders, a German female typewriter and occasional visitors two German Captains of ships which have put in there in early days – in fact as nice a nest of spies as ever was made – The British V. Consul an amiable loquacious person who certainly seemed to think that the war was a passing event and that Germans did not much matter. I am pretty sure that the German submarines have greatly profited by the presence of these people – it is very absurd that we have not proper consuls in war time in these places … I stirred him up to stir the police and I think the gang will be scattered. They were pretty furious at my arrival I could see …'

He travelled on a destroyer to the Dardanelles. 'It was great fun on the destroyer going across,' he wrote. 'The cannonading was not so earsplitting as I should have expected at 2 miles my nearest to it … What a riot the war is but I am not in the least depressed if only we can make up our minds – The Dardanelles people are heroes one and all – I dare not write to you of what I have been at, some day I will tell you if you remind me.' But if he could share nothing of great import, he could continue to regale her with the amusing details of daily life. 'Walter thrives badly on Mediterranean food & won't eat Maccaroni-Yaghourt-Pilaff – which being the only staples, he is getting indigestion on Sardines & bread – he went sick at Salonica & had to be left behind – I have been covered with Bugs & fleas & mosquitoes – Muscatel[18] is quite useless – curse the liar who invented it …'

From Sofia he wrote of meeting Gerald Fitzmaurice, whom he had known since he was chief dragoman in Constantinople. 'I have been shadowed by spies since Syracuse – and have lived among Germans all the time. Fitz Maurice lives between two Germans at Sofia, and they listen at the doors on each side of his room. Here is F & self talking in his bedroom … the Turks under German tuition are committing outrages

they never thought of before. They dug up the dead Russians at St Stefano who were buried during the war and by German order paraded the skulls round C'ople ...'[19]

Staying at Shepheard's Hotel in Cairo, he met Ronald Storrs, who had been a fellow pupil of Professor Browne's at Cambridge, and upon whom he made a lasting impression, particularly his powers of mimicry, which transformed him into 'a first-class music-hall comedian; holding a chance gathering spellbound by swift and complete changes of character, or speaking into my Dictaphone a twenty-five minutes Parliamentary Debate (for which I supplied the interruptions) with the matter as well as the manner of such different speakers as Lloyd George, F. E. Smith, John Redmond, or Sir Edward Carson rendered with startling accuracy ... Mark also dictated for the same instrument a three-act Drury Lane Melodrama, I providing the incidental music and he every other detail, including the trotting of horses, cracking of whips, crash of railway accidents and discharge of revolvers.'[20]

After a week in Cairo, Mark's departure for Aden was marred by what he described to Edith as 'a singular adventure'. 'I, Walter and Albina were arrested as spies by an Egyptian Mulazim who was abominably rude.

We were shut up in a police station – seldom have I been more furious – and we were kept for an hour. When the British officer in command arrived, the Mulazim had fled like the Egyptian he was ...'[21] After a week together, Storrs was sorry to see him leave. 'Mark has left for Aden. It did me good to hear this seasoned soldier and politician cry to his retainer: "Sergeant Wilson! Will you bring me my Shakespeare?" to remind me of an agreeable conceit in the drunken scene from *Anthony and Cleopatra*.'[22]

Travelling across the Red Sea on the SS *Kluva*, Mark was happy to find himself in the company of theatricals. 'Upon this ship I sit opposite the leading lady of the TIGER & THE GIRL Operetta and Illusionist company.

Her husband is less attractive:

and the 'Tyger' poor beast lives forward

in this sort of thing and the temperature is about 103° in the shade.'[23] He found the heat oppressive. 'These are the first heats we have met,' he recounted to Edith, 'and the paper is dabbled with my perspiration. My clothes are now much looser in spite of no exercise – but one does not eat much.' Sergeant Wilson had made friends with the twenty-two Second Class members of the Tiger and the Girl Company, and Mark could hear constant bellows of laughter from below decks, which reminded him of life at Eddlethorpe. 'The leading lady would make you scream with laughter. She is CALTIVEETED END REFAINED beyond words – the only other lady passenger is a Parsee aged 85 of forbidding aspect.'[24]

Mark described Aden, which was then part of British India, as being 'as near like Hell as any place on earth but is inhabited by Arabs both male and female with the most beautiful limbs and bodies imaginable. They are like Greek statues, with the heads of Ramases [*sic*] the II and dress thus

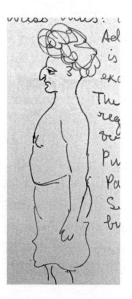

... The whole regime is very Indian, Punkahs, Parsis, Sikhs etc, but very successful.'[25]

In Aden, he found a 'general atmosphere of loyalty and confidence prevailing amongst the Arabs', together with a strong anti-Turkish feeling amongst a number of prisoners of war whom he interviewed. However, in a despatch to the War Office he expressed his disquiet at 'the want of co-ordination in our Arabian policy, owing to Aden being politically and militarily under Bombay in the first place, and the Government of India in the second instead of directly under Egypt. All the moral and intellectual ties between the Arabs and ourselves lie in Cairo rather than in India ... I should therefore imagine that it would tend to facilitate the development of a sound Anglo-Arabian policy if Aden was transferred temporarily to the G.O.C. in Egypt.'[26]

Holding such views, it is scarcely surprising that Mark's arrival in India was greeted in a manner that fell some way short of jubilation. Though requests had been sent to the India Office to give him 100 per cent cooperation, the Viceroy, Lord Hardinge, expressed the view that having a junior official from London going round gathering information and interviewing Anglo-Indians would be a cause of friction, not to mention a duplication of work. In his opinion, 'These amateur diplomatists are ... most dangerous people and Mark Sykes in particular owing to his lack of ballast.'[27] Hardinge was a thoughtful man of great experience, who had formerly been Ambassador to Russia, and he did not take kindly to being lectured by Mark on the entire Eastern situation and how to solve its problems. 'Sykes takes himself very seriously,' he wrote to the journalist Valentine Chirol, 'but seems unduly impressed with the importance of the Syrian Arabs', while telling the head of the India Office, Austen Chamberlain, that he could not go along with Mark's ideas for devolution in the Ottoman Empire, stating, 'Sykes did not seem to be able to grasp the fact that there are parts of Turkey unfit for representative institutions.'[28]

While continuing his task of interviewing prisoners of war, Mark also found time to regale Edith with tales of his social life as he travelled around. 'I have had great fun here. I stayed with Maharajah Bikanir – and to my delight find Indians live on excellent Pilaff & Yaghurt – English people prefer tinned salmon + condensed milk ... Here is Bikanirs Premier noble ...

Bikanir is chok [*sic*] civilisé but very proud of his ancestry.'[29] He described the Maharajah's palace as being 'very fine, of all ages with many treasures, and being Rajput has many strange pagan remains. The day I was there the "ladies of the town" sent a deputation to worship his throne, it being the feast day of Devi or Venus; that sounds almost like Nineveh doesn't it … When Bikanir goes out for a drive in his car the populace acclaim him and shout "Komân" "Mercy", an ancient custom.'[30]

At the prison camp he visited, 'there were Khojas and Mutessarifs and Bombashis and Nedawi and Cadhis and Muftis and Effendis, Syrians, Armenians, Greeks, Kurds, Circassians, etc, and the rule was – if they talked Arabic they were to be fed on curry made of vegetables. If they talked Turkish they were to be treated as Europeans. You may imagine how pleased the pro-English Syrians were and how the Turks smiled at our wise policy. At the prisoners' camp the natives still have bows and arrows so it's pretty out of the way.'[31]

Most of the time Mark found himself billeted with civil servants, whose conventionality he found suffocating. 'The Anglo-Indian of low degree,' he complained to Edith, 'is accustomed to travel with loads of servants, bedding, etc and expects all men to don evening-dress on all occasions, which is disconcerting if one only has a clean uniform. No allowance is made and I had to borrow such things.'

As a man of action and intense energy, nor could he understand the daily routine they all seemed to follow ...

'6.30. Breakfast – ride, swim, sleep, idle.
9.30. Breakfast.
10.45. Go to office.
12.30. Break for tiffin.
1.30. Tiffin.
2.30–4.30. Sleep – I think.
4.30–6.30. Go about.
6.30–8.0. Hang about club.
8.0. Dress for dinner
9.0. Dinner'

'The hours of labour,' he added, 'are also not convenient for anyone in a hurry.'[32]

What depressed Mark most about India was the fact that it seemed to be stuck in the Middle Ages. 'It is a shock to find that Indian towns like Delhi,' he wrote, 'have made obviously less progress in the last thirty years than, say, Konia or Kastamuni; this is a real blow to my ideas ... Of course, India is poor, over-populated and understaffed, but at root the secret of Turkish influence over Hindu Moslems who have been to Stambul is that they have seen there something externally more efficient than they see at home.'[33] While staying in Basra, the next step of his journey, he imparted these views to his host, Arnold Wilson, the Civil Commissioner for Mesopotamia, the efficiency of whose administration in that region had earned him the nickname 'the Despot of Mess-Pot'. They were views he did not share.

'In September, 1915,' he recorded in his diary, 'Colonel Mark Sykes ... was my guest for a few days ... and I retain a vivid recollection of his impetuous energy, his genius for happy but not always accurate generalisations, and his intense interest in everything he saw. Unlike most of his kind, he had been in no way impressed with the efficiency of British administration in India ... All this he told me when we met:

I did not agree then and I do not agree now, but he definitely encouraged the idea of an efficient administration, and impressed on me that in the long run we should stand or fall by our ability to "keep the simple folk by their right: defend the children of the poor, and punish the wrong-doer." He had an intense hatred of injustice and a thoroughly English compassion for the under-dog, but he was too short a time in Mesopotamia to gather more than fragmentary impressions.'[34]

In spite of the 'numerous and evil mosquitoes

that abounded there', Mark loved Basra. 'This place is delightful,' he told Edith. 'The river blue-yellow, between Palms olive green, and sky blue with houses Rosy Yellow and Arabs brown in gondolas ...' He greatly missed his children, however, telling her, 'My dearest darling Edith give all the babies kisses. Tell Freya to be ready to have a fine examination in Philemon Holland's Pliny and in YE HYSTORIE of YE KYNGES of ENGLAND!'[35]

At the end of September, Mark saw action with the Indian Expeditionary Force during its push towards Baghdad, an ill-thought-out campaign which would leave the army with a very thinly stretched supply line of hundreds of miles behind it. He was present when it took the town of Kut-al-Amara and reported on the victory for the *Observer*. It was excellent anti-Turk propaganda. 'Kut the day after its occupation was as Kut of the day before,' he wrote, 'yet with a difference. The Turks had gone and the British had come. The British soldier, the first gentleman in Europe or Asia, and his brother the Sepoy were in possession ... the Turks had fled in haste, our men, both horse and foot, reached the town soon after they had gone. For the last week the Turkish commander had been maintaining his prestige by daily hangings and shootings ... Enter the victors: within an hour the women were chaffering milk, dates and sweet limes, the merchants were offering contracts, policemen were patrolling the dirty little streets, a governor was established in an office ...'[36]

During the six months that he was away on his fact-finding mission, Mark apparently put up a lot of backs. 'Sykes appears to have been amazingly tactless,' wrote Capt. George Lloyd, a fellow MP who visited Iraq in his footsteps, 'and not only to have rather blustered everyone but also to have decried openly everything Indian in a manner which was bound to cause some resentment.'[37] Yet he had seen much and learned a great deal, particularly from his interviews with the great variety of Moslem prisoners he came across, whose opinions he canvassed on how they viewed India, Egypt and Arabia. He was filled with ideas that he transmitted to the War Office, such as a scheme to establish a new bureau in Cairo to wage political warfare against the Turks and the Germans and put an end to their fomenting discontent and anti-British feeling amongst Moslems. Increasingly he believed that the British Government must address its future attitude towards the Arab peoples within areas of British interests, and in a letter to General Calwell he urged that Britain should conclude an agreement with its allies regarding the future of Asiatic Turkey, after which they could 'make proclamation of our intentions and solidify the Arabs of Iraq, Palestine, Syria and Northern Mesopotamia against the Turks'.[38]

Chapter 11

The Sykes–Picot Agreement

On his way back to England from his long trip away, Mark stopped off in Cairo, where he passed on reports of what he had been doing, and learned of the latest developments in the war, the main talking point being the impending evacuation of troops from Gallipoli. One piece of news that particularly interested him was that the British High Commissioner in Egypt, Sir Henry McMahon, had been given the go-ahead by the Foreign Office to continue the wooing of Sharif Hussein. This was good news, since Mark knew that the Turks had made many promises to Hussein in order to persuade him and his followers to take up arms against the British.

What had sparked this off was the discovery by the Sharif in January 1915 of a plot to overthrow him, a decision that he soon discovered was irreversible. Realizing that his only chance of survival was to reignite the idea of leading an Arab revolt against the Turks, a risky move that could leave him isolated in the Arab world, he decided to send his son, Faisal, to Damascus to sound out the leaders of certain secret Arab societies there as to whether they would give him their support. What he found was a strong inclination among them to set up a bidding war for Arab loyalties between Britain and Turkey. The Turks, however, scenting the possibility of rebellion amongst the Arabs, tried to forestall this by attempting to break up the various societies and arrest their leaders, a move that left behind a group of conspirators who made the decision to throw in their hand with Hussein. These men drew up a document, the 'Damascus Protocol', that laid out their demands, in return for the granting of which they would ally themselves with Britain.

The Damascus Protocol was nothing less than a demand for complete independence secured against all foreign interventions, the creation in fact of what Mark was to refer to as a 'Greater Arabia'. The conditions laid out were the minimum on which a call to revolt could be justified, and though Faisal was extremely doubtful that the Allies would accept them, he undertook to hasten to Mecca to show them to his father. Before he left Damascus, he witnessed an oath of allegiance taken by six of the principal leaders binding them to recognize the Sharif as the leader of the Arab race, and pledging that were an agreement reached with Britain on the basis of the Damascus Protocol, the Arab divisions in Syria would all rise with him. As a token of his good faith, the most important of the six, Sheik Baduddin al-Hasani, removed his signet ring and gave it to Faisal to hand over to his father.

Thus it was that in mid-July 1915, the British High Commissioner in Cairo had received out of the blue a letter from Sharif Hussein demanding that almost all of Arab Asia should become an independent kingdom under his rule, an area bounded on the east by Persia, on the south by the Indian Ocean, on the west by the Red Sea and the Mediterranean up to Mersin, and on the north by a line running from Mersin in the west to the Persian border in the east. In return for that agreement the Arab people would enter into an alliance with Great Britain. To the Oriental Secretary, Ronald Storrs, it seemed an exorbitant demand, particularly at a time when the British were still confident of defeating the Turks in Gallipoli and taking Constantinople. 'As I struggled through his difficult writing and even more difficult Arabic,' he wrote, 'I found myself murmuring

> In matters of commerce the fault of the Dutch
> Is offering too little and asking too much.'[1]

With the consequent failure of the August offensive in Gallipoli, however, and increasing Ottoman success, the possibility of internal Arab revolt became more tantalizing, and with it the importance of keeping Hussein and his sons onside.

McMahon's reply, sent on 30 August, opened with a series of 'complimentary titles' which would not have been out of place in a pantomime, and which did little to impress the Sharif. 'To the excellent and well-born Sayyed, the descendant of Sharifs, the Crown of the Proud, Scion of Muhammad's Tree and Branch of the Quraishite Trunk, him of the Exalted Presence and of the Lofty Rank, Sayyed son of Sayyed, Sharif son of Sharif, the Venerable, Honoured Sayyed, his Excellency the Sharif Hussein, Lord of the Many, Amir of Mecca, the Blessed, the lodestar of the Faithful and the cynosure of all devout Believers, may his Blessing descend upon the people in their multitudes.'[2]

It then reiterated the general assurances to the Sharif previously given by Lord Kitchener, regarding both Arab independence and the Caliphate. Otherwise he was evasive, abstaining from saying either yes or no, simply stating, 'As for the question of frontiers and boundaries, negotiations would appear to be premature and a waste of time on details at this stage, with the War in progress and the Turks in effective occupation of the greater part of those regions.'[3] Such elusive posturing greatly annoyed Hussein, as did the 'highly decorated phrases and titles', and he was forthright in his reply, expressing his disappointment at the 'lukewarmth and hesitancy' shown by McMahon 'in regard to our essential clause'. He spoke, he said, not on his behalf, but on behalf 'of our people who believe that those frontiers form the minimum necessary to the establishment of the new order for which they are striving. This they are determined to obtain ...'[4]

It was clear from this letter that Arab territorial ambitions would have to be addressed immediately in order to strike a deal, a fact that became increasingly important as an eventual Allied evacuation from Gallipoli became more likely, which would release large parts of the Ottoman army for deployment elsewhere. On 24 October, McMahon sent his reply in a letter that has been the source of considerable controversy ever since, and has often been cited as proof of the great betrayal of the Arabs by the British. It was a masterpiece of diplomatic language in which he made commitments while being simultaneously non-committal, a necessity since at this time nobody was quite sure what might have to be conceded at a later date to either France or Russia, or indeed to other Arabs of whom Hussein was not the spokesman, namely the Syrian Arabs or the Arabs of Iraq.

Thus he conceded to Hussein that 'subject to the modifications stated above, Great Britain is prepared to recognize and uphold the independence of the Arabs in all the regions lying within the frontiers proposed by the Sharif of Mecca'. But in appearing to promise a lot, he actually promised very little. The 'modifications' were various, and concerned, for example, the Arab sheikdoms of the Persian Gulf, Oman, Qatar, Bahrain and Kuwait, with whom Britain had special relations going back to the early nineteenth century. Hussein's chosen boundaries would be recognized, he stated, so long as it was 'without prejudice to the treaties concluded between us and certain Arab chiefs'. Another area of contention was the oil-rich provinces of Baghdad and Basra, which had come under British control as part of the Mesopotamia campaign. Here '… Great Britain's established position and interests … will call for the setting up of special administrative arrangements to protect those regions from foreign aggression … and to safeguard our mutual economic interests.'[5]

Where McMahon had to be most careful was in making any commitments to the Arabs that might contravene previous agreements made with France, such as their demands, back in March 1915, to annex Syria together with the region of the Gulf of Alexandretta and Cilicia. He knew only too well that should France insist on these ambitions, then it would be the end of any further negotiation with Hussein. So, cleverly, using the rather bogus argument that 'they cannot be said to be purely Arab', he excepted from the proposed delimitation 'the districts of Mersin and Alexandretta, and portions of Syria lying to the west of the districts of Damascus, Homs, Hama and Aleppo'.[6] In this way he removed from the equation territories that might in the future cause problems for Franco-British relations.

The Foreign Secretary, Sir Edward Grey, recognizing France's special interest in the Levant, knew that no final promises could be made to Hussein without her permission. He therefore met with the French Ambassador in London, Jules Cambon, and filled him in with the details of McMahon's dealings with Hussein, suggesting that he get his government to send a delegate over who was 'qualified to settle the extent of Syria's borders with Lord Kitchener'.[7] The man Cambon recommended, 'who knows the Syrian question better than anyone',[8] was Charles François Georges-Picot, the former Consul-General in Beirut. Born in Paris in 1870, Georges-Picot came from a famous colonialist dynasty, his father, the historian Georges Picot, having been a member of both the Comité de l'Afrique and the Comité de l'Asie Française, colonialist societies that had an important influence on the course of French expansion. Tall and fair, with a 'fluting voice',[9] he had begun his diplomatic career in his late twenties, serving in Denmark and Paris, and in 1909 was posted to Peking, where he rose to the post of First Secretary. His posting to Beirut as Consul-General in 1914 only lasted eight months, but in that time he established a powerful reputation among the Lebanese Christians, and when war broke out, the Maronite Patriarch, Monsignor Hoyek, the leading figure in Christian Lebanon, had moved to have him remain in his post. 'There would be nothing to prevent M. Picot, greatly loved in Lebanon,' he had written to the French Foreign Minister, 'from assuming the moral leadership of our national defence.'[10]

Picot had only one unfortunate stain on his career, which was as a result of a wrong decision. When the Turks entered the war, and Beirut was under threat, he failed to take the advice of his American counterpart to destroy all the official files, placing them instead under the diplomatic protection of the US Consulate. A year later, when Turkish troops occupied the Lebanon, they ignored the rules and seized the files, which, when opened, revealed the identities of many Lebanese and Syrians whose sympathies lay with Arab nationalism or with France, rather than with the Ottoman Empire. The Turkish leader, Djemal Pasha, used this information to arrest and charge with treason Arab opponents of the regime, many of whom were subsequently hanged in Damascus and Beirut, earning Picot among the local Arab inhabitants the name of *al-Saffah*, 'the Blood Shedder'. It was an affair that would haunt him for the rest of his life.

Considering his colonialist background, it is not surprising that the party in the French Parliament which Picot represented was the 'Syrian Party', led by the 26-year-old Pierre-Etienne Flandin, who was later to become Prime Minister of France. His manifesto argued that Syria and Palestine were one country, '*la Syrie intégrale*', whose history had been shaped by France, going back a thousand years to the days of the Crusades. 'This French Syria must not be a dwarf state set amidst much bigger foreign possessions, eking out a precarious existence within constricted frontiers and remaining an onerous charge on the metropolitan budget. Our Syria needs extensive borders that will make it capable of earning its own way.'[11] Not only was it vital to France for commercial, historic and geographic reasons, but for strategic reasons too, for he believed that if Syria were to fall into the hands of an imperial rival, French influence in the Middle East would be fatally compromised. When Picot was posted to the London Embassy in August 1915, he set about winning over Cambon to these ideas, the end result being that he was recommended as the man to negotiate a Middle Eastern partition with Britain.

The first negotiations began on 23 November 1915, and were with a British team headed by the Permanent Under-Secretary at the Foreign Office, Sir Arthur Nicolson, along with six senior representatives from the Foreign, India, and War Offices. Picot may have been outranked and outnumbered, but he was in no way intimidated. Amusingly, in order to ensure that 'my instructions are satisfactory' he had drafted them himself, reminding himself from the very beginning that though he foresaw the possibility of compromises, any kind of concession in advance of negotiations was 'deplorable in the highest degree'. 'Our task,' he instructed his negotiating self, 'is to make our demands and to abandon ground only foot by foot if compelled to do so; that way we shall always have some ground left.' With the Syrian Party's manifesto in the forefront of his mind, he wrote, 'You are to insist that our possessions stop only at the Egyptian frontier', and foreseeing that there would undoubtedly be objections to French occupation of the Holy Places, he continued, 'it will be easy for you to reply that the objection which could be made to France would apply equally to any other owner of southern Syria'.[12]

But from the outset Picot was playing the diplomatic game of making big demands in order to strengthen his bargaining power, for in reality the French government did not really want to be stuck with direct rule over the whole of Syria, which, in a time of war, would have put enormous strain on them economically, as well as taking large numbers of troops away from the front line. Once he had impressed the British with the strength of his opposition, he would start to moderate it, in the hope of getting some concession in return. So to begin with he made it quite clear that no French government would survive that was prepared to surrender any French claims in Syria, and from this position he would not budge, in spite of Nicolson pleading that the vital necessity of getting Arab participation in the war against the Turks depended on the promise to them of a large Arab state. 'To promise the Arabs a large state,' commented Picot, 'is to throw dust in their eyes. Such a state will never materialize. You cannot transform a myriad of tribes into a viable whole.'[13] Even when the subject was raised of possible French control over Lebanon and the Mediterranean coast further north, he would not give way, adding 'nothing short of a French annexation of Syria would be admitted by the French public'.[14] With that, impasse was reached and Picot returned to France to submit the British proposals to his government. It was at this point that Mark entered the picture, having returned to England in mid-December and reported directly to Downing Street, meeting on 16 December to present evidence on the Arab question. Present were the Prime Minister, Mr Asquith, Lord Kitchener, David Lloyd George, the Minister of Munitions, and Arthur Balfour, First Lord of the Admiralty.

During the meeting Mark stressed that he felt that Britain should settle with France as soon as possible and get a definitive understanding about Syria. 'What sort of an arrangement would you like to have with the French,' asked Balfour. 'What would you say to them?'

'I should like to retain for ourselves,' replied Mark, 'such country south of Haifa as was not in the Jerusalem enclave ... I think it is most important that we should have a belt of English-controlled country between the Sharif of Mecca and the French.'

'You mean the whole way round from the Egyptian frontier to Haifa?' asked the Prime Minister.

'We have always regarded this 90 or 100 miles of desert upon her eastern side as a stronghold of Egypt;' commented Balfour, 'now you propose still further east of that to give us a bit of inhabited and culti-vated country for which we should be responsible. At first sight it looks as if that would weaken and not strengthen our position in Egypt.'

'I think that what Sir Mark Sykes means,' explained Kitchener, 'is that the line will commence at the sea-coast at Haifa. These Arabs,' he added, pointing at the Arabian peninsula, 'will then come under our control, whereas if we are off the line we lose control over the south.'

'What do you mean to give exactly?' Balfour then asked, regarding the French. To which Mark replied, drawing his finger across the map that lay before them on the table. 'I should like to draw a line from the "e" in Acre to the last "k" in Kerkúk.'

While Lloyd-George saw this as a possible prelude to military action against the Turks, Asquith had a different approach. 'We must have a political deal,' he said, winding up proceedings. 'We must come to terms with the French, which means we must come to terms diplomatically.'[15]

At the end of the meeting, 'Lord Kitchener told me personally,' Mark reported, 'to get hold of the Franco-British negotiations which were at a deadlock, and I worked through Picot the Franco-British agreement on Lord Kitchener's lines.'[16]

When Mark joined the negotiations, he found them deadlocked once again. Picot had returned to London with an offer that he had outlined to the committee when it reconvened on 21 December.

France would agree to forgo direct rule of Syria, even though by rights it was hers, and accept a zone of influence, but in return for this she expected Britain to make considerable concessions. In the first instance Picot was happy with Britain's agreement to accept French rule over a 500-mile band of territory from Cilicia in the west to the Persian frontier in the east, as well as over the Mediterranean ports of Alexandretta and Latakia. What he rejected outright, however, was the British proposal for Lebanon, which was that it would become a nominal part of the new Arab State under the administration of a French governor. His argument was that the large community of Maronite Christians that resided there would never accept even the nominal sovereignty of Sharif Hussein, and that only French rule would prevent the outbreak of religious war. As Cambon wrote, somewhat prophetically, to the French Prime Minister, Aristide Briand, 'It is enough to know the intensity of rivalries between the various rites and religions in the Orient to foresee the violence of the internal strife in Lebanon as soon as no external authority is there to curb it.'[17]

Mark now met with Picot on an almost daily basis, negotiating with him at the French Embassy, and it was not long before a friendship developed between them that grew out of mutual respect and lasted throughout the war. Each evening he would report back to Oswald Fitzgerald at the War Office, and through him to Kitchener, of whom sightings were rare. 'During this work,' he later reported, 'I saw Lord Kitchener occasionally – about 3 times in all ... one worked a sort of triangular equation; I acted, Fitzgerald spoke, he inspired.'[18] It is difficult to know exactly whose ideas presided, particularly since Mark later said of Kitchener, 'I could never make myself understood: I could never understand what he thought, and he could never understand what I thought', but gradually a deal was hammered out.

The first thing Mark did was to drop the British demand to make Lebanon and Mediterranean Syria a nominal part of the proposed new Arab State. He also agreed to include Mosul in the French zone, thereby extending the French sphere of influence eastward from Syria, something that Picot had been very keen to achieve. For this 'concession' he and Kitchener had very sound reasons. At a time when the 'Great Game' was still very much a reality, the new French Zone would create a buffer between the British and Russians that might help avoid future friction. In return for Mosul Picot agreed to concede the ports of Haifa and Acre to the south of Beirut together with a territorial belt on which Britain could construct a planned trans-Asian railway. The only stumbling bock was Palestine, which both parties wanted for themselves, Picot for its prestige, and Mark in order to complete his plan for a line of Imperial defence. In the end it was agreed that it should have an international administration.

Of course, Sharif Hussein and the Arabs who supported him were not consulted during the course of these negotiations because Kitchener and his Allied partners knew perfectly well that it was impossible to reconcile their claims with his, and so they made the decision to keep both the talks a secret and the treaty that came out of them. 'The Sykes–Picot Agreement', which was concluded on 3 January 1916, effectively defined areas of colonial domination in Syria and Mesopotamia in which France and Great Britain were 'at liberty to establish such direct or indirect administration or control as they may desire or as they may deem fit to establish after agreement with the Arab State or Confederation of Arab States'.

The treaty, as drawn up by Mark and Picot, took into account the Acre–Kerkúk line that Mark had described to the Cabinet back in December. Territory to the north of this line, the 'blue area', came under French protection, and included the coastal areas of modern Syria and Lebanon down to the port of Tyre, as well as, to the north, an extensive part of eastern Anatolia. Territory to the south, the 'red area', was under British control and took in the Iraqi provinces of Basra and Baghdad. Apart from Haifa and Acre, already promised to Britain, Palestine was to form a 'Brown' zone under an international administration, the make-up of which was to be decided after consultation with Russia and the representatives of Islam, but it was stipulated that whatever happened, the requirements of Christianity,

Judaism and Islam must be accommodated. The vast desert hinterlands that lay between these coloured zones were nominated as independent Arab states, with the northern one, designated A, under French protection. This included the major inland cities of Syria – Aleppo, Homs, Hama, and Damascus. The southern one, designated B, spanned the deserts of Northern Arabia from Iraq to Egypt, and fell under British protection. 'France and Great Britain,' stated the Agreement, 'are prepared to recognize and uphold an independent Arab State or a Confederation of Arab States in the areas shown as A and B on the annexed map, under the suzerainty of an Arab Chief.' It is not surprising that the Allies were so keen to hide the treaty from Hussein, since its contents fell far short of McMahon's pledges to him, something that, among the members of the British Cabinet, only the Prime Minister seemed to be aware of, stating at a meeting on 23 March that he 'thought the Arabs would not be content with the A and B areas'. His mind was, however, put at rest by the Foreign Secretary. 'Sir Edward Grey pointed out that the four cities Homs, Damascus, Hamma and Aleppo have been assigned to them which would satisfy them.'[19]

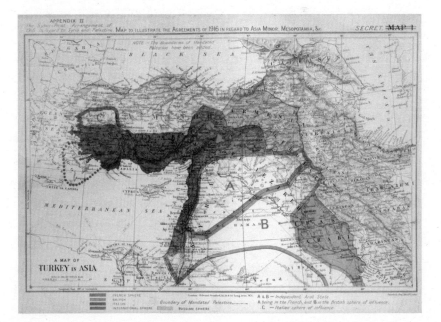

Two conditions were still attached to the Sykes–Picot Agreement, the first being that the British insisted that it would not be put into effect until the Arab Revolt was proclaimed. Secondly the terms of the wartime alliance necessitated the agreement of Russia, which is how Mark, accompanied by the faithful Walter Wilson, found himself travelling to Petrograd in the middle of March. The first leg of the journey, by boat, was miserable as the seas were high and he was sick thirty times 'i.e once every hour'. When they finally reached Stockholm, he found time to write Edith a short letter. His correspondence with her was far less regular during this period, mostly owing to the war and his hectic timetable, and what he could say was limited. However, he continued to amuse her with his observations. 'Walter is still in this state,' he wrote on 3 March from the Grand Hotel Royal, 'and seems to refuse all comfort while awake but sleeps most of the time as usual.

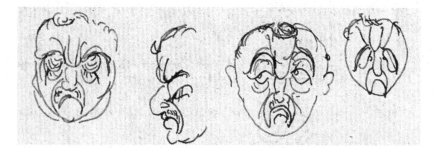

I cannot understand anyone taking no interest whatever in anything.' He apologized for the lack of interesting news. 'I can say very little as there is a strict censorship both in and out – I saw some fine pictures today by a Swede who I think paints men better than Sergeant[20] – incredibly better – he paints women too but only paints this sort of woman:

i.e. Swedish peasant women with no clothes on. It is a very great pity as his men with clothes on are as grand as Velasquez.'[21]

A few days later, Mark arrived in Petrograd, where he enjoyed an audience with the Tsar. 'General Calwell has come from England,' wrote Tsar Nicholas to Tsaritsa Alexandra, on 7 March, 'together with another very interesting man, Major Sykes, who has travelled all his life in Asia Minor and Mesopotamia, and knows the Turks and Arabs well, He has told me many strange and noteworthy things.'[22] The Tsar struck Mark as being like a well-informed schoolboy of fifteen, though one with a prodigious memory. He was impressed by his recalling the exact position of every unit in the Russian army, and by the fact that as he passed down the line of officers drawn up in the ante-room before dinner, he remembered exactly what each one had done. Mark in turn impressed the Tsar enough for him to make him a Commander of the Order of St Stanislaus, an award that honoured service to the Tsar.

On 10 March, Mark and Picot met up to present their draft agreement to the Russian Foreign Minister, Sergei Sazonow, who saw no problems with the British demands, their area of interest being so far to the south. He did, however, express extreme surprise that Britain had allowed France so much territory on the Persian border. After several days of negotiation, the Russians came up with counter-proposals, claiming for themselves what the French had been given on their borders in return for giving them a share of Turkish Armenia. This more than satisfied Picot, who told Albert Defrance, the Secretary of State for War, that the negotiations had 'achieved everything I could have hoped for',[23] while Mark wrote to Nicolson: 'P is in the highest spirits over his new Castle in Armenia.'[24]

Writing from the Hotel Astoria in Petrograd, Mark told Edith, 'Since I last wrote I have had wonderful luck, settled everything and should be soon back after you get this. Information by mouth – now only personal details for your amusement. Petrograd delightful, all sorts of funny old things.

One drives in sleys [sic]

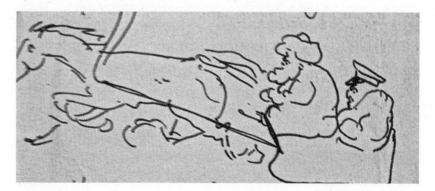

but this hotel is nothing but a Brothel and consequently very noisy. The reading room is like the Empire promenade and full of officers and other persons. I am reading Johnson's life again – he would make the same observation about this hotel as he did about the Green Room at Drury Lane; "The silk stockings of your actresses disturb me ..."

I have not been anywhere (been so busy) except to the opera last night & the Ballet tonight. Opera a foolish one with poor music by Tshaikowsky [*sic*] ... and is long and tiresome. The opera however is well staged with splendid scenery – the baritone was amusing in his dress A also the tenor B both dresses correct for 1820 which is the period ...

The Rusks fancy themselves in art and produce Carmen from photographs of modern Seville to be as like as possible – consequence absurd. The Matador appears in the first act thus

done up as the Bullfighter of 1905 and Carmen in a Paris frock – very ridiculous …'[25]

However happy Mark may have been with the agreement that he had come to with Picot, he returned home to find it being regarded with some scepticism within government circles. George McDonogh, the Director of Military Intelligence at the War Office, typified this sentiment when he wrote, 'It seems to me we are rather in the position of the hunters who divided up the skin of the bear before they had killed it.'[26] The head of intelligence at the Admiralty, Captain Reginald Hall, made another point, which was that the Jews, who had 'a strong *material*, and a very strong *political* interest in the future of the country', might well oppose any promises made to the Arabs. This latter view gave cause for thought to Mark, who up till now had not considered the Jews at all in his calculations.

Chapter 12

Zionism

On 9 November 1914, the Home Secretary, Herbert Samuel, a leading member of a distinguished Jewish family, and the first practising Jew to serve as a Cabinet Minister in the British Government, recorded in his diary, 'I spoke to Sir Edward Grey today about the future of Palestine. In the course of our talk I said that now that Turkey had thrown herself into the European War and that it was probable that her Empire would be broken up, the question of the future control of Palestine was likely to arise. The jealousies of the great European Powers would make it difficult to allot the country to any one of them. Perhaps the opportunity might arise for the fulfilment of the ancient aspiration of the Jewish people and the restoration there of a Jewish State.'[1] What Samuel was talking about to Grey was the long-held goal of the Zionists, the Jewish Nationalist movement, that they should one day find suitable territory in which to create their own independent State.

Up till now Mark's views on the Jews were the anti-Semitic opinions of a man of his time and class. He saw them as a secret society who were spread around the world, yet always in touch with one another, conspiring to control global events, both financially and politically. 'Sykes sees Jews in everything',[2] his former professor at Cambridge, E. G. Browne, had said of him. But Mark was intrigued by what Captain Hall had said regarding their interest in Palestine and knowing of, but little about, Zionism he decided to ask Samuel to enlighten him on the subject. Before he left for Russia to meet up with Picot, Samuel gave him a copy of 'The Future of Palestine', a memo he had presented to the British Cabinet in January 1915. This suggested that the time was not yet ripe for an independent, autonomous Jewish State in Palestine, the reason being that 'If the attempt were made to place the 400,000 or 500,00 Mahommedans of Arab race under a Government which rested upon the support of 90,000 or 100,000 Jewish inhabitants, there can be no assurance that such a Government, even if established by the authority of the Powers, would be able to command obedience. The dream of a Jewish State, prosperous, progressive, and the home of a brilliant civilization, might vanish in a series of squalid conflicts with the Arab population.' The solution he suggested 'which would be much the most welcome to the leaders and supporters of the Zionist movement throughout the world would be the annexation of the country to the British Empire'.[3]

Mark found a thriving Zionist movement in Russia held in great suspicion by the Tsarists, who saw them as a hostile power, maintaining neutrality while demonstrating complete loyalty to Turkey and therefore liable to support Germany. But he realized that the Jews were dangerous only if they were alienated, in which scenario, because their power and influence were worldwide, they might do damage to the Allied cause. The answer, he believed, was to win them over, and, with that, their support for an Allied victory. 'If they want us to win,' he wrote to Nicolson, 'they will do their best, which means they will (A) Calm their activities in Russia (B) Pessimise in Germany (C) Stimulate in France, England and Italy (D) Enthuse in the U.S.A.' On the other hand, 'With Great Jewry against us there is no possible chance … it means optimism in Berlin – dumps in London, unease in Paris, resistance to the last ditch in C'ople – dissension in Cairo – Arabs all squabbling among themselves – as Shakespeare says "Untune that string and hark what discord follows …"'[4]

Mark knew, from a telegram he was shown by Sir George Buchanan, the British Ambassador to Russia, that there was some support within the British government for a Jewish settlement in Palestine. It had come from the former Secretary of State for India, Lord Crewe, and suggested that any formula for such a settlement 'might be made far more attractive to the majority of Jews if it held out to them the prospect that when in course of time the Jewish colonists in Palestine grow strong enough to cope with the Arab population they may be allowed to take the management of the internal affairs of Palestine (with the exception of Jerusalem and the Holy Places) into their own hands'.[5]

While the Russians had every reason to support this idea, the dilemma for Mark was that though he managed to persuade his friend Picot of the 'inestimable advantages to allied cause of active friendship of Jews of the World',[6] he found little enthusiasm from him for the Jewish desire that the country should be under British rule, rather than French or international rule. So together they concocted a plan that they hoped might be acceptable to all parties, including the Jews and the Arabs. To placate the latter, for example, they suggested appointing an Arab Sultan, possibly one of the Sharif's sons, as titular head of Palestine, who would be under both French and British protection. Then they came up with the idea of establishing a chartered land company to purchase territory for Jewish colonists, who would then become citizens with equal rights to Arabs. So far as the Holy Places were concerned, the three great powers must come to an agreement over how best to administer them.

Such ideas cut little ice with London, however, who saw a danger that they might end up alienating both Jews and Arabs, and Nicolson telegraphed Mark telling him to keep all such thoughts to himself. Even if what he had discussed with Picot had been relatively harmless, the fact was that the Allies still needed the Arabs to revolt against Turkey and this could well be endangered if they got an inkling that not only was France laying claim to the coastal areas of Syria, but France and Britain were both considering some gesture towards the Jews in Palestine. Mark agreed that it was necessary to 'keep actual terms of provisional agreement from knowledge of Arab leaders'.[7] When 'we bump into a thing like Zionism, which is atmospheric, international, cosmopolitan, subconscious, and unwritten – nay often unspoken – it is not possible to work and think on ordinary lines'.[8] In such circumstances, he believed, secret diplomacy was the order of the day.

On his return to England in April 1916, Mark decided that he needed to further his knowledge about Zionism. Once again he contacted Samuel, who introduced him to Dr Moses Gaster, the Chief Rabbi of the Sephardic Jews in England. Tall and bearded and born in Romania, from where he had been deported, Gaster was striking in appearance and quarrelsome by nature. He was also a brilliant scholar of Jewish and Middle Eastern history, mythology, and English folk-lore, and spoke ten languages. Mark was deeply impressed and told him his ideas, which Gaster and Samuel then discussed with two other Jewish leaders, Chaim Weizmann and Nahum Sokolow, at a meeting at Gaster's home, 193 Maida Vale, on 11 April. 'H.S.'s meeting of far-reaching and momentous importance,' Gaster wrote in his diary on 16 April. 'It practically comes to a complete realization of our Zionist programme. We are offered French-English condominium in Palest. Arab Prince to conciliate Arab sentiment and as part of the Constitution a Charter to Zionists for which England would stand guarantee and which would stand by us in every case of friction …'[9]

This was all fine, except that it appears that Mark had failed to mention that none of these proposals had been approved by the Foreign Office. He hoped to move things forward by introducing Picot to Gaster, when he returned to London in early May, but the Frenchman did not fall under his spell and was thus disinclined to support Mark's suggestion that France and Britain should cease to be rivals in the Middle East, but should work together in support of Arabs and Jews. Mark was also genuinely worried that if the Allies failed to offer the Jews a place in Palestine, then this might tip the scales for them in favour of the Turks and Germany, wherein lay the possibility of an Allied defeat. Though he did his very best to persuade Picot to present this argument to his government, he was only inter-ested in formally concluding the Sykes–Picot agreement as it had been agreed on in Russia in April, so for the time being the Jewish question was put aside. On 16 May 1916, six months after they had begun their negotiations, the two men finally put their signatures on the map that they had drawn up. The dividing line, territories and zones were all marked up in coloured pencil, and they placed their names in the bottom right-hand corner just below Basra, Picot signing F. Georges-Picot in black ink, Mark signing Mark Sykes in pencil, an indication perhaps of how much faith each had in what they had achieved.

Now that Mark's work with the Foreign Office was over, he needed to find himself a new base, preferably a job that did not have him stuck working in one department, something that was anathema to a man as restless as he was. The lifeline came from Maurice Hankey, an important civil servant who was secretary to the Committee of Imperial Defence, which was responsible for research on issues of military strategy. He appointed Mark as one of his assistants, and gave him a desk in the department's offices in Whitehall Gardens. His brief was to act as liaison officer for Middle Eastern affairs between the Foreign, War and India Offices. The information that he gathered together from the relevant sources was then published in a weekly *Arabian Report*, the London counterpart to the *Arab Bulletin*, founded on the initiative of T. E. Lawrence to provide a secret magazine of Middle East politics. The *Report* was a compilation of secret papers, made up of telegrams, memoranda and reports of operations, relating to Eastern affairs, with a commentary on them written by him for the guidance of the War Committee, and it was only issued to about twenty people, who included the King, the members of the Committee and various senior officials.

There was much to think about, not least the fact that on 5 June Lord Kitchener, on a diplomatic trip to Russia, put to sea from Scapa Flow on the Royal Navy's battle-cruiser H.M.S. *Hampshire*, bound for Archangel. Three hours into the journey, the ship struck a mine and went down with almost all hands, including Kitchener. Ironically, considering that he had done as much as any man to promote it, on the very same day, Sharif Hussein finally proclaimed his Arab Revolt, launching a number of attacks against various Turkish positions across the length of the Hijaz. Unfortunately it turned out to be something of a damp squib, drawing nothing like the support throughout the Arabic-speaking Moslem world that the Arab Bureau in Cairo had predicted. Hussein and his son Feisal had first intimated that they expected to be joined by about a third of the Ottoman army, amounting to 100,000 Arabic-speaking troops, later increasing this number to 250,000 troops joining them. In the event, no more than a few thousand tribesmen supported the Revolt.

Mark now did his utmost to try and persuade the War Committee to throw their weight behind Hussein's Revolt, warning them that if it did not succeed, the Ottoman Empire could end up as little more than a German colony. In a secret memorandum entitled 'The Problem of the Near East' he stated, 'The rising of the Sharif of Mecca is an event of importance as it brings us face to face with the necessity of adopting a definite policy with regard to the Arabs, and consideration of our contingent intentions in the Middle East.' On the bright side of things, he suggested, the Arab Revolt might spread of its own accord into Syria and North Mesopotamia and help bring Turkey to its knees. But just as, if not more, likely was that the Turks would crush the Revolt, small as it was, the practical results of which would be disastrous: 'if our protégé is successful all will be well, but if he is driven out of the holy places and they are retaken by the Turks a terrible ferment will be set up among Mohammedans, we shall have played with fire and probably have set our house in a blaze. The Turks will be in Mecca for good and will use it as a fountain of sedition, excitement and anarchy. This will be as serious for France as ourselves, and almost as serious for Russia. Having launched the Sharif on his rebellion it is imperative that we should see that he keeps his head above water ...'[10] But the War Committee seemed unimpressed by Mark's arguments and however much he urged them to think again, his cause was not helped by the fact that the newly appointed Chief of the Imperial General Staff, Field Marshal Sir William Robertson, would not contemplate diverting troops or efforts from the Western Front.

While he gnashed his teeth in frustration, Mark put his time to good use, his former tutor, Egerton Beck, describing a typical day as thus. 'Day after day he made what he called his rounds: first to the War Office to interview various high officials and to visit the Arabian section of the Intelligence Department, which was at that time the high-water mark of "intelligence": then to the India Office and the Foreign Office to get the latest news from Egypt, from the Persian Gulf and Eastern Arabia, to say nothing of the doings for good or ill of our Allies. And this was not all, there were interviews with generals home on leave, with intelligence officers from one front or another. With ambassadors, with politicians, with Arabs, Syrians, Armenians and Jews, and speeches in the house. His day began with an early mass in Westminster Cathedral, which he often served, and ended, it might be, at midnight.'[11]

He lived almost permanently at Buckingham Gate, with the occasional weekend visit to Sledmere. At the beginning of August he was obliged to forgo one of these much anticipated northern trips, but was, as he wrote to Edith, 'rewarded ... at 02.15 I was aroused from a dream of Lloyd George moving all our furniture & throwing it downstairs by finding that shells were bursting on both sides of the house, say about 1½ miles away. Out of your window I only saw shells, but I crossed to the other side & saw a Zep very clearly with shells bursting near it. In about 5 minutes it made off due north and disappeared ... suddenly the sky from the north began to light up until it was like daylight just after sunrise only bright red ... everywhere you could hear little distant cheers. The light lasted by my calculation about 35 seconds ...'[12]

Later in the morning he and a friend jumped on a train and went in search of the destroyed Zeppelin, which had come down near the village of Cuffley to the north of London. Since the train was crowded with other 'delighted' people, they travelled in the guard's van with fifteen others. 'By the time we got to Cuffley,' he wrote, 'there were 40 in the guards van, children, Mrs Nuggins, clerks, farmers, all agog with joy ... it was Goodwood on the big day and crowds and crowds, bicycles, motors, dog-carts, vans full of girls and men, and converging streams of people on foot, all in the highest spirits. I cannot estimate crowds. But every road was blocked and people were pouring over the fields, and I remember every platform of the 12 stations between Finsbury Park and Cuffley had been crowded – so to a little field where some 200 Scots Guards held the ground, and in the midst the wreckage. The Zep had been dealt with thus ...

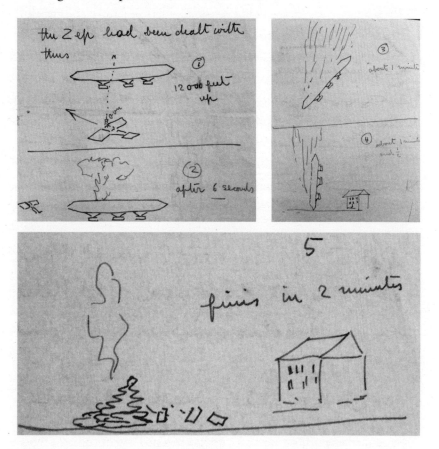

Much was fished out of the wreckage, one gondola complete, barely scorched, and a great deal of other stuff including 15 German bodies which looked very much like Ramases [*sic*] at the Bulak Museum ... A most interesting afternoon I think, don't you? I am sending each of the children a piece of Zep, but they must keep them.'[13]

As well as being an exciting story to tell his children, this was a timely reminder of the war that was raging in Europe. Another piece of news came from the front, to remind Mark of just how far removed he was from his regiment of Yorkshire 'Terriers'. This was the death in action of his friend Edward Bagshawe, killed at Flanders on 22 July. It was a difficult loss for him, since they had been friends since boyhood, and Bagshawe had been a witness at the trial of his mother for fraud. What made it worse, however, was the sense of guilt he felt, particularly since he was aware that after he had left the Terriers to work for Kitchener, there had been accusations in certain circles that abandoning his regiment was an act of cowardice. The news about Bagshawe sent him into a deep depression that was only lightened by a trip to Sledmere to see Edith and the family, a visit made more joyous by the fact that Edith was six months pregnant with her sixth child, conceived during one of their increasingly rare and ecstatic reunions.

It had been in the first half of 1915 that the family had moved from Eddlethorpe back into the big house, work on which was nearing completion. 'While our troops retreated from Mons and choked out their lives in Flanders,' the youngest daughter, Angela, was later to recall, 'work continued at a leisurely pace on the rehabilitation of Sledmere House. It was noticeable that the workforce were on the mature side, but nobody seemed to find their work inappropriate in time of war.' The first parts to be finished were two enormous servants' wings that extended from the back of the house and it was decided that the young family and their household should move into these until the main house became habitable. Edith had the housekeeper's room, the children slept in the maids' wing, and the servants took over the men's wing. They used the new kitchen as a dining-room, while the scullery next door became the kitchen, and soon the bake-house, dairy, laundry, boot-room, gun-room, butler's pantries and still-room were all in full use.

For a young child like Angela, aged just four, it was a dramatic change. 'Left behind at Eddlethorpe,' she wrote, 'were those dark, cosy interiors, the protective womb of my existence till the move. Light poured in through Sledmere's huge eighteenth-century windows, reflecting light again on the pale Adam decoration; gone were the thick oriental carpets, the floors were of ice-cold stone. No nooks and hidey-holes were to be found, but seemingly endless passages with terrifying, angry-looking grey doors frowning at one. I used to run past one particularly horrible door at the top of the secondary stairs on the way to the nursery. Although my surroundings were so different I soon accepted them …'[14] Nor was it just the surroundings that were so unlike anything she had known, for the war had brought other changes. Women now dominated the household, rather than men. There were parlour-maids rather than butlers and footmen, a female cook rather than a chef. Aunts and godmothers came to stay, while on the farm droves of land-girls had appeared to replace the lads who had all gone to the front.

Slowly but surely new life was breathed into the house as the children began to get used to it, realizing that this was now their home, with no grumpy old grandfather to tell them where or where not they could roam. They chased Petsy through the half-finished rooms playing hide-and-seek, while the Library, with its polished floor and numerous tall windows, was the perfect setting for endless games of 'Rats and Ferrets, played in the dark'. Richard discovered Tatton's old wheelchair, and the long passages on the ground floor echoed to Petsy's screams of terror as she was raced up and down them blindfolded. 'The rubble in front of the house,' she later recalled, 'was a wonderful place to toboggan down on trays, and when Papa was at home on his brief leaves, we had a wonderful time.'[15]

'My father was now mostly away,' remembered Angela, 'and when he appeared was dressed in uniform, which made him somehow different. When he returned, usually from the Middle East, briefly all would be transformed, great excitement prevailed, suddenly the house was filled with uniformed men, raised voices, impromptu games of football or archery, cavalcades of horses would be mounted and go galloping down the dales, while indoors my father would thunder out music on the American Organ in the Music Room.'[16] Her cousin, Nino Hunter, a frequent visitor to Sledmere as a child, also recalled how 'He imprinted on us children the vividness of his personality, the ebullience and irrepressibility of his humour. He was the mainspring at the centre of all the fun we had, acting endless charades at his insti-gation.'[17] On his trip up in August 1916, Mark had written to Edith to make a special request. 'Please have Gray's Elegy hung at the end of the dining-room. I want to see it.' He was referring to a painting by W. Hamilton, RA, of a group of people gathered round a tombstone in Stoke Poges Church, the famous setting for Thomas Gray's 'Elegy Written in a Country Churchyard'. An old man is regaling a child and two women with a story, and they are leaning over him, resting on a walking stick. This was the inspiration for one of his favourite cartoons, 'What would happen if the stick broke'. It depicted the old man and child lying on the ground, beneath the winsome, respectable females who, with their legs up in the air, were displaying a wealth of frilly undergarments, and it would make the children roar with laughter.

Long after he died Mark's children would wax lyrical about what a wonderful man their father was, but the truth is they scarcely knew him as he was almost permanently away, and particularly so during the latter half of the war, a period in which he became a man possessed with the belief that only he could solve the Arab problem. This became more important to him as his frustration grew at the apparent lack of support for the Arab Revolt, which, in spite of initial successes, includ-ing the taking of both Mecca and Taif, along with the capture of a number of Red Sea ports, was faltering, mostly due to a lack among many of the Bedouin volunteers of any ideological commitment to the movement for Arab independence. They were more interested in grabbing as much booty as they could from their former Ottoman rulers before going home.

In many speeches Mark made during the latter half of 1916 he emphasized the danger of a German takeover of the east in the event of the collapse of the revolt, illustrating his talks with a huge map denoting 'German War Aims', and adopting the term '*Drang nach Osten*', an expression that was the motto of the German nationalist movement in the late nineteenth century, meaning 'drive towards the east'. During these talks he made common use of the expression 'Middle East'. Though this was not of his own invention, it having been first used by General Gordon in March 1900 in an article he wrote titled 'The Problems of the Middle East', it was seized upon by the national press and thus gained common currency.

What changed the game so far as Middle Eastern policy was concerned was a change of government. The war was going badly, with the disastrous campaign in the Dardanelles, in which around 58,000 Allied soldiers had died, being followed by the appalling losses of the Somme offensive, which accounted for 420,000 British casualties. Asquith's large and unwieldy War Cabinet of twenty-four held lengthy and inefficient meetings in which they appeared to debate endlessly and decide nothing. Lloyd George, the Minister for War, frustrated by Asquith's constant procrastination, told Maurice Hankey in despair, 'We are going to lose this war.'[18] In the end Asquith was forced to resign by a combination of revolution within his own government and the power of Lord Northcliffe, owner of both *The Times* and the *Daily Mail*, who used their leaders to give strength to the argument that Asquith and his Cabinet were preventing the military from attaining victory. On 7 December he was succeeded as Prime Minister by Lloyd George, who immediately cut the War Cabinet down to a group of five, creating effectively the first parliamentary dictatorship since the days of Oliver Cromwell.

Maurice Hankey was now appointed as Secretary to the War Cabinet, an important position, since it was his job to see that its decisions were carried out. With his promotion came Mark's opportunity to rise in political circles, beginning with Hankey's suggestion to the Prime Minister that he be appointed his chief political assistant. 'It is true that you know him mainly as an expert on Arab affairs,' wrote Hankey to Lloyd George, 'but he is by no means a one-sided man, has a considerable knowledge of industrial questions and an almost unique position in the Irish question as practically a conservative Home-Ruler. He also has a most extraordinary knowledge of foreign policy, and has views very similar to yours in regard to Turkey. He has a breadth of vision and a knowledge that may be invaluable in fixing up the terms of peace, which is a task that is sooner or later bound to fall to your lot.'[19] The Prime Minister only partly took Hankey's advice, appointing Mark as one of three political assistants, along with Leo Amery, a Conservative back-bencher, and William Ormsby-Gore, a keen Zionist.

Lloyd George made the destruction of Turkey one of his premier war aims and amongst his first moves on taking office was to order his armies in Egypt under General Murray onto the offensive, and to carry the war across the Turco-Egyptian frontier. He wanted a major victory to impress public opinion. Thus by the spring of 1917 the War Cabinet had committed itself to an aggressive policy designed to lead first to the capture of Jerusalem, and then to the total expulsion of the Turks from Palestine. The idea of capturing the Holy Land appealed to Lloyd George's deeply religious upbringing. Britain, he told C. P. Scott of the *Manchester Guardian*, 'could take care of the Holy Places better than anyone else'.[20] And he intended that she should do so free from France.

In his later memoirs, Lloyd George made it clear that he never believed in the Sykes–Picot Agreement. It was, he wrote, 'a crude hacking of a Holy land … The country was to be mutilated and torn into sections. There would be no more Palestine. Canaan was to be drawn and quartered.' Then, 1917, he continued, 'saw a complete change in the attitude of the nations towards this historic land … the attention of her warriors was drawn to the mountains of Judea beyond. The zeal of the Crusaders was relumed in their soul. The redemption of Palestine from the withering aggression of the Turk became like a pillar of flame to lead them on. The Sykes–Picot Agreement perished in its fire. It was not worth fighting for Canaan in order to condemn it to the fate of Agag and hew it in pieces before the Lord. Palestine, if recaptured, must be one and indivisible to renew its greatness as a living entity.'[21]

Though Lloyd George may have had no intention of sharing a conquered Palestine with France, he was not yet in a position to openly disown the Sykes–Picot Agreement, and at an Anglo-French conference held at the end of December 1916 it was agreed that both British and French 'Political Officers' should be attached to General Murray's staff, in the persons of Mark Sykes and Francois Georges-Picot. At 3.30 p.m. on 3 April 1917, the day before his departure for Cairo, Mark was summoned to Downing Street to discuss his instructions. Asked by the Prime Minister what actions he proposed to take, he replied that he hoped to open up relations with the various tribes in the area, and, if possible, to try and raise an Arab rebellion in the region of Jebel Druse with a view to attacks on Turkish lines of communication.

'The Prime Minister and Lord Curzon,' ran the memo of the meeting, 'both laid great stress on the importance of not committing the British Government to any agreement with the tribes which would be prejudicial to British interests. They impressed on Sir Mark Sykes the difficulty of our relations with the French in this region and the importance of not prejudicing the Zionist movement and the possibility of its development under British auspices … The Prime Minister suggested that the Jews might be able to render us more assistance than the Arabs.' Lloyd George laid most stress on the importance 'of securing the addition of Palestine to the British area'.[22]

It satisfied Mark that the Zionist movement had been brought up in this meeting, as it was still his ambition to somehow incorporate Zionism into the whole Anglo-French-Arab melting pot. For this reason he had been recently furthering his knowledge of the subject by widening his acquaintance with leading Zionists in London. In addition to Herbert Samuel and Rabbi Gaster, whom he already knew, he had effected introductions to Dr Chaim Weizmann, a Russian Jewish biochemist and head of the London Bureau of the Zionist Federation, and the journalist Nahum Sokolow, Executive Chairman of the Zionist International Committee. In a memorandum, they had laid out for him exactly what their aims were. 'Palestine to be recognized as the Jewish National Home, with liberty of immigration to Jews of all countries, who are to enjoy full national, political, and civic rights; a charter to be granted to a Jewish company; local government to be accorded to the Jewish populace; and the Hebrew language to be officially recognized.'[23] His response to this, which was governed by what had already been laid down in Sykes–Picot, whereby the Holy Places were all to be placed under an international administration, was that any Jewish body in Palestine should be under Anglo-French rule. At an unofficial meeting on 7 February, however, which took place at Rabbi Gaster's home, Mark met with Weizmann and other British Zionists, who made it quite clear that they wanted Palestine to be ruled by Britain, not an Anglo-French condominium. France, they believed, would never allow the Jews to develop their own way of life, but would gradually try to make Frenchmen of all of them. Mark knew this would never wash with the French, who stubbornly refused to recognize that concessions to Zionism might help win the war. It was an attitude he simply did not understand. 'What was their motive?' he asked the Zionist leaders.[24]

The following day, Mark introduced Sokolow to Georges Picot, who was also in London. The meeting took place at 9 Buckingham Gate: 'the latter place,' Sokolow later recalled, 'had already become an important centre for matters concerning the new and at that time scarcely completed plan of a Kingdom of the Hedjaz, concerning Armenia and Mesopotamia, and was equipped with all such material as files of correspondence and telegraphic communications etc. It was then that Zionism took its place in the system and came to dominate the situation more and more as our labours progressed. One was liable to be called upon at any moment, early in the morning or late at night. It became a joke with us to name his sudden telephone calls "brain-storms". Sir Mark had a "brain-storm" which meant: danger in sight. This may appear as somewhat far-fetched to outsiders, but those who were in the thick of the work knew well what formidable obstacles stood in the way and how well founded were Sir Mark's doubts and fears. At every moment dangers had to be guarded against ... The cause of Zionism was in the same dire case as Laocoön in the grip of snakes. Every day brought a fresh indication of some hostile movement, a new suspicion of enemy schemes each of which caused Sir Mark to sound a warning. These were the "brain-storms".'[25]

Picot was impressed by Sokolow, and though he was somewhat wary on their first meeting, when they met for a second time the following day he let him know that France might be sympathetic to the Zionists if she were to have a role in Palestine equal to that of Great Britain. They continued their dialogue in Paris in April, when Mark stopped over there on his journey out to Egypt to join General Murray. 'Very stiff journey,' he wrote to Edith from the Hotel Lotti in the Rue Castiglione on 4 April, '– went across in a boat loaded like Noah's Ark – so to G.H.Q., did my business and more ... then at 10 PM motored to Paris, 5 hours open car, 35 miles p.h. freezing – so to bed very cold – Today saw Picot – things seem a bit easier, but many difficulties ... I am very tired indeed.'[26]

To say there were many difficulties was something of an understatement, but Mark thrived in such circumstances. His latest scheme was to create a Middle Eastern entente between Arabs, Zionists and Armenians, British support for which would be consistent with Allied propaganda that called for the liberation of the oppressed peoples of the Middle East from the Turk. This was epitomized by the proclamation that had been issued to the people of Baghdad on 11 March 1917, when it was occupied by General Maude's Mesopotamia Expeditionary Force, in order to restore order and halt looting following its evacuation by Ottoman forces the previous day. Drafted by Mark in flowery language, it pledged that 'our armies do not come into your cities and lands as conquerors or enemies, but as liberators', going on to state that it was the hope of the British Government 'that the aspirations of your philosophers and writers shall be realised and that once again the people of Baghdad shall flourish enjoying their wealth and substance under institutions which are in consonance with their sacred laws and their racial ideals'.[27] To help promote the 'entente', Mark had asked a London acquaintance of his, James Malcolm, to accompany Sokolow to Paris. Malcolm, a wealthy Armenian fixer, had been instrumental in helping Mark meet the Zionist leaders, and as he had influential acquaintances everywhere, it seemed a good idea for him to be in Paris, where he might foster cooperation between Armenian and Jewish Nationalists. The strategy appears to have paid off, Sokolow writing some weeks later to Weizmann, 'You are of course acquainted with Mr M's idea of an entente between Armenians, Arabs and Jews. I regard the idea as quite fantastic.'[28]

First of all Mark had to continue working to persuade Picot of the importance of supporting Zionism. 'If the great force of Judaism,' he wrote to him, 'feels that its aspirations are not only considered but in a fair way towards realization, then there is hope of an ordered and developed Arabia and Middle East. On the other hand, if that force feels that its aspirations will be thwarted by circumstance and are doomed to remain only a painful longing, then I see little or no hope for our own future hopes.'[29] There was also another factor on the horizon, which was that America was now on the brink of entering the war. Given the powerful economic and political force that the Jews were in the US, Mark suggested to Picot that support for Zionist aspirations could only be good for the entente cause over there. The French response to this, however, was suspicion that if the United States began to play a part in the Middle East as patrons of Zionism, she might easily become France's commercial rival there.

Sokolow met with Picot, and back and forth went the discussions with France yielding little to begin with, stating unequivocally that neither an Anglo-French, nor an Anglo-American condominium would be acceptable, even refusing to contemplate international control. 'The French are determined to take the whole of Palestine,' he reported back to Weizmann. There were many forces at work – French businessmen trying to protect their interests in Syria and Palestine, the Imperialists who wanted to see Syria annexed, French Catholics who opposed Zionist plans for Palestine, and there were even French Jews who were anti-Zionist. 'This work is very difficult,' Sokolow told Weizmann, 'but not impossible.'[30] And persistence did pay off. By the time Mark arrived in Paris, Sokolow was able to report that he had persuaded the Foreign Office in Paris to study a statement of Zionist aims which he had every confidence they would endorse. He was to meet with the French Foreign Minister, Jules Cambon, and other officials, including Picot, on 9 April.

Sokolow began that day by walking from his hotel, the Meurice, on the Rue de Rivoli, to meet Mark at the Lotti, where they closeted themselves away and studied all the information that was required for the meeting. 'Sykes was impatient,' he recalled in his memoirs; 'in spite of his complete confidence in us, he could not refrain from remaining near me, always ready with advice and help. We worked together for some hours. I departed on my mission and we arranged for him to wait for me at the hotel. But as I was crossing the Quai d'Orsay on my return from the Foreign Office I came across Sykes. He had not had the patience to wait. We walked on together, and I gave him an outline of the proceedings. This did not satisfy him; he studied every detail; I had to give him full notes and he drew up a minute report. "That's a good day's work," he said with shining eyes.'[31] The meeting had indeed gone well, with the French having agreed to meet the Zionists more than halfway. 'I was told,' Sokolow reported back to Weizmann, 'they accept in principle the recognition of Jewish nationality in the capacity of National Home, local autonomy, etc. It is beyond my boldest expectations …'[32] Yet, as Mark found out from a little judicious intelligence work, it was not the whole story. He persuaded an Irish friend, Valentine Hussey-Walsh, who was married to a French aristocrat, to use his position to gain an interview with Etienne Flandin, and gauge the feelings of the Syrian Party. 'Flandin rose like a trout on a dull day,' Mark reported of their meeting; '…

Picot was a fool who had betrayed France – France required the whole
of the Mediterranean Littoral ... A small international conclave of
Jaffa, Jerusalem and Bethlehem might be arranged in which France
should predominate ... but for the rest, the country should be absolute French territory as far east as the Euphrates.'[33]

'Since I wrote to you, I have done a good deal of work,' Mark
reported to Edith, going on to describe a family lunch at the Georges-
Picots, which featured 'Picot brother=Picot only fatter – Madame
Picot – enjoys bad health but improving, gave me a multitude of
instructions re. his health – and Picot's daughter 13 and extremely
beautiful – and Picot's belle-mère, the kind of vivacious old body you
only see in command of a French family, 5ft nothing, slight cavalry
moustache, and in supreme control. Sokolof [*sic*] and all Jewry in a
great to do. I cannot quite fathom their anxiety and excitement.'[34]

Before his arrival in Egypt, Mark stopped off in Rome,' He travelled
there by sleeper. 'In the train,' he recounted, 'I met the Japanese Naval
Attaché in Paris who was very pleasant. He showed me his sword, 250
years old, of his ancestor, the Lord High Admiral of Nippon.

The sword was perfectly lovely, took a year to make and the man who made it had to fast before beginning to make it. It rather surprised me when he said "Our population subsist chiefly on LICE!" It was only when he said "What will be the LESULT of the LUSSIAN LEVOLUTION?" that I understood what he was driving at!'[35]

On arrival in Rome, Mark checked into the Hotel Excelsior, where he found an interesting collection of fellow guests: 'the Russian Ballet … seems to be staying in this hotel, from the odd people I see about, viz …

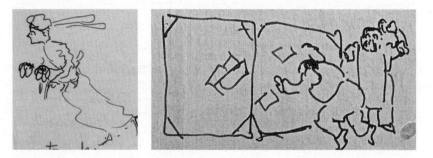

maids with Pekingeses, immense trunks

excited men of managerial aspect, and an occasional glamourpuss.'[36]

The true point of the visit to Rome was that it contained the Vatican, whose good will might prove important to the Zionists. 'Went to the Vatican this morning,' he reported, 'to see the assistant undersecretary of state previous to seeing His Holiness tomorrow. A.U.S.O.S. very pleasant, quick & keen, so this afternoon round some churches & the Colloseum [*sic*] – pestered by guides who are fierce and staring and come up like menacing demons.

BUYA POSCAR SHEEP SAIR they cry very fiercely. Poor things they have not had any tourists for 3 years.'[37] He evidently worked his charm on the Assistant Under-Secretary of State, Thomas de Salis, who stated that 'Sir M. Sykes's visit has been the best thing that has happened to me since I have been here.'[38] Sir Rennel Rodd, however, the British Ambassador in Rome, found him a trickier customer, complaining that he 'opened fire on questions which I have been guarding as closely as the riddle of the sphinx'.[39] Nevertheless he smoothed the way for Mark to meet with the Pope's Assistant Under-Secretary for Foreign Affairs, Monsignor Pacelli, a man who had the Pope's ear.

'I spoke to the Monsignor,' he wrote to Sir Ronald Graham, a diplomat at the British Foreign Office who was a supporter of the Zionist cause, 'of the immense difficulties which surrounded the question of Jerusalem, the Arab Nationalist movement, the Moslem Holy Places, Zionism and the conflicting interests of the Latins and Greeks, beside the aspirations of the various powers ... Although he did not say as much, the Monsignor ... let it be easy to see that the idea of British patronage of the Holy Places was not distasteful to Vatican policy. The French I could see did not strike him as ideal in any way. I also prepared the way for Zionism by explaining what the purpose and ideals of the Zionists were, and suggested that he should see Sokolow when he came to Rome.'[40]

When he eventually arrived there, three weeks later, Sokolow did indeed find that Mark had paved the way for him. 'He had gone to the East,' he later wrote. 'I put up at the hotel; Sykes had ordered rooms for me. I went to the British Embassy; letters and instructions from Sykes were waiting for me there. I went to the Italian Government Offices; Sykes had been there too: then to the Vatican, where Sykes had again prepared my way. It seemed to me as if his presence was wherever I went, but all the time he was far away in Arabia.' He met with Pacelli, an encounter which, much to Sokolow's delight, was followed by a long and fruitful meeting with Pope Benedict XV, in the course of which, in answer to Sokolow's request that the Pope accept his assurance of the loyalty of the Jews and accord them his moral support, he told him, 'Yes, yes, I believe we shall be good neighbours.'[41] Sokolow now returned to Paris with his head held high, and no higher than at the moment when, on 4 June 1917, Jules Cambon, Secretary-General to the Foreign Ministry, signed a formal document accepting the principle of Jewish colonization in Palestine. 'You consider that,' it ran, 'circumstances permitting, and the independence of the Holy Places being safeguarded at the same time, it would be a deed of justice and reparation if the Allied Powers, by lending their protection, were to assist the renaissance of Jewish nationality in that land from which the people of Israel were exiled many centuries ago ... I am happy to give you herewith such assurance.'[42] Honeyed words indeed, which is what they turned out to be.

Chapter 13

The Balfour Declaration

'The complexities of my work,' Mark wrote to Edith on 15 April 1917, are to me appalling – just look.

'Anglo-India v. Anglo-Egypt.
Latins v. Greeks.
Army v. Civilians.
French v. British.
French v. Italians.
Christians v. Moslems.
Jews v. Christians.
Arabs v. Arabs.
Syrians v. Hejaz.

And as a presiding Genius the great War Cabinet plus the F.O. This will I hope disentangle itself somehow.'[1]

He finally arrived in Egypt on 23 April 'after an abominable journey'. The first boat he set out on, a 3rd Class cruiser, 'built for Chinese navy, taken on by the Greeks and stolen by the French', was in a filthy state, had a hopeless captain and nearly rolled over because she would not answer her rudder. Two days out she broke down and had to put in for repairs. Picot, who had organized the transport, was 'very ashamed'. 'It was decided that the party should separate,' recounted Mark, 'and that I should go on one of the accompanying French torpedoe [*sic*] boats, not a destroyer. 48 hours of gale, like a kettle floating in Niagara:

French torpedo-boat crew delightful, no room below, all sat night &
day like starlings on a rail, very amusing, excellent dinners cooked no
one knows how ... here is a French sailor.'[2]

Regarding his work ahead, he opined, 'Prospects not brilliant to my
mind – however time will tell', but of one thing, he told Edith, he was
certain: 'the intense happiness of our meetings after separation, and
anticipation of that happiness, is an immense solace. Your face is
always before me, and you are never out of my mind. Dearest H.W.B
Co-relig. How wonderful is our love for each other. I feel now writing

to you even more intensely than when we first met, if such a thing were possible. God has given us a happiness given to few I think ... So much are you to me that I feel you by me every instant.'[3]

There is no doubt that through the hard and tortuous negotiations between French, Russians, Arabs and Jews, Mark was kept going by thoughts of home. 'Truly Darling,' he wrote, 'the day I look forward to seeing you again, I look forward to with as great a joy and intensity as the day we married, & keep wondering and picturing when and where it will be; It is worth parting for the happiness of coming back.'[4] That day was to be months ahead. In the meantime he had to take up his post as the British Political Officer on General Murray's staff, and the situation was not good. General Murray had so far failed in his attempts to invade Palestine, with two attacks on Gaza repulsed. In Cairo, reported Mark, 'the atmosphere is very bad – recriminations – gossip and mistrust'. 'I wish I felt some confidence in the General Sir A. Murray,' he admitted, 'but I am afraid he is lacking in imagination and leadership. By all accounts he is very unpopular with his troops ... Personally I should not hesitate to change the General ... because he is at a fag end of his work and a fresh broom is needed ...'[5] As it happened, Murray was relieved of his command within weeks, the Palestine offensive being postponed until the autumn, when it would be reignited under the leadership of General Sir Edmund Allenby.

With the Turks still undefeated, Mark worried that forging ahead with Zionist and Arab projects might lead to reprisals against those seeming to side with Allied causes, and advised the Foreign Office that for the time being they should go quietly in these areas. Meanwhile he and Picot held meetings in Cairo with various Arab representatives to sound out 'Syrian and Arab desiderata', and to try and bridge the gulf between French Imperial designs in Syria, and Britain's pledge to Syrian independence, a task that was simplified by the fact that the Syrian delegates were unaware of such a gulf. 'Main difficulty,' explained Mark in a cable to London, 'was to manoeuvre the delegates, without showing them a map or letting them know that there was an actual geographical or detailed agreement, into asking for what we are ready to give them.'[6] They were more straightforward about Palestine, persuading the Arabs that the Jews should be recognized as a nation there, so long as equal recognition was accorded the actual population.

Mark now received a request from Sharif Hussein, who since October 1916 had styled himself 'King of the Hejaz', for a meeting, an appointment he had every reason to jump at, especially since he had never met the man on whose behalf he had apparently been working for the past year and a half. More importantly he was under instruction from Sir Reginald Wingate, the British High Commissioner in Egypt, to finally inform Hussein of the general lines of the Sykes–Picot Agreement, which up till now had been kept secret from him. 'I am off to Jeddah tomorrow morning,' he told Edith, 'to see the Grand Sharif – then back here – many negotiations and much hard work, uphill much of it, but so far successful.'[7] En route he stopped at Wejh, where he met with Hussein's son, Faisal, on 2 May, meeting Hussein in Jeddah on 5 May, and bringing with him a message of solidarity from the King of England, George V. Dressed in his full regimental

uniform for such a formal meeting, he undoubtedly envied the Sharif, who was wearing Arab dress of cool, flowing robes. The temperature was a stifling F120° ...

That Mark carried out Wingate's instructions is confirmed by the contemporary testimony of Hussein's secretary, Fu'ad al-Khatib, who stated that the King was given 'a hasty perusal and explanation ... of the Sykes–Picot agreement'.[8] He also later told the Islamic scholar Rashid Rida that at that time Hussein had expressed satisfaction with the terms of the agreement.[9] Thus Mark was able to report back to Wingate that at his meeting with Hussein, 'In accordance with my instructions, I explained the principle of the agreement as regards an Arab confederation or State ... I impressed upon the King the importance of Franco-Arab friendship and at least got him to admit that it was essential to Arab development in Syria, but this after a very lengthy argument.'[10]

Now that Mark's visit to Hussein was seen to have been a success, Wingate suggested that he should take Picot to meet him, an encounter that took place on 19 May. In spite of the meeting getting off to a poor start, 'M. Picot being unfavourably impressed by the King', a second conference took place the next day, which concluded with Hussein's secretary, Fu'ad, reading out a declaration, the gist of which was that since the King now believed that the French supported Arab national aspirations, he was ready to accept that they should have a role in the Lebanon similar to that of the British in Baghdad. In agreeing to this, Hussein was naturally under the impression that that role was still to be, as had been discussed with Henry MacMahon back in 1915, that of a short-term leasing arrangement until it was handed back for inclusion in an independent Arab nation. 'Monsieur Picot received this very well,' Mark cabled to Wingate, 'and relations became cordial.' Both sides now appeared to have got what they wanted, though neither in fact had.

Back in London, the Zionists gave not a thought to Hussein and his armies in the Hejaz and Syria. Their sole interest was, by the use of skilful diplomacy, to persuade the British government to support them, and when Mark returned home in June 1917, he immediately became involved again in their aspirations. It was quite clear to Weizmann that they needed some definite statement with regard to Palestine that went beyond the mere verbal assurances they had been given thus far. Working with Sokolow, it was decided to compose a Zionist statement, which would be sent to Arthur Balfour by Lord Rothschild, head of the leading Jewish family in England, who would present it to the War Cabinet for approval. While a number of his colleagues believed that the Zionists should ask for as much as possible in this statement, Sokolow knew exactly what the British government would accept and what it would not. 'Our purpose,' he stated, 'is to receive from the Government a general short approval of the same kind as that which I have been successful in getting from the French Government.'[11]

Mark was instrumental in helping work out the draft of this first statement, working occasionally from 9 Buckingham Gate, but mostly from his office in Whitehall. During those summer days, Harold Nicolson, a young diplomat also working alongside Mark, remembered 'Dr Sokolow would visit us daily, slow, solemn, patri-archal, intense.' The first statement worked out by him and his advisers, and shown to Mark, was deemed too long and to contain too much detail. They then set to work on a second draft declaration 'encouraged by the dynamic optimism of Mark Sykes, inspired by the dogged perseverance of Nahum Sokolow', who 'gave the impres-sion not of a prophet or a politician, but of a very industrious science student who was interested, not in fantasies or irony, but in hard ascertainable facts. Mark Sykes's blustering, gay manner disconcerted him.'[12] The new draft was much simpler, a single paragraph, and this was passed by Lord Rothschild to Balfour, along with a note that read, 'At last I am able to send you the formula you asked me for. If His Majesty's Government will send me a message on the lines of this formula, if they and you approve of it, I will hand it on to the Zionist federation and also announce it at a meeting called for that purpose.'

Rothschild was mistaken in believing that a statement of support from the government would arrive forthwith, for there followed months of argument from a strong anti-Zionist group, led by two prominent Jews, the scholar Lucien Wolf and the Secretary of State for India, Edwin Montagu, that came close to swaying the British Government in the opposite direction. When Mark discovered that to a man the Cabinet were ignorant of the fact that France had already given her support to the Zionists, he went to Paris to see Picot. 'One day, Sir Mark Sykes came to see me at the Embassy,' he later recalled. '"The discussion has taken a turn for the worse. There are growing doubts because the British Government is totally ignorant of the position taken up by the French Cabinet. Is it possible for you, without asking Paris for instructions, to come today to Downing Street and to tell our Ministers what your Government has done?" I replied "I am prepared to go with you and to read our formula …" I arrived and told the people I saw "here is what has been done. I have never been able to understand its having been kept secret."'[13]

Cambon's declaration thus came as a surprise to the Cabinet, but they finally made up their minds to support the Zionists, and on 2 November 1917, the following declaration was sent to Lord Rothschild by Balfour. 'His Majesty's Government view with favour the establishment in Palestine of a National Home for the Jewish people, and will use their best endeavours to facilitate the achievement of this object, it being clearly understood that nothing shall be done which may prejudice the civil and religious rights of the existing non-Jewish communities in Palestine or the rights and political status enjoyed by Jews in any other country.' Mark was present at the War Cabinet meeting during which the 'Balfour Declaration' was sanctioned and, as soon as pen had been put to paper, rushed off to give the good news to Chaim Weizmann, who was anxiously waiting outside. 'Dr Weizmann, it's a boy,' he told him joyfully. 'Well,' wrote Weizmann in his memoirs, 'I did not like the boy at first. He was not the one I had expected. But I knew that this was a great event.'[14] Any disappointment that Weizmann may have felt that the Declaration had not promised any specific action was soon put aside as he climbed into a taxi with his secretary, Shmuel Tolkowsky, to go and spread the news. He 'behaved like a child,' Tolkowsky recorded in his diary: 'he embraced me for a long time, placed his head on my shoulder, and pressed my hand, repeating over and over *mazel tov*'.[15] The day ended with an impromptu party at the Weizmanns' home at which he, his wife Vera and their friends danced a Hassidic dance in celebration.

The Balfour Declaration was published in the British Press exactly one week later, and news of it was not welcomed in all quarters. On 28 November, Mark received a telegram from General Sir Gilbert Clayton, now Director of Army Intelligence in Cairo, stating that 'Recent announcement by His Majesty's Government on Jewish question has made profound impression on both Moslems and Christians who view with little short of dismay prospect of seeing Palestine and eventually Syria, in hands of Jews, whose superior intelligence and commercial abilities feared by all alike.'[16] This was troubling to Mark, who had gone out of his way to impress upon the Zionist leaders his conviction that the success of their cause depended so much upon their reaching an understanding with the Arabs, whose national aspirations must be reconciled and linked with their own. It was equally important, he told Clayton, that Arab leaders should join the combine. Clayton was not convinced that this was workable, writing, 'I quite see your arguments regarding an Arab–Jew–Armenian combine and the advantages that would accrue if it could be brought off. We will try it, but it must be done very cautiously and, honestly, I see no great chance of any real success It is an attempt to change in a few weeks the traditional sentiment of centuries.'[17]

At a meeting of Jews held at the Manchester Hippodrome on 9 December, to thank the British Government for its support of Zionism, he reiterated his views. 'Today the Arabs ... were one in blood and in tongue,' he said. 'There were seven or eight millions of them; they were prolific ... Arab civilisation was coming; no Sultan or Kaiser could prevent it, and when it came no imperialists and financiers would be able to control it. It was the destiny of the Jews to be closely connected with the Arab revival, and co-operation and goodwill from the first were necessary or ultimate disaster would overtake both Jew and Arab. Therefore he warned Jews to look through Arab glasses.'[18]

At the same time he tried to encourage the Arabs to think similarly about the Jews, writing in a letter to Feisal, 'I know that the Arabs despise, condemn and hate the Jews, but ... those who have persecuted or condemned the Jews could tell you the tale. The Empire of Spain in the old days and the Empire of Russia in our time show the road of ruin that Jewish persecution leads to ... Believe me, I speak the truth when I say that this race, despised and weak, is universal, is all powerful, and cannot be put down ... In the councils of every state, in every bank, in every business, in every enterprise there are members of this race ... And remember, these people do not seek to conquer you, do not seek to drive out the Arabs of Palestine ... Look on the Jewish movement as the great key to Arab success, as the one guarantee of strength when the nations come together in council ... and, above all, recognize that the Jews desire to live their national life in Palestine; recognize them as a powerful ally.'[19] Feisal replied, 'I have a perfect notion of the importance of the Jews' position, and admiration of their vigour and tenacity and moral ascendancy, often in the middle of hostile surroundings ... On general grounds I would welcome any good understanding with the Jews.'[20]

Sokolow recalled that after the Manchester meeting, one of the largest ever held there, 'we sat down, tired out, to tea'. Not so Mark, however. 'Sykes hurried in in his raincoat; he had no time to stay, as he had to catch the night train. He was due in London next morning to send urgent telegrams to Palestine.'[21] This was the crux of his character. He had no time to sit still, to drink tea, to rest, while there were urgent tasks to complete, and the urgent task which relentlessly gripped him, of which he would not let go and which he believed he was the only man capable of solving was that of settling, to everyone's satisfaction, the question of Arab, Jewish, Armenian and French aspirations in the Middle East. Chaim Weizmann wrote of him, 'He was not very consistent or logical in his thinking, but he was generous and warm-hearted.'[22] He could also be naïve, in that his optimism often led him to believe that everyone supported the politics of idealism that he espoused, when the truth was that there were more against him than with him. They did not share his dreams, the fight to achieve which would eventually overwhelm him.

Prospects for an invasion of Palestine had been looking up since July 1917, when Aqaba, a tiny port at its southern tip, defended by heavy gun batteries pointing out to sea, was captured in an audacious raid from across the desert led by Auda abu Tayi, chief of the Northern Arabian Bedouin, and T. E. Lawrence. This was a great coup for the Hejaz rebellion since it opened up the possibility of the Royal Navy transporting Arab tribesmen to Palestine in order to fight alongside British forces. General Murray's replacement, Sir Edmund Allenby, began his new offensive in October and soon had the Turks on the run, capturing Beersheba, an important Ottoman garrison, in early November, then finally taking Gaza a few days later, before moving forward relentlessly towards Jerusalem, which fell on 11 December. On Mark's advice, Allenby and his officers and companions, including Lawrence and Georges-Picot, entered the Holy City on foot, through the Jaffa Gate, and to avoid anything that smacked of triumphalism no British flags were flown. Martial law was established and Allenby made it quite clear that the ultimate disposition of Palestine would have to wait until he considered that the military situation allowed a return to civil administration. As for Picot, 'he arrived,' wrote Clayton, 'in the full conviction that he was to be the French representative in a joint Anglo-French provisional administration which was to govern occupied enemy territory in Palestine until the end of the war – when some sort of international arrangement would be made ... If this is so, I cannot protest too strongly against any such unworkable and mischievous arrangement. The country is under martial law and under martial law it must remain for a long time to come.'[23]

It did not help matters that Allenby took the decision not to publish the Balfour Declaration in Jerusalem while it was under military rule for fear of it raising problematic issues while there was still a war being fought. Applications from foreign Jews to settle in Palestine were for the time being to be turned down, and little was done by the military to foster good relations between the native Arabs and Jews who were already living there. There was in fact a tendency to treat the Moslem population differently. 'One can't help noticing,' wrote William Ormsby-Gore, a fellow assistant secretary to the War Cabinet, to Mark, 'the ineradicable tendency of the Englishman who has lived in India or the Sudan to favour quite unconsciously the Moslem both against Christian and Jew.'[24] It was a complicated situation that Mark must have understood was not going to be solved in a hurry, as Ronald Storrs, appointed military Governor of Jerusalem, told him, 'It will take months, possibly years, of patient work to show the Jews that we are not run by the Arabs, and the Arabs that we are not bought by the Jews', adding, 'it is one thing to see clearly enough the probable future of this country, and another thing to fail to make allowances for the position of the weaker and probably disappearing element. The results of the changes will be more satisfactory and more lasting if they are brought about gradually with patience, and without violent expression of ill will, leaving behind them an abiding rancour.'[25]

At the turn of 1918, after years of war, there was change in the air, in particular a groundswell of opinion against imperialism. After the overthrow of the Tsar in Russia, the Bolsheviks had sacked government offices and released all the secret papers they had discovered, and these included the Sykes–Picot Agreement. The British people first got wind of it on 26 November 1917, when the *Manchester Guardian* published a story headlined 'RUSSIA AND SECRET TREATIES'. It ran, 'M. Trotsky, Commissioner for Foreign Affairs, had published a series of secret telegrams and documents, dating partly from the year 1915 … The Allies put forward a series of claims to which the Russian Government consented. According to these demands Constantinople was to become a free port for goods neither going to nor coming from Russia. The Allies further demanded the recognition of their rights over Asiatic Turkey, as well as the preservation of the sacred places in

Arabia under Mussulman sovereignty, and the inclusion of the neutral zone in Persia within the sphere of British activity.'[26] A few days later, in Beirut, Djemal Pasha, one of the Ottoman military leaders, divulged the terms of the agreement to a stunned audience, hoping that evidence of such treachery would bring back the King of the Hejaz and his sons into the fold, though it was to no avail, since Hussein was already aware of the treaty and its contents.

In Britain, however, the divulging of the secret treaty caused some embarrassment to Lloyd George, who now bent over backwards to assure the Labour Party that his views had changed. On 5 January 1918, he addressed the delegates of the Trades Union Congress, meeting at the Central Hall, Westminster, issuing a statement of British War Aims. These were no longer the conquering and annexation of countries, but the restoration of their independence. 'Outside Europe,' he told them, 'we believe that the same principles should be applied. While we do not challenge the maintenance of the Turkish Empire in the homelands of the Turkish race with its capital at Constantinople ... Arabia, Armenia, Mesopotamia, Syria and Palestine are in our judgement entitled to a recognition of their separate national conditions.'[27] On 8 January the American President, Woodrow Wilson, set out his own ideas about how a post-war world might work in his 'Fourteen Points' speech which outlined principles for world peace, number XII of which stated, 'The Turkish portion of the present Ottoman Empire should be assured a secure sovereignty, but the other nationalities which are now under Turkish rule should be assured an undoubted security of life and an absolutely unmolested opportunity of autonomous development ...'

In December 1917, keen to be in a position where he could stay on top of Middle Eastern affairs, Mark requested from his boss, Maurice Hankey, a transfer to the Foreign Office, a wish that he was granted on the condition that he continued to keep up his work on the *Eastern Report*. Lord Robert Cecil tried to persuade Lord Curzon to put him in charge of a new Middle Eastern Department, but without success, since Curzon was running his own Middle Eastern

Committee. Instead he was given the title of 'Acting Adviser on Arabian and Palestine Affairs' and was responsible to Lord Hardinge, Permanent Under-Secretary for Foreign Affairs, and former Viceroy of India. When he moved, Hankey wrote jokingly to him that 'When you look down from the sublime heights of your Under-Secretaryship at the Foreign Office, you will discern no snow or ice on these lesser peaks!'[28] There were no 'sublime heights' so far as the new office was concerned, it being situated in the basement of the back wing of the Foreign Office building in Whitehall, where it was connected to the upper storeys by a lift. This, recalled Sokolow in his memoirs, was 'never used by Sir Mark, who mounted the stairs about twenty times daily at a lightning speed, which made it impossible for me to keep pace with him in spite of my most strenuous efforts'.[29]

Going on to describe the office, he recalled, 'The first large room was dark because the big window was blocked with sandbags as a protection against possible air-raids: it had long tables and was illuminated artificially. I had to be there often and for long periods at a time: my work, indeed, required my attendance there more than at the Zionist offices, and sometimes I had to go there three times a day and to remain there till late at night. On one of these occasions Sir Mark said to me "Does not this subterranean room look like a medieval inquisition chamber, with those long tables upon which victims of the Inquisition might be stretched for torture? Who knows," added he humorously, "whether some of your forefathers had not to undergo treatment in chambers of this kind?" I answered "Yes, as Scripture has it: 'I will make the desolate valley into a door of hope.'" After that we often used to call this room the "Door of Hope".'[30]

The first room opened into another, in which Mark worked with his 'young and energetic' secretary, Dunlop, while his faithful servant, Sergeant Wilson, passed to and fro between the two. 'It was like a hive,' described Sokolow; 'there was a constant coming and going of Foreign Office men, M.P.s, Armenian Politicians, Mahommedan Mullahs, officers, journalists, representatives of Syrian Committees, and deputations from philanthropic societies. In the midst of this busy world Zionism maintained its prominent position. Everything had to pass through Sykes's hands. In order to avoid confusion and divergence of effort he insisted upon what was readily conceded him, namely that he should pass an opinion on every question and every detail, and in this there was no hesitation, no delay.'[31]

From these two rooms, Mark did his best to put his Palestine policy into effect. With the support of the Foreign Secretary he had set up a Zionist Commission, made up of leading Jews from the Allied countries, with the intention of sending it out to tour the Middle East to soothe uneasiness that existed there regarding Zionist aims and intentions, and to pave the way for carrying out the Balfour Declaration. Chaim Weizmann headed the British delegation. 'Sir Mark Sykes,' he later recalled in his memoirs, 'suddenly had the idea that it would be useful for the prestige of the Commission if I, as its chairman, were to be received by His Majesty the King before we left … Arrangements were made for me to be taken to the Palace on the Saturday morning preceding the departure. I bought, and put on, my first and last top hat … And so I was presented to … King George V … He showed great interest in our plans. Knowing me to be of Russian birth he also spoke at some length on the Russian Revolution – then front page news – saying at one point "I always warned Nicky about the risks he ran in maintaining that régime; but he would not listen."'[32]

The Commission set out for Alexandria at the beginning of March, and thence to Palestine, arriving there in April, where they met with General Allenby, a member of whose staff, Alan Dawnay, arranged for Weizmann a meeting with Prince Feisal. Having listened to his account of Zionist aims, he saw no reason why the two men should not establish a friendly relationship. This was just the kind of meeting that Mark had envisaged. Weizmann set out in June, accompanied by William Ormsby-Gore, and after a gruelling journey of nearly two weeks arrived at GHQ high up on the Transjordan plateau. Here he was greeted by Colonel Joyce, the senior British officer with Emir Feisal, who advised him to take a good rest, before seeing the Emir the next day. 'So that evening found me wandering about the camp,' he wrote. 'It was a brilliant moonlit night – Palestinian moonlight – and I looked down from Moab on the Jordan Valley and the Dead Sea and the Judean Hills beyond, I may have been a little light-headed from the sudden change of climate, but as I stood there I suddenly had the feeling that three thousand years had vanished, had become as nothing. Here I was, on the identical ground, on the identical errand, of my ancestors in the dawn of my people's history, when they came to negotiate with the ruler of the country for a right of way, that they might return to their home ...'[33]

The following morning Weizmann was taken to meet Feisal, who was surrounded by a forbidding-looking band of warriors, and was also accompanied by T. E. Lawrence, 'probably making arrangements for the night, when they would go forth on their destructive mission to blow up a few kilometres more of the Hedjaz railway'.[34] Feisal impressed him immediately. 'He is the first real Arab Nationalist I have met,' he wrote to his wife. 'He's a leader! He's quite intelligent and a very honest man, handsome as a picture! He is not interested in Palestine, but on the other hand he wants Damascus and the whole of Northern Syria.'[35] Colonel Joyce reported back that the meeting went well, though Feisal was not at liberty to make any decisions without authorization from his father.

When Weizmann reached Jerusalem, he found the military still unwilling to openly announce the Balfour Declaration for fear of stirring up unrest. General Clayton supported Feisal's point of view that the way forward for the Zionist issue was to link it to that of an Arab Syria. 'The two important points,' he explained to Leo Amery, 'are not to make too much of a splash locally with Zionism until the Arabs have got a slice of the cake themselves, i.e. Damascus, and to get the French to come out clearly with the declaration disavowing any ideas of Colonial annexation and emphasizing their adherence to the idea of Arab Autonomy.'[36]

By now Mark was aware that the Sykes–Picot Agreement was out of kilter with the new idealism expressed by Lloyd George and President Wilson. In March 1918, he admitted to Wingate that the

Agreement was 'dead and gone, and the sooner scrapped the better', while to Clayton he wrote, 'For the time at which it was made, the Agreement was conceived on liberal lines but the world has marched so far since then that the Agreement can only be considered as a reactionary measure.'[37] And when Sharif Hussein feigned indignation at Djemal Pasha's revelation of the documents published by the Bolsheviks, Wingate assured him that they 'do not constitute an actually concluded agreement but consist of records of provisional exchanges and conversations between Great Britain, France and Russia', going on to say that Djemal 'has … ignored the fact that the subsequent outbreak and the striking success of the Arab Revolt, as well as the withdrawal of Russia, had long ago created an altogether different situation'.[38] In so many words it was thus being hinted that the British government was disowning the Sykes–Picot Agreement.

Mark now had to persuade Picot of the importance of French policy being brought into accord with the new war aims of Lloyd George and President Wilson. 'It is no use thinking in terms of the past,' he told him; '… President Wilson's voice is now the important one, and ideas which do not fit in with his speeches won't have much influence on the Peace Conference. Any question of annexation or direct control as a post-war form of settlement I think is now fairly disposed of.'[39] They met in London in June, when Picot made it clear that abolishment of the 1916 Agreement 'would raise violent opposition and ill-feeling among the colonials in France and give great strength to the pro-Turkish elements'. Mark retorted that it could only survive in a radically changed form, because as it stood it 'was regarded by the democratic forces of the Entente as an instrument of capitalistic exploitation and imperialistic aggression'.[40] They thus devised a new preamble to the treaty stipulating that 'a period of tutelage must supervene before the inhabitants of the area are capable of complete self-government', and that this 'tutelage' should only be effected 'on the sanction of the free nations of the world and with the consent of the governed'.[41]

Thanks to Curzon's Middle Eastern Committee, Mark's influence was beginning to dwindle, and when he sent the new drafts for approval, they simply sat on them. He was not prepared to give up, however, on his efforts to reach an Anglo-French accord and at the beginning of August he submitted a new 'Joint Declaration by Great Britain and France to assist Arabs', which also fell upon deaf ears. Frustrated, and eager to support any organization that promoted *entente*, he joined the fledgling League of Nations Society, in a debate on which he made what was to be his last speech in the House of Commons, on 1 August. Without a League of Nations, he said, '– if a League of Nations is the label of the machinery to prevent wars taking place – we shall not only sink into material barbarism but into spiritual barbarism as well: the grass will grow in the streets and we shall destroy present-day civilization and the great mass of the human race as well. Therefore a League of Nations … carries the good wishes of practically the whole of the civilised world.' Towards the end of his speech he made another, then very topical, point. 'The idea of annex-ation and conquest which urges people on to war … seems to be growing more and more remote', citing Germany meeting huge resist-ance in the Ukraine, 'active resistance, passive resistance, and revolu-tionary resistance. That in fact is a blow at the evil kind of imperialism … which hopes to conquer a place, annex it, and make it one's own.'[42]

By the time the summer recess began, Mark was physically exhausted and suffering from a bad cold. He was due to travel to Yorkshire for a three-week break, and his secretary, Walter Wilson, fearing for his health, wrote to his election agent in Hull, Mr Hallmark, giving him strict instructions not to bother him. 'I write to you privately to say that Sir Mark is going to Sledmere on Saturday for 3 weeks *rest & quietness* – he badly needs it I am sure – so I do not want you to bother him at all while he is up there. You understand I'm certain what I mean, but if Sir Mark does not take a rest it will pay him out, so do not fetch him to Hull will you?'[43]

When he arrived at the local station at Fimber, he was greeted by the children, though, to his disappointment, there was no sign of Edith, who, they explained, had had to stay at home. Since petrol was rationed, the family coach had come to collect him rather than the

Daimler, and climbing aboard he noticed a bearded coachman whom he did not recognize. The old coachman had had to leave, the children told him, and this was his replacement. A few minutes into the journey, however, he noticed the shoulders of the coachman quivering and heaving as if with laughter, which was followed by howls of mirth from the children as he turned around and revealed 'himself' to be Edith in coachman's livery and a false beard. It was an incident that became part of family history.

While Mark was recuperating at Sledmere, Picot spent the summer in diplomatic efforts to modify the views of French colonialists, to bring them more into line with the new thinking of Lloyd George and President Wilson. It was an uphill task, not helped by continuing silence from the Eastern Committee. 'People here can't understand why there is no response,' wrote Picot, 'the spiteful see it as evidence of hidden intentions ... the colonial party is already on its guard. Meetings are being held, representations to the government are being prepared. The government must have something with which to reassure the delegations.'[44] Suspicion abounded and as General Allenby resumed his advance in September, there was a feeling close to panic in some quarters that France might be pushed out of Syria altogether. After all, had not the British done something very similar at the end of the nineteenth century, when they pushed her out of Egypt?

Their fears were not unfounded. After Damascus finally fell to Allenby on 1 October, Jules Cambon had a meeting with Balfour, in the course of which he 'had pointed out that General Allenby's army had now entered the French sphere of influence, as defined in the Sykes–Picot Agreement of 1916, and that arrangements should be made as regards the administration'. When this was reported to Lloyd George, 'The Prime Minister said he had been refreshing his memory about the Sykes–Picot Agreement, and had come to the conclusion that it was quite inapplicable to present circumstances, and was altogether a most undesirable agreement from the British point of view. Having been concluded more than two years ago, it entirely overlooked the fact that our position in Turkey had been won by very large

British forces, whereas our Allies had contributed but little to the result.'[45] Moreover, in the superior position that the British now found themselves in, Lloyd George had even contemplated leaving France out of Syria altogether, though in the end it was to be a complete revision of Sykes–Picot that he proposed.

The flames of fear that flickered in the minds of the French coloni-alists were increased after the fall of Damascus, and a few days later of Aleppo, when, on the orders of the Foreign Office, the flag of the King of the Hejaz was raised over both cities. Designed by Mark, its colours – black, white, green and red – had been chosen to signify the past glories of Moslem Arab empires, and having it flying gave out two messages. It strengthened Sharif Hussein's claim to leadership of Arab Syria, and reminded the French that Arab independence was on the cards, and there was little they could do about it. They did object strongly, however, when a few days later the flag was raised in Beirut, to such an extent that Allenby ordered it to be taken down again, an act which in turn infuriated Feisal. Once again rumour and suspicion swept the country, igniting the possibility of mutiny within the Arab ranks. Feisal then made it clear that unless the Allies came out with a firm statement of their intentions, he could not be held responsible for the consequences.

The result was the Anglo-French Declaration, an agreement origi-nally drawn up by Picot and Mark, and modified by the Foreign Office, which proclaimed the principle of the consent of the governed. While actually omitting any specific reference to Arab independence, it stated the goals of the two governments to be 'the complete and final liberation of the peoples who have for so long been oppressed by the Turks, and the setting up of national governments and administra-tions that shall derive their authority from the free exercise of the initiative and choice of the indigenous populations'. It went on to nobly declare that the only concern of the two Allied governments was 'to offer such support and efficacious help as will ensure the smooth working of the governments and administrations which those popu-lations will have elected of their own free will to have ...'[46] Its publi-

cation resulted in the dousing of the flames, and for the time being a
rupture between Britain and her Arab allies was staved off.

By the time of the Ottoman defeat in Syria, peace was in the air.
Two million American soldiers had helped the Allies to a string of
victories on the Western Front, and Germany had approached
President Wilson to mediate a ceasefire with Britain and France. In a
long letter to Lord Robert Cecil, Mark set out his views on the situation as it now stood in the Middle East.

> The present prospect in the Middle East is not unfavourable
> compared to what it was in the early days of 1916 when the
> following situation obtained:
>
> Anglo-French relations in Eastern affairs were very much
> strained, and east of Brindisi the Entente hardly existed in name.
>
> The Arab movement was regarded as a dangerous and
> visionary idea.
>
> The Dardanelles had been evacuated with a terrible blow to
> our prestige.
>
> A considerable reverse had overtaken us in Mesopotamia.
>
> A huge immobile and unorganized force was isolated in
> Egypt.
>
> Turkish prestige was high, with the natural result that it
> menaced us in India, Afghanistan and Egypt.
>
> Now ...
>
> 1. We have been able to foster the Arab movement till it has
>   become a considerable military-political asset.
> 2. We have been able to occupy Palestine and a great part of
>   Syria without unduly straining French susceptibilities.
> 3. We have occupied Mesopotamia effectively.
> 4. We have been able to wear down Turkish resistance to so fine
>   an edge that General Allenby's victory in Palestine has, by
>   accounting for 80,000 men, reduced Turkey to temporary
>   impotence in the field.

Peace, or at least armistice, seems now to be imminent, and I think you will agree that it is of the greatest importance both to this country and to humanity in general that we should now exert ourselves to the utmost in order to obtain as satisfactory a settlement of the Middle Eastern question as military and political circumstances will permit. The problems which confront us in those parts are thorny, complicated and even dangerous, but if so good a result could be brought about in 1918 out of the bad situation which subsisted in 1916, I think that one would be a pessimist indeed if one could not hope to build a sound settlement on the existing state of affairs.[47]

In typical Mark fashion, he optimistically believed that only he could solve the thorny problems of easing the path of Zionism in Palestine, and smoothing over Franco-Arab frictions in Syria, and with these in mind he decided to set off once again on a long tour of the Middle East. It was a trip that was to be the death of him.

Chapter 14

Worked to Death

Syria was now divided into three zones, each of which had been placed under a separate administration, the first being the British zone of Palestine, known as *Occupied Enemy Territory Administration South*, or *O.E.T.A.* for short; the second, *O.E.T.A. East*, was Arab and consisted of the interior of Syria from Aqaba to Aleppo, while the third was *O.E.T.A. West*, and was French, comprising the Lebanon and the Syrian seaboard from Tyre to Cilicia. With the prospect of a Peace Conference in the near future, Mark was only too keen to return to the area to ensure that the proper administrative regimes were being put in place, and to gather any fresh information that might prove useful when peace was being discussed After ensuring that he had the support of both the Foreign Office and the War Office, both of whom agreed to sponsor the mission, he laid out his ideas in a memorandum, emphasizing the importance of the fostering of good relations between Arabs and French, and submitted it to Lord Curzon's Eastern Committee. While they were mulling over its contents, he left for Sledmere to break the news to Edith and the family that he was about to depart again for the East. As a treat, he planned a special surprise for the children, which did not go down as well as he might have hoped.

'It was announced,' recalled Angela, 'that there was to be a grand presentation of some kind by papa to all of us in the Hall. He summoned us to line up before a table covered with a cloth under which were hidden objects. Excitement was intense and expectation fierce when with a flourish he whisked away the cloth and revealed what lay beneath: a row of five beautifully bound Roman Missals, each one with the owner's Christian name in gold letters on the cover. What had we expected? What had our father thought our reactions would be? It is odd but I do not think he had at all foreseen the blinding disappointment that each would feel, or realised how near to tears of disappointment that were in the choking words of "Thanks awfully!" and the hugs that hid true feelings. Poor Papa, I don't think he realised to what an extent his gifts had misfired. Nor need they have if they had been given in a different way, individually with a personal explanation. It was the build up that was the fatal flaw ...'[1]

On his return to London, Mark was happy to find that the Eastern Committee had agreed to his mission, and had received a telegram from General Allenby stating: 'I should be glad to see Sir Mark Sykes who should come to my HQ direct.'[2] His only disappointment was that the War Office turned down his request that, in order to give his mission more authority, he should be temporarily promoted to the rank of Major-General! He left London as a mere Lieutenant-Colonel on 30 October, the day that, in the Mediterranean, the Turkish armistice was signed on aboard HMS *Agamemnon*. Travelling with him were his secretary, Walter Wilson, Major Ronald Gladstone, a soldier from the Yorkshire Regiment, whose task was to make a record of the trip, and the two young Arab officers, Capt. Husheimy and Capt. Abdul, whose presence on the mission he felt would be of great value. They travelled first to Paris, where he had a brief meeting with the French Foreign Minister, Pichon, and from there to Rome, having accepted an offer from Jean Gôut, chief of the Asiatic section of the Foreign Ministry, of a French cruiser to take them to Egypt. From Rome he told Edith, 'I have not had a moment to write to you, interviews, rushing in cabs hither and thither. We are going to a High Mass at the Sistine Chapel which is a great privilege. I must say after 18 months in an office this is a real holiday viz: change of occupation. The general temper here is one of great enthusiasm … Processions, cheers, shouts and cries. Food is intolerably dear. 10 francs for two alleged quails which were really thrushes is the limit I think … The Americans are very popular, chiefly by reason of their terrific expenditure. They are knows as the Golden Geese.'[3]

Mark held talks with a number of Vatican officials regarding the welfare of the Holy Places in Palestine, before visiting the British Ambassador, Sir Rennell Rodd, at whose residence he was introduced to General Townshend, who had been taken prisoner by the Turks after the siege of Kut-al-Amara in 1916, and held captive ever since in a luxury villa on the Island of Heybeliada. Since thousands of his troops had been simultaneously imprisoned in terrible conditions, many of them dying, his reputation was tarnished, and Mark was convinced he had been brainwashed. In his report, Gladstone noted 'General Townshend told Sir Mark the Turks were in great spirits in regard to the Armistice and had promised the Allies a great reception on their entry into the Dardanelles. Sir Mark thought it expedient that His Majesty's Government would be well advised if strict orders were issued to the effect that all Turkish Hospitality should be refused by the Allies on the occupation of the Straits.' Gladstone added, 'at a later date it was gratifying to note the suggestion had been promptly acted upon'.[4]

He also met with the Armenian Committee, to whom, recorded Gladstone, 'Mark gave his views in an eloquent and carefully-worded speech in French in regard to the future of Armenia in relation to Turkey, a speech which left no misconception behind it as regarded the suzerainty of Turkey over Armenia, in which he gave a lucid description of the conditions under which the Armenians had existed under Turkish rule, and of the atrocities committed upon this Christian people, which was almost obliterated by the cruel, wanton and organized massacres of the Turks.'[5] Mark was angry because he believed that under the terms of the Armistice, Turkey should agree to give independence to Armenians who were living in areas still unoccupied by the Allies, a stipulation that had been left out of the final document. 'You will have observed,' he pointed out to Edith, 'that the Armenians have been completely let down by the Armistice. Armistice is not Peace but we shall have a hard struggle I make no doubt, but prayers and energy ought to secure victory.'

'I hope you are not feeling too lonely,' he continued. 'I do not see how my mission can keep me very long, but I am certain that work on the spot and first hand information is essential.' He told her he would wire her his arrival in Egypt, after a journey he expected to be 'detestable'. He ended the letter on an ominous note. 'By the way, the Flu is awful here ...'[6] The epidemic of influenza, first reports of which had emerged from Spain in May, had swept through Europe in the summer, killing thousands in its path, and the outbreak in Rome in October had been particularly deadly, with a 172 per cent rise in mortality rates. Mark was thus only too keen to board the train down to Taranto, from where the French cruiser would take him to Port Said. Unfortunately he was delayed by another day: 'so went to the Sistine Chapel at leisure,' he reported to Edith; 'viz. not having a train to catch did not suffer from distractions. The picture is very beautiful: (the ceremony was the annual requiem for the last Pope). The Chapel is very tall and spacious ... The whole lined with the famous cartoons, which are if a little foggy and faint still very beautiful – as to the general impression, it is amazing – you find yourself suddenly in the

Chapel amidst Swiss Guards and Chamberlains of say the early 17 century …'

Behind rows of scarlet Cardinals, and 'well fenced in' were 'the famous choir and a conductor more exquisite, more intense, more preoccupied and more sympathetically magisterial than even Sir Henry Wood …'[7]

What he was most taken by were 'the colours. Hazy frescoes, gold grill [*sic*], green benches, Red Cardinals, black, white and grey orders, white surplices at the top, heavy velvet curtains of dark crimson, then a movement among the surplices and enters His Holiness in a black and gold Cope and a mitre of white silk … It was real and wonderful and grand, I only wish you and the babies had been there, even Walter was moved to admiration. Beside me sat a little American novice from a seminary evidently writing it up I suppose for a U.S. paper,

so the catholicity of the church was punctuated and underlined and accented, for the boy was wrapt [*sic*] with delight and fervour which resulted in the scratching of his pencil on paper and occasional little gasps of "Say!" "My!" "Well!" "Cute!" "Fine!" which of course is just as it should be. Off I hope tonight, but the French navy is a weapon rather of art and drama than precision and science so we shall get there when we do ...'[8]

Mark and his colleagues sailed into Port Said on the morning of 11 November, the very day that the Germans signed the armistice, an occasion that was marked by 'a fusillade of innumerable fog signals and a display of Very lights by the Royal Air Force'.[9] The following morning he reached GHQ at Bar Salim, where he met with General Allenby to discuss the purpose of his mission. Though they had never met, Allenby wrote to Field Marshal Sir Henry Wilson, the Chief of the Imperial General Staff, 'I know him, fairly well, from hearsay.'[10] 'I hope Mark Sykes behaves himself,' replied Wilson. 'He is a good fellow but cracked and his blessed Sykes–Picot Agreement must be

torn up somehow.'[11] Allenby and Mark appear to have hit it off –
'Allenby is splendid,' Mark told Edith'[12] – and the meeting ended with
him being given a staff car and driver and agreeing to submit all
reports and interviews back to Allenby for his personal supervision.

'We left General Headquarters the same afternoon and proceeded
by motor to Jerusalem,' reported Gladstone, 'a two hours run and
passed through Ramleh by the old coach road which winds through
rocky undulations and brings one to the Damascus Gate of the ancient
and holy city.'[13] Mark paid a hurried visit to the Church of the Holy
Sepulchre, built on the site of the Crucifixion, before leading his party
to the home of the Military Governor, his old friend, Ronald Storrs,
where they were billeted for the night. 'Mark with me again,' Storrs
noted in his diary, 'giving as always a maximum of trouble and a
maximum of delight', while in his later memoirs he wrote of him that
'he found affairs politically far more complicated than he had hoped,
and I had never known him so uncertain of the practical truth of his
dearest convictions'.[14]

'The situation is very complex,' Mark told Edith, and just how can
be judged from the content of some of General Allenby's correspondence around the time that Mark had his meeting. 'The future, when
martial law no longer prevails, is not so cloudless,' he wrote to Field
Marshal Wilson on 9 November. 'Distrust of the French is not, in any
way, abated. The Moslems are suspicious that the whole littoral will be
given to the French; and I think that the French military governors
think so too. If the Arabs have no access to the sea, there will be
endless trouble. Feisal has already asked to be allowed to resign. If he
did so, there would be blood, fire and ruin throughout all Arabia and
Syria. All communities and creeds have absolute faith in the English,
and, if we act up to our declared principles regarding the rights of
self-determination of peoples, we shall retain that confidence. If not,
there will be chaos.'[15]

The Zionist question further muddied the waters, since, egged on
by Jews in America, and with the Peace Conference about to begin,
they had begun to be more aggressive in their demands. Allenby

expressed his worries on this subject in a cable to the War Office, sent on 5 December. 'In Palestine non-Jews number approximately 573,000 as against 66,000 Jews. In view of above considerations, consider it essential that Zionists should avoid increasing apprehension by indiscreet declarations of policy and exaggerated demands which can only militate against their success by arousing permanent hostility and laying them open to charge of securing their aims by force. The Zionists realise their legitimate aspirations provided that they carry out their programme patiently and show sympathy for what is today a very large majority of Palestine's population. If they force the pace now insecure foundations will be the basis of the whole structure.'[16]

Tricky as the situation was, Mark remained absolutely determined to achieve the solution he believed in. 'I have always been an optimist,' he told Edith, and he began, while he was in Jerusalem, by consulting both Jewish and non-Jewish leaders, and making motor trips through Palestine to review how things stood. These were long and tiring journeys. On 15 November, for example, 'At 4.a.m … we set out to Es Salt by motor car, a distance of 120 miles, we travelled from Jerusalem via Jericho and the Jordan Valley through the mountains of El Belka, following the route of the Turkish army over almost impossible roads cut up by motor lorry traffic and damaged by recent rains, we arrived at Es Salt at midday. In the short space of one hour … Sir Mark summed up the situation with remarkable rapidity and we returned to Jerusalem the same afternoon and reported to General Headquarters at Ramleh … On the morning of the 16th we motored into Jaffa there to meet the Zionist Commission at Tel Aviv … returning to General headquarters the same evening to acquaint the C-in-C on the Zionist position.'[17] He wrote to Edith, 'Tell Mr Sokolow that if possible he ought to come out here and judge for himself as to the situation. He is the only person I know who could produce a better atmosphere.'[18]

In a cable to the Foreign Office, he spelled this out, echoing the views of Allenby. 'Situation is that non-Jews under pan-Arab and Effendi influence are getting into an irritable state. Jews drifting into hostile attitude. Both under influence of world armistice feel moment propitious to make good rival claims … I do not attempt to judge of relative importance of situation here as compared with wider issues nor do I suggest that Zionists should ask for less than is necessary to enable them to achieve their objects. However I feel present situation arises rather from misunderstanding than permanent incompatibility of views.'[19]

While all this was going on, there were politics back home to be considered, in that there was an upcoming General Election, which would be the first ever run in which women of thirty and over would have the vote. Though his constituency anticipated a landslide victory, especially since the local Labour Party were not putting up a candidate, Edith was keen to know Mark's views. He, however, had other things on his mind. 'I am absolutely in the dark as to what is going on or how the Election arose. Anyway I cannot bother my head about it now as I have more important things to do …' He needed to leave as soon as possible for inland Syria, O.E.T.A. East, to check the situation there and hopefully to meet with Prince Feisal, and for this purpose Allenby had put two cars at his disposal.

'We left General Headquarters at 5.00am on 19 November,' reported Gladstone, 'collecting the other members of the mission from the Political Camp, including Sir Mark's old Arab servant Jacob who had arrived from Jerusalem … Devoted he was to his Master as in turn his Master was no less devoted to him. The route selected was Jerusalem, Nabulus, Nazareth, Tiberias, el Kuneitra to Damascus. Equipped for all eventualities we arrived at Nazareth the same night where the Franciscans gave us quarter. For the greater part of the journey the road was strewn with the wreckage of Turkish war material, dead horses, broken limbers, and ammunition wagons, motor lorries and ambulances, circassian carts and all appurtenances of the recent flight of the Turkish Army. The following day we journeyed through Tiberias along the shores of the sea of Nazareth and made our way into Damascus … and on arrival we were informed of the impending departure of the Emir Feisal for Marseilles.'

Feisal was heading to France at the instigation of T. E. Lawrence, who believed that it was important for Sharif Hussein's representative to attend the upcoming Peace Conference, which would include discussion relating to the future of the Middle East. That the Royal Navy was prepared to send one of its cruisers, HMS *Gloucester*, to deliver him and his entourage to Europe was indicative of the high standing in which he and his family stood in the eyes of Britain. So far as Mark was concerned, however, he would have been better off staying at home, and during the course of a brief meeting he told Feisal, 'he regretted very much his departure to Europe at a time when he was most wanted for the Governing of his people in Syria'.[20] In his report back to the Foreign Office, Mark told them, 'Damascus and district is pro-Feisal … Anti-French feeling runs high and to impose French advisers now would invite disorder. Government working very feebly, vitality and cohesion are lacking and intrigue is rampant …' He also suggested that they should not be fooled by apparent Anglophilia amongst the Arabs, since this was often just a way of expressing their anti-French feelings. 'Arabs,' he wrote, 'love to set partners by the ears.'[21]

On 24 November, the mission set off for Aleppo, spending the first night in Homs as the guests of the Australian Desert Corps, and arriving the following day at Hama, famous for its numerous *norias*, large water wheels driven by the currents of the Orontes river and used for irrigation. 'The native Governor had been acquainted of Sir Mark's coming,' recorded Gladstone, 'and a great reception lay in store for him. Approaching the city a mounted escort of Arabs came out to meet him, and they cantered in front of the cars and conducted the mission to the local Serai[22] where a guard of honour of local Arab troops was drawn up at the Present to the strains of an Arab band playing "God Save the King".'

Mark was now in his element, made welcome by the Civil Governor and local chiefs, many of whom remembered him from the days when he had travelled through their lands as an unknown undergraduate. Now he, who had designed the flag that flew over their town, came as an official representative of the British Government. Having placed his residence, on the banks of the Orontes, at the disposal of the Mission, the Governor summoned all the notables in the district to a special dinner in their honour. 'Previous to the dinner, the guests assembled in a finely carpeted room where each in turn addressed warm expressions of welcome to the Chief … and at the conclusion and before proceeding to dinner Sir Mark, in thanking them for their great welcome, addressed them with words of encouragement and gave them advice in regard to their future, pointing out how necessary it was for the whole community of Hama to work very hard in order to show the Allied Powers their ability for municipal self-government … We then partook of a sumptuous repast consisting of no less than twenty dishes.'[23]

Before leaving for Aleppo, on the morning of 26 November, Mark made it known to the Arab Governor, Gilani, how impressed he was at the businesslike way he was running the Municipality. 'On our departure,' reported Gladstone, 'the Guard of Honour was again drawn up with the Syrian Flag flying, and on Sir Mark saluting this National Emblem as we passed, tremendous cheers burst forth from the assembled crowd.' One cannot help but think that he must have felt that an occasion such as this represented one of the highlights of his life. 'The wildest dreams of his youth were taking place,' wrote his first biographer, Shane Leslie. 'He had never nursed more ambition than to be an explorer of the Middle East. The war had made him a disposer of boundaries and an abettor of nationalities, a weaver of flags. Wherever he appeared in those absorbing days, the peoples rose up to acclaim him. The recorder of history found himself making history … Every day he lived to the full as he struggled to bring order out of the chaos, and to leave his name as a great peacemaker among the peoples who already trusted him as a heaven-sent arbiter of their destinies.'[24]

Considering that the Turks had only left Aleppo at the end of October, Mark found it in a remarkably calm and organized state, mostly due to the expert control exerted by Major-General Henry

McAndrew and the 5th Cavalry Division who were overseeing the transition. He decided to make the city his headquarters, and began the setting up of a provisional administration under the Governor-Generalship of Shukri Pasha. When this task was completed, he travelled to Hama on 9 December to meet Allenby and bring him back the following day for his official entry into the city, where the Field Marshal addressed local dignitaries and a great crowd of people from the steps of the Government Serai. For Mark it was a far cry from his undergraduate days when he had first visited Aleppo and found it 'not altogether a pleasant town'.

Only one event distracted Mark from his Middle Eastern duties, and that was the news that, with the election due to be held on 18 December, he had come under a vicious attack in his constituency from his Liberal opponent, the Rev. R. M. Kedward, a Wesleyan minister, who had as good as accused him of cowardice. 'Sir Mark,' he had said in a speech, 'would have had a better claim to support if he had been risking his life with the boys in France.'[25] Indignant, Mark immediately cabled his reply to the charges, stating that his work in the Middle East had been 'on the imperative order of Kitchener', who realized that 'twenty years previous study and specialisation, combined with mapping of 5,000 miles of military roads in Middle East, made it essential I be employed in sphere of hostilities where my knowledge could be used ...'[26] Moreover, he said, he had served on four fronts during the war, crossed the Mediterranean five times, and the North Sea twice.

Lloyd George himself weighed into the war of words, writing to Edith, 'I have had frequent opportunities of seeing the result of Sir Mark's work, which was of an exceptionally arduous and difficult character, both at home and abroad on special missions to the eastern fronts.'[27] As for Edith herself, she had the Prime Minister's letter circulated throughout the constituency, and in an interview with the *Leeds Mercury* she spoke passionately in her husband's defence. 'No one can say he has been a shirker. He has been working very hard since the war began. In fact, he has hardly ever had a day to go home, and has hardly seen anything of his children. I know there is no man in England who works harder than he has, or longer hours.'[28] At the election, polled in a single day on 18 December, Mark swept back into his seat with a majority of over 10,000. In reply to Edith's cable announcing the results, he sent her a one-line message, 'ADJUTRIX MEA ET LIBERATRIX MEA ES TU.'[29] 'That is what I like to think I was and am,' commented Edith, adding that the words 'touched me deeply and will remain forever imprinted on my heart'.[30]

Soon after Allenby had left, some disturbing news filtered through from Aintab, a town ninety-five miles to the north and which was still occupied by the Turkish army, who were supposed to be demobilizing in accordance with the terms of the Armistice. A member of the American Mission in Aleppo had heard on good authority 'that the Turks had assumed a very threatening attitude towards all Europeans and Armenians and desired it to be known that they fully intended to oppose the approach of the British troops should they come near ...'[31] Mark decided that the lives of the American Mission and the Armenians were sufficiently in jeopardy that immediate action to protect them should be taken.

After consultation with General McAndrew, it was decided that a strong patrol of armoured cars should be despatched to Aintab without delay: 'on the morning of December 15', recorded Gladstone, 'a fleet of armoured cars was drawn up outside Aleppo, consisting of five heavy armoured cars with a Patrol of seven light Ford cars armed with Lewis guns under command of Major May. The weather conditions were very adverse and we were confronted with driving sleet and rain with intense cold throughout the whole journey ... we came, about three in the afternoon upon Aintab, when speed was increased and within a few minutes we were within the heart of the city, to the utter amazement of the inhabitants. The populace flocked into the streets, a hue and cry was set up that the British had arrived, Turkish soldiers appeared from all quarters and the patrol came to a standstill.'[32]

Mark now showed the mettle that the Rev. Kedward had doubted. He called out the Military Governor and Council, who were fraught and angry at the scene unfolding before them, and demanded from them the safety of all the Christians in Aintab. 'No guarantees were given,' reported Gladstone, 'but before leaving ... Sir Mark gave them strictly to understand he would make each one of them responsible for any further atrocities which might be committed, an edict which created an impression among them and which apparently had the desired effect.'[33] In spite of the ultimatum issued by Mark, he and his men felt in no way secure, and could not wait to get out of Aintab, spending the night at the American missionary school, which Major May surrounded with his fleet of armoured vehicles, before returning to Aleppo the following day. Still, however, fearful for the lives of the Christians in Aintab, after reporting on the situation there to General McAndrew, he received permission to return and keep an eye on things until reinforcements were to arrive a fortnight later.

Over the next month Mark kept up a hectic schedule in his attempts to pull all sides together, travelling hundreds of miles up and down the country, by jeep and by train, holding meetings at all hours of the day and night. 'The whole of his time,' wrote Gladstone, 'was devoted to promoting the welfare of the people. He allowed himself no relaxation from the work he had undertaken in his endeavour to create a more satisfactory state of affairs. All nationalities thronged to the house from early morning till late at night in pursuit of his counsel and advice, Arabs, Armenians, priests, Archbishops, Staff-Officers, Ex-Consuls, dervishes, Kurdish Chiefs, Missionaries, Notables of the city, Merchants, Refugees, and others too numerous to mention. None were allowed to be turned away and interviews often continued to the small hours of the morning. In spite of the intensity of the work, no one ever found it of any avail to remonstrate with Sir Mark or ask for a more equal division of the task.'[34] Though Gladstone also wrote that, apart from him occasionally complaining at the end of a long day of being tired, his hectic schedule did not seem to affect his health, it was a point of view that was contradicted by his old friend Edmund Sandars. He recorded in his diary that Mark had contracted a virus while in Aleppo and had been unable to hold down solid food for three weeks, surviving instead on a diet of three tins of Ideal condensed milk per day, as a result of which he had lost a great deal of weight.

Mark finally left Aleppo on 11 January, travelling to Damascus, where he addressed the Arab Club, made up of members of the most prominent Arab families and politicians of the city, encouraging them to forget rivalries and think as one, and to try and look upon France as a helping hand. With this in mind he organized a reception for Georges-Picot, as well as setting up a meeting between Arabs and Zionists. The last leg of his journey was to Haifa, where lay the advance Headquarters of Field Marshal Allenby, to whom he was to report on all he had achieved. Allenby was impressed. 'I arrived in Haifa yesterday morning,' he wrote to Reginald Wingate, 'after a useful tour. – I visited Aleppo, Jerablus, Adana, Bozanti, Mersin, Alexandretta, Tripoli, and Beirut. Things are quieter, and the situation is easier, than I had expected. Mark Sykes' influence at Aleppo has been for good ...'[35]

One of the last people to see him off was Ronald Storrs. 'We were at Haifa when he left Palestine,' he recorded. 'After a long walk, during which he favoured me with inimitable renderings of a French priest pronouncing Latin, an Orthodox Bishop taking a service, the Indian Government's spelling of Moslem names, and the sort of "crusted" Service Member who might be expected to be returned at the next Khaki Election, he stepped into a boat and was rowed through the gathering dusk to a French Cruiser continuing the conversation until his voice was lost in the distant knocking of the rowlocks.'[36] He did, however, find him thin and worn, and a little harassed at the growing Arab–Jew tension, and was happy that he would at least have five days enforced rest aboard ship en route to the Peace Conference taking place in Paris. 'How I rejoice that I rose at four and journeyed till eleven to spend a few precious hours with him,'[37] he later wrote to Edith.

Allenby had told Mark that he agreed absolutely with his views and that he was to write up his report on the ship and present it at once on arrival to the General Staff Officer. This turned out to be more difficult than might have been expected, beginning with a crossing that was less than smooth. 'He said he had had an awful crossing on the French cruiser,' noted his friend Edmund Sandars in a memo; 'the topmast smashed off by the gale & the French Captain calling him into his cabin, peeled with his hand a large flake of metal from some stanchion (reduced to softness with age) & said "the trouble is that her bottom is like that!"'[38] Despite its ancient condition, the ship survived the crossing and Mark managed to write his report, entitled *Appreciation of the Situation in Syria, Palestine, and Lesser Armenia.* If this document is remarkable for one thing, it is that it shows that Mark's thinking had evolved considerably since the days when he had put his signature to the Sykes–Picot Agreement. 'Whoever takes over Syria,' he opined, 'ought to realise that to have a purely native admin-istration running things badly but with prospects of improvement represents more real progress than having a European staff doing things properly but the natives learning nothing and getting accus-tomed to having things done for them.'[39]

When he finally got to Paris, Mark was sent on a wild goose chase. 'He got here,' described Sandars, '& the GSO was not here. Saw Balfour who understood & sent him to England. There he saw Curzon who also understood & told him to go back to Paris … When he got to Paris he was sent for by Military Intelligence & cursed & ticked off in the presence of that whipper snapper D**** who said that Mark had quoted M.I. as having sent him to England. Mark protested that he had never said he came from M.I. but, as was the fact, direct from Balfour – the best he could get "the old fart" to say was that "he was prepared to believe there had been a misunderstanding" – "and will you believe it I have not seen GSO yet".'[40]

One person he did spend time with in Paris was Nahum Sokolow. 'One evening there was a telephone call,' recalled the latter. 'On taking up the receiver I heard Sykes's voice telling me that he had just arrived in Paris, and was staying as usual at the Hotel Lotti opposite us. I invited him at once to dinner and he came. He was the same lovable fellow, full of life and humour, but now frightfully thin … he had suffered much from digestive troubles.' The two men had a lot to discuss. In his report, Mark had shown wisdom on the subject of the Zionists, his approach to the subject having been profoundly influenced by the intense bitterness he had found it provoked in the Holy Land. He had written that while he believed that every opportunity for the growth of Zionism should be provided in Palestine, it should be done so 'while securing the rights of the existing population and the integrity of the Moslem and Christian Holy Places' even when 'Zionists had become a majority'. Moreover Damascus must not be allowed to become 'a breeding ground of discontent and agitation' against Zionists and the way to prevent this happening was for them not to 'ask for more than justice or reason can demand'.[41]

'It was two hours after midnight when he left us,' wrote Sokolow; 'he had so much to tell about the ordinary incapacity for proper administration of the local Syrian population and their marked capacity in that direction under suitable guidance, about the prospects for Palestine, about the steps he had taken against anti-Zionist intrigues in Syria and other matters. From that time forward we saw each other every day ... He had a thousand ideas and had brought reports and instructions from Syria that had to be elaborated. Our days were filled with appointments for visits, interviews, etc.'

Mark was excited by the thought of what kind of new world might emerge from the war. In his election address, cabled to the constituents of Hull from Jerusalem, he had told them, 'I stand for a League of Nations ... the establishment of international relations on basis of guaranteed security of states from aggression, permitting disarmament and the abolishment of war.' He saw the 'continuation of pre-war system of secret diplomacy and military preparation' as 'fatal to future of civilisation ... In the peace terms I stand neither for aggrandisement nor revenge but for justice, reparation and security.'[42] These were the ideas he intended to take to the Peace Conference, where he was determined to make all those attending see a new vision for the future of the Middle East. But it was not to be.

Early in February, Edith, who had joined him at the Lotti Hotel, fell ill with the flu that was still wreaking havoc across Europe. Writing on 10 February, Edmund Sandars described how Mark told him that 'Edith was ill with influenza. I urged him to keep her in bed. He said he had done so & hoped he was not too late, that yesterday he had thought her ill but had no thermometer & she denied having a temperature, but today had a definite touch of fever & he had laid her to bed.'[43] That night Mark had tickets for the opera and invited Sandars and his wife, Mary, to join him and a friend, Sir Arthur Hirtzel. They dined beforehand at a popular restaurant, Henri. Before Edith fell ill, Mark and she 'had been to the Grand Guignol & were much impressed with one of their horrors in which there was a lunatic who gouged out a fellow prisoner's eye'. According to Mark the lunatic reminded them both of someone they all knew, 'a quiet determined man', and he amused them greatly by pretending to be him and leaning across the table moaning, 'I'll be wanting one of your eyes – yes, one of your eyes, yes, I'll be wanting one of your eyes ...'[44]

At the opera Mark 'chuckled a good deal at being in the Rothschild box ... and as usual facially acted the music & we laughed over the play & cast (neither of us had heard Thais before). Mark and I went out to smoke in the intervals. He remarked two or three times how much that was good in Paris was due to Napoleon III in art, building and organisation. We met a Major in the Hull Garrison Artillery to whom we talked & Mark rather tried to scare him as to the dangers of a revival of war activity on the part of the Turk if not of the Boche. Sir Arthur Hirtzel took us all in his car to the Lotti where Mark jumped out of the car & left us.'[45]

Mark's bonhomie that night had masked a fearful truth. 'I've got it,' he told his faithful secretary, Walter Wilson, as he went to bed, and Sandars finished his memo with the melancholy sentence, 'He never got out of bed again after that night.' The following morning, Edith rose from her own sickbed to nurse him, convinced then that he had nothing worse than a chill. The hotel sent up supplies of Bovril, Oxo, and various patent medicines to her, but when the chill developed into full-blown flu, she sent for their doctor from England. He arrived too late. By then, Sunday, 16 February, pneumonia had set in, together with a severe infection of the ear that caused him terrible pain, and obliged Edith, by the end, to have to shout at her 'Terrible Turk' to be heard. He died at 6.30 p.m., a month to the day before his fortieth birthday. Many years later, his daughter Petsy was to confide to a friend, Coote Lygon, that her father appeared to her in London at the very moment he passed away.

Edith wrote immediately to the children. 'My darling Children, a very very heavy blow has fallen upon us all. You will have been told that your darling Papa died last night at 6.30. Darlings we have got to face this great sorrow that God in his wisdom has sent upon us. Papa was everything to me and life without him seems very difficult. But you my darlings will help me. We shall always have his memory and the example of his noble, Christian, spotless life to help us ... No man has more truly laid down his life for his country, for weakened by his work and journey in Syria he had not the resistance to overcome the illness which attacked him. I am bringing him to Sledmere. Bless you darlings and pray for Papa's soul ...'[46]

'Mark Sykes dead!' wrote his cousin, Shane Leslie. 'A genuine cry of grief ascended from strange places ... English Catholics mourned him in Westminster Cathedral. Jews in Morocco heard his panegyric from the lips of their Chief Rabbi. In Aleppo and Jerusalem his solemn Requiem was sung. The Armenian nation symbolized their grief by sending a wreath of red roses from "*La Nation Arménienne reconnaissante.*" The King sent gracious word of his regret ... And the First Minister of the Crown said well "During the War he gave his energy and his strength ungrudgingly and to the utmost. Had he lived, he must surely have attained great heights."'[47]

He undoubtedly left a yawning gap in the lives of all those he left behind. 'So,' wrote his childhood friend, Tommy Ellis, now Lord Howard de Walden, 'the one man that I had met who seemed to me to have in him the seeds of greatness was not to attain it after all.'[48] Nor was he to achieve his ambition to live to a ripe old age and, as he had once told his brother-in-law, Harold, 'end his days at Sledmere as a patriarch, after the Italian fashion, with all his married sons and their families living in the house with him'.[49] 'I shall always for the rest of my life live largely in the past because of Mark,' wrote John Hugh Smith to Edith, 'and there is little in my mind which is not what it is because of him. His conversation was surely the best that one has ever heard; its interests, whether one agreed with his ideas or not, was mastering; its imagination never failed nor its unique humour. And what I feel myself will I know be felt by hundreds of men – not only his friends but his own people at Sledmere and his constituents at Hull and his soldiers: Bedawin, Druses, Kurds and Turks.'[50] Mark's friend Ronald Storrs, who had been Oriental Secretary in Cairo at the beginning of the war, said simply, 'I do not like to think of England without him; it will never be the same place.'[51]

On the evening of Saturday, 22 February, Mark's coffin, encased in lead, arrived at Sledmere, where it was placed in the new family chapel and covered with a Union Jack. Three wreaths were placed upon it. One was from the villagers and read, 'He who never rested, rests'. The others were from the children – 'To darling Papa' – and Edith – 'Adjutor Meus Liberator Meus Fuistis'.[52] The funeral service was held three days later in the presence of family and close friends, and afterwards an enormous crowd joined the procession to the graveyard. At its head were the Abbot and monks of Ampleforth Abbey, bearing lighted tapers as they walked in front of the flag-draped coffin, borne on a gun carriage. Behind the coffin came Punch, Mark's favourite charger, carrying an empty saddle, with his field boots reversed in the stirrups. Edith, flanked by her two oldest boys, Richard and Christopher, followed closely behind, leading the rest of the mourners. As the cortège passed through the gates of the church, a band of the 5th Yorkshires struck up Chopin's 'Marche Funèbre'.

A reporter from the *Eastern Morning News* described the burial, which took place with full military honours. 'The Father Abbot pronounces the committal service, and the body of Sir Mark is in its last resting place, close to that of his father and mother. The firing party fire three rounds into the northern sky, and following each the drums roll and the air seems to tremble with their sadness. Then bayonets are fixed and Buglers sound the Last Post. Each of the clergy sprinkle Holy Water on the coffin. The church has completed its offices. The widowed mother and fatherless boys fall on their knees, and the hearts of the multitude are filled with a great compassion, and their eyes brim over with tears as they watch their silent prayer.'[53]

So Mark was laid to rest in the shadows of both the church, built by his father, and the great house rebuilt stone by stone by him. His image was also given a more permanent residence, where it could be looked upon for generations to come. During some of the darkest days of the war, when horrendous losses occurred at Passchendaele in 1917, and in the German offensives into France and Flanders in the spring of 1918, Mark had made a vow to commemorate some of the friends he had lost, both in his battalion and elsewhere. His father, in 1896, had erected, outside the gates of his new church at Sledmere, an Eleanor Cross, being a replica of one of the monuments built by Edward I to commemorate the resting places of the body of his wife, Eleanor of Castile, as it travelled from Nottinghamshire to London. Into its niches, Mark had inserted memorial brasses depicting his departed heroes, each dressed in the garb of a crusading knight, treading underfoot the barbaric Hun, and chivalrously slaying the evil dragon of German imperialism with the sword of St George.

The first of eight panels had been in memory of his boyhood friend Edward Bagshawe, 'Captain of the 5th Yorkshire Regiment, killed in Flanders on July 22, 1916, *"Preux chevalier sans peur et sans reproche"*'. Others were remembered by their trades and ranks. 'Ye who read this remember Walter Barker, a footman of Sledmere and a Private in the 5th Yorkshire Regiment', 'Harry Agar, an Agriculturist and a Private', 'Thomas Frankish, a Carpenter and a Sergeant', 'William Watson, a Saddler and a Lance Corporal', along with many others, officers and men of the same regiment, who died with them. By coincidence he had left one panel unfilled, and in this his own effigy was engraved in brass, bearing sword and shield, trampling underfoot the prostrate figure of a Saracen, for scroll the *Laetare Jerusalem*,[54] and in the background the Holy City itself.

It made a fitting memorial to a man whose loss, wrote George Antonius, the first historian of Arab Nationalism, 'for Jews, Arabs, and British alike, to say nothing of the French ... was little short of a calamity'. This from a man who was no fan, who had described the Sykes–Picot Agreement as 'a shocking document ... not only the product of greed at its worst, that is to say, of greed allied to suspicion and so leading to stupidity', but also, 'a startling piece of double-dealing'. But he accepted that Mark's views on the treaty had undergone a profound change, that 'he had become convinced of its inadaptability to actual conditions and of the futility of trying to execute it ... He had hurried back to Paris bent upon doing all he could to correct false hopes and put a brake upon ambitions which now seemed to him insensate.' His sudden death had brought these plans to a halt. 'Without going so far as to suppose', concluded Antonius, 'that one individual, however genuine, talented and forceful, could have infected the Versailles peacemakers with his own sense of justice, there is little doubt that, had he lived, his recital of facts and his forecast of consequences might have filled the minds of the politicians with those anxieties which are often, in politics, the beginning of wisdom'.[55]

Epilogue

The Legacy

'PEACE AND PRAYER BE UPON THE MESSENGER OF GOD! AND HIS FAMILY AND COMPANIONS AND HIS ALLIES! GOD IS GREAT!' It is August 2014 in Raqqa, Syria, and three turbaned warriors, wearing long robes with bulletproof vests and carrying automatic rifles, punch the air chanting, showing off to the cameraman and reporter of Vice News. They climb into a flatbed truck loudly singing: 'OH IRAQ THE WAR IS ON. WHAT ARE YOU WAITING FOR? FIGHTING IS THE ONLY WAY TO GET YOUR RIGHTS BACK. RAISE YOUR SWORD AGAINST THE CROSS WHICH IS ALREADY FADING OUT!' They then set out on the journey to the Iraq border, a distance of some 200 miles. One masked soldier says 'I'm from Syria and I'm twenty-eight years old. This is the first time I've entered Iraq without a passport.' 'I'm from Tunisia,' says another, also masked, 'and it's my first time entering Iraq without using a passport, a visa or anything else.' 'Now we are one state, the Islamic State,' says a third, 'with the Caliph, Prince of the Faithful, Abu Bakr al-Baghdadi.'

These young men are soldiers of the Islamic State, or IS, an ancient form of government based on the rigid application of Sharia law which had a resurgence in the Middle East after what has become known as the Arab Spring, the series of democratic uprisings that exploded throughout the Arab world in 2011. After consolidating their power-base in Syria, IS set about creating their Caliphate – hard-line, religious, and recognizing no borders. In June 2014, they began a rapid military expansion into Iraq, pushing the army back to Fallujah, just forty-five miles from Baghdad. Within weeks they were in control of huge areas of two countries, shocking the world at the speed of their advance and the ease with which they brushed aside an American-equipped and trained army.

'Thanks to God,' says a black-turbaned fighter, 'we are now on the border between Syria and Iraq. Syria is right in front of you. We've brought a bulldozer to take down the barricades to open the route for Muslims. Thank God. We don't believe in the Sykes–Picot Agreement.' Just a few weeks earlier the place where he is standing had been a checkpoint manned by Iraqi soldiers. Then IS overran it, and, as is common, they filmed the action and published the results. 'Break the borders!' they cried. Visibly terrified, the Iraqi guards, stripped of their uniforms, were piled in their underwear into the back of a flatbed truck. 'We're going to chop your heads off with a knife,' crowed their captors, and from the looks on the faces of the captives it was quite clear that they did not doubt for a moment that this was to be their fate. They were driven away, putting on an unconvincing performance of cheering for the Islamic State.

Now a large red bulldozer begins the work of demolishing the border, its twin exhaust pipes belching dark and acrid fumes into the desert air. 'We've broken Sykes–Picot,' yells one the of the IS fighters. Another walks over to a metal sign lying on the ground which has the words 'COMMANDOS BATTALION BORDER' written on it. He says: 'The only commandos here now are the Battalion of Islam.' He steps on the sign. It lets out metallic creaks and groans. He adds: 'And as you can see, it is under our feet right now. We are the breaker of barriers, Inshallah, and we shall break the barrier of Iraq, Jordan, Lebanon, all the countries, Inshallah. This is the first of many barriers we shall break.' Later the same warrior, brandishing and slapping his Kalashnikov, exclaims: 'For God's sake, if any of the infidel countries or the Christians decided to build a church to practise their false religion, will anyone stop them from doing that? Will anyone fight them? Will anyone prevent them? We Muslims are the ones who want to enforce Sharia in this land. I swear Sharia can't be established without weapons.'[1]

The Middle East occupied by these foot-soldiers of the Islamic State is a complicated and extremely violent place. As I write these words, thirty-two people have been blown to pieces by an Islamic State suicide bomber at a football match in Iraq. The dead included seventeen young boys, as well as members of the local security forces and the mayor of the village of Al-Asriya, where the attack took place. Such events are a regular occurrence in a country where tensions are rife between the Shiite majority, the minority Sunnis, and the Kurds in the north. The threat of civil war is never far away, especially as there is the ever-present danger of a spillover from the one raging in neighbouring Syria, where over 150,000 people have died in the conflict. The Lebanon is a deeply fractured state, tensions between Sunni and Hezbollah having been exacerbated in the wake of the Syrian war, while Palestine and Israel are constantly at each other's throats. It is a far cry from the Middle East that was imagined by Mark Sykes, who would be turning over in his grave were he able to follow its history since his sudden and unexpected death.

To begin with, if he had had any faith that the lofty sentiments expressed in the Anglo-French Declaration of November 1918 would influence the decision-making of the Peace Conference that convened in Paris in 1919 then he would have been sorely disappointed. That may have promised 'the complete and definitive liberation of the peoples so long oppressed by the Turks and the establishment of National Governments and Administrations drawing their authority from the initiative and free choice of indigenous populations', but the reality was that the rivalries and clashes of the great powers, all eager to make the best deals for themselves in the aftermath of victory, dominated the proceedings, and pushed the issue of the rights of small nations into the background.

The Arab delegation at the Peace Conference was headed by Emir Feisal, and he was completely out of his depth. He spoke little English, was unused to the ways of European diplomacy, and had no mandate from his autocratic father to negotiate, only orders that he must accept nothing less than the fulfilment of the pledges made by Great Britain with regard to Arab independence. He also felt very strongly the hostility of the French towards both him and his mission. As he saw things, his best chance of achieving his aspirations for independence lay with America, hopes which were embedded in a series of resolutions set out by the General Syrian Congress, which met in Damascus in July 1919, with the purpose of defining Arab aims in regard to Syria, Palestine and Iraq. 'We rely,' the delegates asserted, 'on President Wilson's declaration that his object in entering the War was to put an end to acquisitive designs for imperialistic purposes.'[2]

These resolutions were an authoritative statement, by a genuinely representative assembly, of Arab attitudes towards the issues of the day. They demanded the repudiation of the Sykes–Picot Agreement and the Balfour Declaration and of any plan for the partition of Syria or the creation of a Jewish Commonwealth in Palestine; the recognition of the independence of Syria and Palestine as a sovereign state with Feisal as king, and recognition of the independence of Iraq. The resolutions were concluded with a statement that 'The lofty principles proclaimed by President Wilson encourage us to believe that … we may look to … the liberal American nation, who are known for their sincere and generous sympathy with the aspirations of weak nations, for help in the fulfilment of our hopes.'[3]

Feisal had also proposed that the Peace Conference should set up a commission to visit Syria and Palestine for the purpose of ascertaining the wishes of the population. It was a proposal that appealed greatly to President Wilson, though less so to the British and the French, the result being that though the King–Crane Commission, named after its delegates, did take place, it was finally a purely American affair. This was no bad thing since it meant that the inquiry was undertaken by a body with no national ambitions to promote and who approached their task with open minds. For two months, in June and July 1919, Charles Crane, a Chicago businessman, and Dr Henry King, an American theologian, travelled through Syria and Palestine interviewing hundreds of Arab notables and making themselves accessible to every shade of opinion without restriction. Their eventual report, delivered to President Wilson at the beginning of September, was shrewd in its findings and honest in its recommendations.

They favoured the mandatory system in Syria–Palestine and Iraq, the latter to be treated as one country, so long as the mandates were for a limited time, with independence to follow as soon as conditions allowed. Syria–Palestine should be under a single mandate granted to neutral America, while Great Britain should undertake that for Iraq. As for the forms of government in each, the suggestion was that they should be constitutional monarchies, with Feisal as king in Syria, and another Arab sovereign to rule over Iraq. Opposition to France was so powerful throughout the region that they felt unable to recommend a French mandate. Similarly they felt that Zionist ambitions in Palestine should be severely limited. The Jews made up only 10 per cent of the population of Palestine, so any attempt to support their national rights there would have meant denying them to the Arab majority, which would have constituted a gross violation of their rights.

Wise though these observations may have been, the commission was in the end a futile exercise, since the consulting body had no authority to act on its recommendations. The latter made uncomfortable reading for the Versailles peacemakers and this, combined with President Wilson's sudden departure for the US, abandoning what he termed 'the whole disgusting scramble', and his subsequent severe stroke, meant that the Crane–King Report was pigeonholed and ignored. Feisal was left to the mercies of the colonial powers, and when the Supreme Council of the Peace Conference met in San Remo in April 1920, they agreed on a new map for the Middle East. Instead of the Arab nation-state that the British had once promised Sharif Hussein in return for his loyalty, the victorious powers divided the Middle East into four countries. Britain received the mandate for Iraq and Palestine, including the buffer state of Transjordan. France took the mandate for Syria and the Lebanon.

The decisions made at San Remo were viewed in Arab eyes as nothing less than a betrayal, provoking deep resentment throughout the region, and in the annals of Arab history 1920 is known as '*Am al-Nakba*', 'the year of catastrophe'. Violence flared up all over the place, with armed uprisings in Syria, Palestine and Iraq, where a full-scale rebellion broke out, lasting from July to October with up to 10,000 casualties. Though British reaction, as an imperial power, was to stamp the trouble out ruthlessly, it was also realized that some kind of plan had to be formulated to try and keep the lid on the cauldron. In an attempt to calm the mounting Arab nationalist fervour, Winston Churchill, Secretary of State for the Colonies, advised by T. E. Lawrence, decided to hand over the administration of Iraq to an Arab government and secure the nomination of Emir Feisal to be king. Meanwhile his elder brother, Abdullah, was given the Emirate of Transjordan. Both these rulers, of course, being imported and having no power-base of their own, would always be dependent on Britain.

A further cause for friction was the arbitrary and autocratic manner in which borders were delineated, with little regard for division along linguistic or religious lines, but entirely to suit the Allies' political, strategic and commercial interests, the latter more and more influenced by the increasing demand for oil. The example of Iraq was typical, with Kurds to the north, Sunni Muslims in the centre and Shiite Muslims to the south. As one contemporary observed, 'Iraq was created by Churchill, who had the mad idea of joining two widely separated oil wells, Kirkuk and Mosul, by uniting three widely separated peoples, the Kurds, the Sunnis and the Shiites.'[4]

The problem of the new Middle East, created out of the ruins of the old order, was that it was a constant reminder to Arab nationalists of the betrayal of their aspirations. They regarded the system of mandates as merely imperialism in disguise, a fact that was borne out in their eyes by the constant military presence and the exploitation of their raw materials. Moreover the Allies had fashioned it in their own image, creating a state system, with arbitrary frontiers and governors whom they nominated, that was based on European ideas and as such held no legitimacy in the eyes of local people, both secular and religious. This has been the cause of turmoil and instability in the region ever since, at the root of uprisings, territorial disputes, revolutions and wars. The Versailles Peace Conference should have left a better world for the former subjects of the Ottoman Empire. Instead, what it ended up doing was best summed up by Field Marshall Wavell, who was the Brigadier-General of the General Staff in Palestine in 1919. 'After the war to end war,' he said, 'they seem to have been pretty successful in Paris at making a Peace to end Peace.'[5] These turned out to have been prophetic words indeed.

Acknowledgements

In the writing of this book, I have been greatly helped by various people, of whom I would particularly like to mention Professor John Oxford for his invaluable information on the Spanish flu and the exhumation of Sir Mark Sykes, Judy Burg and her successor, Simon Wilson, Chief Librarians at the Hull History Centre, and their excellent and helpful staff, and my brother, Nicholas Sykes, for his advice and help in passing on to me articles on the subject of the Sykes–Picot Agreement. I am also indebted to the staff of the London Library, where most of this book was written.

Bibliography

Adelson, Roger, *Mark Sykes: Portrait of an Amateur*, London, Jonathan Cape, 1975

Allenby, Field Marshal Viscount, *Allenby in Palestine: The Middle East Correspondence of Field Marshal Viscount Allenby, June 1917– October 1919* (ed. Matthew Hughes), Sutton Publishing/Army Records Society, 2004

Amery, L. S., *The Leo Amery Diaries*, vol. 1: *1896–1929* (eds. John Barnes and David Nicholson), London, Hutchinson, 1980

Amery, Leo, *My Political Life*, London, Hutchinson, 1953

Anderson, Scott, *Lawrence in Arabia*, London, Atlantic, 2014

Andrew, C. M., and A. Kanya-Forstner, *The Climax of French Imperial Expansion, 1914–1924*, Stanford, Calif., Stanford University Press, 1981

——, *France Overseas*, London, Thames and Hudson, 1981

——, *The French Colonial Party and French Colonial War Aims, 1914–1918, Historical Journal*, vol. xvii, 1974

Antonius, George, *The Arab Awakening*, London, Hamish Hamilton, 1938

Bell, L. G., *Syria: The Desert and the Sown*, London, William Heinemann, 1919

Bell, Lady (ed.), *The Letters of Gertrude Bell*, London, Ernest Benn, 1927

Bowles, Sydney, *Diary of Sydney Bowles*, Chatsworth Papers, Chatsworth House

Budworth, Julia M., *Never Forget: A Biography of George F. S. Bowles*, Stowmarket, J. M. Budworth, 2001

Burgoyne, Elizabeth, *Gertrude Bell, 1889–1914*, London, Ernest Benn, 1958

Busch, B. C., *Britain, India, and the Arabs, 1914–1921*, Berkeley, Calif./London, University of California Press, 1971

Cooper-Busch, Briton, *Hardinge of Penshurst: A Study in the Old Diplomacy*, Hamden, Conn., Archon Books, 1980

Fairfax-Blakeborough, J., *Sykes of Sledmere*, London, Philip Allan, 1929

Fitzherbert, Margaret, *The Man Who was Greenmantle*, London, John Murray, 1983

Fromkin, David, *A Peace to End All Peace: Creating the Modern Middle East, 1914–1922*, London, André Deutsch, 1989

Gilbert, Martin, *Winston S. Churchill*, vol. 3: *1914–1916: Companion*, London, Heinemann, 1972

Gorst, Harold. E., *Much of Life is Laughter*, London, George Allen & Unwin,1936

Hansard, various vols

James, M. R., *Eton and King's: Recollections, Mostly Trivial*, London, Williams and Northgate, 1926

Kedourie, Elie, *Arabic Political Memoirs and Other Studies*, London, Frank Cass, 1974

——, *England and the Middle East: The Destruction of the Ottoman Empire, 1914–1921*, London, Mansell, 1987

——, *In the Anglo-Arab Labyrinth*, Cambridge, CUP, 1976

Kingsmill, Hugh, *Frank Harris*, London, Biografia, 1987

Lawrence, T. E., *Seven Pillars of Wisdom*, London, Jonathan Cape, 1973

Leslie, Shane, *Mark Sykes*, London, Cassell and Co., 1923

Lloyd George, D., *Memoirs of the Peace Conference*, New Haven, Conn., Yale University Press, 1939

Lubbock, S. G., *A Memoir of Montague Rhodes James*, Cambridge, CUP, 1939

Monroe, Elizabeth, *Britain's Moment in the Middle East*, London, Chatto & Windus, 1963

Morris, The Rev. M., *Yorkshire Reminiscences*, London, Humphrey Milford, 1922

Murray's Handbook for Travellers in Syria and Palestine, London, Edward Stanford, 1903

Nicholas, Tsar, *Letters from Tsar Nicholas to Tsarita Alexandra*, www.alexanderpalace.org/letters

Oxford Dictionary of National Biography

Reinharz, Jehuda, *Chaim Weizmann: The Making of a Statesman*, New York/Oxford, OUP, 1993

Samuel, Rt Hon. Viscount, *Memoirs*, London, The Cresset Press, 1945

Schneer, Jonathan, *The Balfour Declaration*, London, Bloomsbury, 2010

Sokolow, Nahum, *History of Zionism, 1600–1918*, London, Longmans, Green & Co., 1919

Stein, Leonard, *The Balfour Declaration*, London, Vallentine, Mitchell, 1961

Storrs, Ronald, *Orientations*, London, Nicholson & Watson, 1945

Sumner, Ian, *The Wolds Wagoners*, Sledmere Estate, 2000

Sykes, Christina Anne Jessica, *Algernon Casterton*, London, Bickers & Son, 1903

——, *Mark Alston*, London, Eveleigh Nash, 1908

Sykes, Christopher Simon, *The Big House*, London, HarperCollins, 2004

——, *Two Studies in Virtue*, London, Collins, 1953

Sykes, J., *Sidelights on the War in South Africa*, London, Fisher Unwin, 1900

Sykes, Mark, *The Caliph's Last Heritage*, London, Macmillan and Co., 1915

——, *Dar ul Islam: A Record of a Journey through Ten of the Asiatic Provinces of Turkey*, London, Bickers & Son, 1904

——, *Narative of a Journey East of Jebel Ed-Druse*, Palestine Exploration Fund Quarterly Statement, 1899

———, *Through Five Turkish Provinces*, London, Bickers & Son, 1900

Things Political. IV, Malton, 1909

Weizmann, Chaim, *Trial and Error*, London, Hamish Hamilton, 1949

Wilson, A. T., *Loyalties: Mesopotamia 1914–1917*, Oxford, OUP, 1930

Newspapers and Journals

Army and Navy Illustrated, The, 14 February 1903

Beaumont Review, December 1894

Daily Express, 4 October 1902

Daily Mail, 4 June 1912

Daily News, 7 November 1902

Daily Sketch, 2 April 1914

Eastern Morning News, 26 February 1919

Manchester Guardian, 22 November 1915

Hull Daily Mail, 25 January 1907

IDEAS, Manchester, 6 June 1914

Journal of Contemporary History, vol. 3, no. 3, July 1968

Journal of Modern History, December 1994

Morning Post, The, London, 4 August 1874

Saturday Review, The, 28 March 1914

Snarl, The, no. 2, 14 November 1899

Spectator, The, 21 February 1903

Sunday Chronicle, 20 April 1913

Things Political, IV, Malton, 1909

Times, The, 14 January 1898

Vanity Fair, 8 August 1874

Victorian Studies, vol. XI, 1968

World, The, 26 January 1898

Yorkshire Herald, 29 October 1903

Yorkshire Post, 17 May 1902

References and Notes on Sources

U DDSY refers to the papers of the Sykes family of Sledmere Hall held by Hull University Archives in the Hull History Centre. SCP ERA refers to the Strickland-Constable Papers held in the East Riding County Archives in Beverley. References for images by Mark Sykes correspond to the references for written correspondence unless otherwise stated, and are used with the kind permission of Christopher Simon Sykes and the Hull History Centre. Cartoons on p.74 and pp.197–198 illustrated in Leslie, Shane, *Mark Sykes*, London, Cassell & Co., 1923, p.44. and p.232 respectively. Map on p. 259, *The Sykes–Picot Agreement of 1916 in regard to Syria and Palestine*, used with kind permission of The National Archives. All photographs are courtesy of the author.

Prologue: An Exhumation
1. Interview with the author, April 2014.

Chapter 1: The Parents
1. M.S. to E.G., 1 September 1900, U DDSY2/1/1/50.
2. M.S. to E.G., 17 April 1900, U DDSY2/1/2a.
3. Ibid., p. 222.
4. This nickname was to distinguish him from his cousin Sir George Bentinck, known as 'Big Ben'.
5. *Morning Post*, 4 August 1874.
6. SCP ERA.
7. Prudence Penelope Cavendish-Bentinck to J.S., August 1874, SCP ERA.
8. Venetia Cavendish-Bentinck to J.S., 30 August 1874, SCP ERA.
9. U DDSY(5)/42/30-[TEMP].
10. Christina Anne Jessica Sykes, *Algernon Casterton*, Bickers and Son, London, 1903. p. 44.
11. 'What a dream for a young woman.'
12. Sir George Wombwell to J.S., 9 April 1879, SCP ERA.
13. Jessie's diary, 1883, SCP ERA.
14. Bay Middleton to J.S., 25 August 1881, SCP ERA.
15. Ibid.
16. J.S. to Lady Herries, 5 November 1882, SP.
17. Ibid.
18. J.S. to C.M., 20 November 1882, SP.
19. J.S. to C.M., 24 December 1882, SP.
20. J.S. to L. de H., July 1885, SCP ERA.
21. J.S. to L. de H., 4 November 1885. 'I am deeply unhappy to leave my child, who is truly the only being in this world

except you who I passionately wish to see again', SCP ERA.
22. Ibid.
23. J.S. to L. de H., 15 December 1885, SCP ERA.
24. J.S. to L. de H., 20 December 1885, SCP ERA.
25. Ibid.
26. Ibid.
27. J.S. to L. de H., 8 January 1887, SCP ERA.
28. J.S. to L. de H., 22 January 1887, SCP ERA.
29. Portia Cavendish-Bentinck to J.S., 14 December 1886, SCP ERA.
30. Ibid.
31. J.S. to L. de H., 25 January 1887, SCP ERA.
32. J.S. to L. de H., 24 February 1887, SCP ERA.
33. Shane Leslie, *Mark Sykes: His Life and Letters*, London, Cassell, 1923, p. 30.
34. M.S. to E.G., 13 April 1900, quoted in Leslie, *Mark Sykes*, p. 32.
35. Mark Sykes, 'How I Achieved Success', *Ideas*, Manchester, 6 June 1914.
36. Ibid.
37. Leslie, *Mark Sykes*, p. 9.
38. Julia.M.Budworth, *Never Forget: A Biography of George F. S. Bowles*, Stowmarket, J. M. Budworth, 2001.
39. Sykes, 'How I Achieved Success'.
40. Leslie, *Mark Sykes*, p. 33.
41. Ibid.
42. Ibid., p. 32.
43. Ibid., p. 35.
44. Ibid.
45. Ibid., p. 31.
46. Ibid., p. 36.
47. Mark Sykes, 'Night in a Mexican Station', *Beaumont Review*, December 1894.
48. Leslie, *Mark Sykes*, p. 10.
49. Ibid., p. 37.
50. Ibid., p. 11.
51. Ibid., p. 10.
52. Ibid., p. 37.
53. J.S. to C.M., 24 December 1882, SP.
54. J.S. to L. de H., 31 December 1886, SCP ERA.
55. H. J. Dyos, 'The Slums of Victorian London', *Victorian Studies*, vol. XI, Summer 1968, p. 19.

Chapter 2: Trials and Tribulations
1. Leslie, *Mark Sykes*, p. 33.

2. Christopher Simon Sykes, *The Big House: The Story of a Country House and Its Family*, London, HarperCollins, 2004.
3. Diary of Sydney Bowles. Chatsworth Papers, Chatsworth House.
4. Leslie, *Mark Sykes*, p. 38.
5. M.S. to E.G, 1 September 1900, U DDSY2/1/1/50.
6. Interview with the author, June 2003.
7. Roger Adelson, *Mark Sykes: Portrait of an Amateur*, London, Jonathan Cape, 1975, p. 52.
8. Leslie, *Mark Sykes*, p. 48.
9. Ibid., p. 51.
10. Ibid., p. 52.
11. S. G. Lubbock, *A Memoir of Montague Rhodes James*, Cambridge University Press, 1939. p. 17.
12. M. R. James, *Eton and King's: Recollections, Mostly Trivial*, London, Williams and Norgate, 1926, pp. 221–3.
13. M.S. to E.G., 25 July 1902, U DDSY2/1/2a.
14. Sykes Family Papers (SFP).
15. *Morning Post*, 13 January 1898.
16. The palatial residence on Piccadilly of the Duke of Devonshire.
17. *Morning Post*, 13 January 1898.
18. Ibid.
19. Ibid.
20. Ibid.
21. *The Times*, 14 January 1898.
22. *Morning Post*, 14 January 1898.
23. Ibid., 15 January 1898.
24. *The Times*, 15 January 1898.
25. Ibid., 18 January 1898.
26. Ibid., 19 January 1898.
27. *The World*, 26 January 1898.
28. *The Times*, 19 January 1898.
29. Diary of Sydney Bowles, Chatsworth Papers, Chatsworth House.

Chapter 3: Through Five Turkish Provinces
1. Leslie, *Mark Sykes*, p. 52.
2. Ibid., p. 56.
3. M.S. to H.C., U DDSY2/1/1.
4. M.S. to H.C., February 1898, U DDSY2/1/1.
5. M.S. to H.C., March 1898, U DDSY2/1/1.
6. M.S. to H.C., March 1898., 'Letters. Mark Sykes', MS. book in Sledmere House Library.

7. Mark Sykes, *Narative of a Journey East of Jebel Ed-Druse*, Palestine Exploration Fund Quarterly Statement, 1899, p. 47.
8. Ibid., p. 48.
9. *Murray's Handbook for Travellers in Syria and Palestine*, pt I, London, Edward Stanford, 1903 [1858], p.186.
10. Sykes, *Narrative of a Journey East of Jebel Ed-Druse*, p. 51.
11. Ibid., p. 54.
12. Ibid.
13. Ibid., p. 55.
14. Leslie, *Mark Sykes*, p. 59.
15. M.S. to E.G., 16 April 1900, U DDSY2/1/2a.
16. M.S. to H.C., 6 December 1898, U DDSY2/1/1.
17. M.S. to E.G., 20 October 1900, U DDSY(2)/1/2a.
18. Mark Sykes, *Through Five Turkish Provinces*, London, Bickers and Son, 1900, p. 1.
19. Ibid., p. 2.
20. Ibid., p. 3.
21. Ibid., p. 22.
22. Ibid., p. 23.
23. Ibid., p. 33.
24. Ibid., p. 35.
25. Ibid., p. 54.
26. M.S. to H.C., 23 February 1899, U DDSY2/1/11.
27. Ibid., p. 63.
28. Ibid., p. 66.
29. Ibid., p. 76.
30. Ibid., p. 82.
31. Ibid., p. 86.
32. Ibid., p. 87.
33. L. G. Bell, *Syria: The Desert and the Sown*, London, William Heinemann, 1919, p. 4.
34. Sykes, *Through Five Turkish Provinces*, p. 105.
35. Ibid., p. 117.
36. M.S. to E.G., 20 October 1900, U DDSY2/1/2a/1-77.
37. M.S. to E.G., 20 October 1900, U DDSY/2/1-2a.
38. M.S. to H.C., 8 August 1899, U DDSY2/1/1/1-46.
39. M.S. to H.C., 13 August 1999, U DDSY2/1/1/1-46.

Chapter 4: South Africa
1. M.S. to H.C., U DDSY2/1/1.

2. *The Snarl*, no. 2, 14 November 1899.
3. M.S. to H.C., early 1900, U DDSY2/1/1/18.
4. Ibid.
5. About £1,288,000 today.
6. M.S. to E.G., 26 February 1900, U DDSY/2/1/2a.
7. M.S. to E.G., 23 March 1900, U DDSY2/1/2a.
8. M.S. to E.G., 24 March 1900, U DDSY2/1/2a.
9. M.S. to E.G., 1 April 1900, U DDSY2/1/2a.
10. M.S. to E.G., 11 April 1900, U DDSY2/1/2a.
11. Ibid.
12. M.S. to E.G., 17 April 1900, U DDSY/2/1/2a.
13. M.S. to E.G., 21 April 1900, U DDSY/2/1/2a.
14. M.S. to E.G., 22 April 1900, U DDSY2/1/2a.
15. M.S. to E.G., 26 April 1900, U DDSY2/1/2a.
16. M.S. to E.G., 16 May 1900, U DDSY2/1/2a/36.
17. M.S. to E.D., 24 June 1900, U DDSY/x2/1/3b/1.
18. Ibid.
19. Ibid.
20. M.S. to E.G., 29 July 1900, U DDSY2/1/2a/43.
21. M.S. to E.D., 24 June 1900, U DDSY/x2/1/3b/1.
22. M.S. to E.G., 9 July 1900, U DDSY2/1/2a/40.
23. M.S. to E.G., 21 July 1900, U DDSY2/1/2a/42.
24. M.S. to E.G., 15 July 1900, U DDSY2/1/2a/41.
25. M.S. to A.D., 8 August 1900, U DDSY2/1/3b/2.
26. M.S. to E.G., 29 July 1900, U DDSY2/1/2a/43.
27. 'God is Great.'
28. M.S. to R.D., 8 August 1900, U DDSY2/1/3b/2.
29. M.S. to H.C., 5 August 1900, U DDSY2/1/1/20.
30. M.S. to E.G., 11 August 1900, U DDSY2/1/1/45.
31. M.S. to E.G., 20 August 1900, U DDSY2/1/1/47.
32. 'Praise be to Allah.'
33. M.S. to E.G., 1 September 1900, U DDSY2/1/1/50.

34. M.S. to E.G., 7 September 1900, U DDSY2/1/1/52.
35. Ibid.
36. M.S. to E.G., 16 September 1900, U DDSY2/1/1/55.
37. Ibid.
38. M.S. to E.G., 20 September 1900, U DDSY2/1/1/56.
39. M.S. to E.G., 6 October 1900, U DDSY2/1/1/58.
40. M.S. to R.D., 14 October 1900, U DDSY/x2/1/3b/3.
41. M.S. to E.G., 13 October 1900, U DDSY/x2/1/2a/59.
42. M.S. to E.G., 1 December 1900, U DDSY/x2/1/2a/68.
43. M.S. to E.G., 19 December 1900, U DDSY/x2/1/2a/72.
44. Ibid.
45. M.S. to R.D., 1 January 1901, U DDSY/x2/1/3b/5.
46. M.S. to E.G., 29 December 1900, U DDSY/x2/1/2a/74.
47. M.S. to R.D., 1 January 1901, U DDSY/x2/1/3b/5.
48. M.S. to E.G., undated.
49. M.S. to E.G., January 1901, U DDSY/x2/1/2b/2.
50. M.S. to R.D., 28/29 January 1901, U DDSY/x2/1/3b/6.
51. M.S. to H.C., 28 April 1901, U DDSY/x2/1/1/25.
52. M.S. to R.D., 28/29 January 1901, U DDSY/x2/1/3b/6.
53. M.S. to E.G., spring 1901, U DDSY/x2/1/2b/29.
54. M.S. to R.D., spring 1901, U DDSY/x2/1/3b/7.
55. M.S. to E.G., April 1901, U DDSY/x2/1/3b/18.
56. M.S. to E.G., 5 July 1901, U DDSY/x2/1/3b/32.
57. M.S. to E.G., July 1901, U DDSY/x2/1/3b/33.
58. M.S. to E.G., 5 March 1901, U DDSY/x2/1/2b/10.
59. M.S., to H.C., 18 April 1901, U DDSY/x2/1/1/25.
60. M.S. to E.G., 26 February 1901, U DDSY/x2/1/2b/7.
61. M.S. to E.G., spring 1901, U DDSY/x2/1/2b/26.
62. M.S. to E.G., April 1901, U DDSY/x2/1/3b/18.
63. M.S. to E.G., 12 March 1901, U DDSY/x2/1/2b/11.
64. *Kaffir*, which is today considered an offensive ethnic slur, was in 1900 a neutral term for South African blacks.
65. M.S. to E.G., 1 April 1901, U DDSY/x2/1/2b/14.
66. M.S. to E.G., 15 May 1901, U DDSY/x2/1/2b/25.
67. M.S. to E.G., 6 November 1901, U DDSY/x2/1/2b/41.
68. General Louis Botha, General-in-Chief of the Boer army.
69. M.S. to E.G., 9 November 1901, U DDSY/x2/1/2b/42.
70. Ibid.
71. M.S. to E.G., November 1901, U DDSY/x2/1/3b/45.
72. M.S. to E.G., 22 November 1901, U DDSY/x2/1/3b/46.
73. *Mieleipap*: a porridge made from maize, and the traditional staple food of the Bantu.
74. M.S. to E.G., 13 December 1901, U DDSY/x2/1/3b/48.
75. Ibid.
76. M.S. to E.G., 31 January 1902, U DDSY/x2/1/2c/1.
77. M.S. to E.G., 16 March 1902, U DDSY/x2/1/2c/6.
78. M.S. to E.G., April 1902, U DDSY/x2/1/2c/8.
79. M.S. to E.G., 25 March 1902, U DDSY/x2/1/2c/7.
80. M.S. to E.G., April 1902, U DDSY/x2/1/2c/8.
81. M.S. to R.D., 25 March 1902, U DDSY/x2/1/3b/9.
82. M.S. to E.G., 21 May 1902, U DDSY/x2/1/2c/10.

Chapter 5: Coming of Age

1. M.S. to E.G., 15 May 1902, U DDSY/x2/1/2c/9.
2. *Yorkshire Post*, 17 May 1902.
3. M.S. to E.G., 2 February 1902, U DDSY/2/1-2c.
4. M.S. to E.G., 21 May 1902, U DDSY/x2/1/2c/10.
5. M.S. to E.G., 22 May 1902, U DDSY/x2/1/2c/11.
6. M.S. to E.G., 9 June 1902, U DDSY/2/1-2c/15.
7. M.S. to E.G., 27 June 1902, U DDSY/2/1-2c./20.
8. Hugh Kingsmill, *Frank Harris* (rev. edn), London, Biografia, 1987, p. 94.

9. M.S. to E.G., 20 September 1901, U DDSY/x2/1/2b/37.
10. M.S. to E.G., summer 1902, U DDSY/x2/1/2c/45.
11. M.S. to R.D., 28–29 January 1901, U DDSY/2/1/3b/6.
12. M.S. to E.G., 17 September 1902, U DDSY/x2/1/2c/30.
13. Maj.-Gen. G. D'Ordel, *Tactics and Military Training*, eds. M. Sykes and E. Sandars, London, Bickers and Son, 1902.
14. *Daily Express*, 4 October 1902.
15. *Daily News*, 7 November 1902.
16. M.S. to E. G., summer 1902, U DDSY/2/1-2c.
17. *Oxford Dictionary of National Biography*, London Library Electronic catalogue.
18. M.S. to E.G., 17 September 1902, U DDSY2/1/2c/30.
19. M.S. to E.G., 19 September 1902, U DDSY2/1/2c/31.
20. M.S. to E.G., September 1902, U DDSY2/1/2c/32.
21. M.S. to E.G., 19 September 1902, U DDSY2/1/2c/31.
22. M.S. to E.G., September 1902, U DDSY2/1/2c/32.
23. M.S. to E.G., 30 September 1900, U DDSY/x2/1/2a/57.
24. M.S. to E.G., 1 November 1902, U DDSY/x2/1/2c/56.
25. M.S. to E.G., 3 November 1902, U DDSY/x2/1/2c/57.
26. M.S. to E.G., 6 November 1902, U DDSY/x2/1/2c/58.
27. M.S. to H.C., 17 December 1902, U DDSY2/1/1/4.
28. M.S. to E.G., 13 November 1902, U DDSY/x2/1/2c/60.
29. M.S. to E.G.B., 20 November 1902, U DDSY 2/1/2c.
30. Ibid.
31. M.S. to E.G., 13 November 1902, U DDSY/x2/1/2c/60.
32. M.S. to E.G., 20 November 1902, U DDSY/x2/1/2c/61.
33. M.S. to H.C., December 1902, U DDSY2/1/1/30.
34. Mark Sykes, *Dar ul Islam: A Record of a Journey through Ten of the Asiatic Provinces of Turkey*, London, Bickers & Son, 1904, p. 20.
35. M.S. to E.G., 11 April 1903, U DDSY/2/1/2d.
36. A very high official.
37. The husband of an Imperial Princess.
38. M.S. to E.G., May 1903, Kerkúk, U DDSY/x2/1/2d/6.
39. 'The English Jew.'
40. Sykes, *Dar ul Islam*, p. 219.
41. Ibid., p. 225.
42. A civilian and military title in the Ottoman Empire, meaning 'Chief' or 'Lord'.
43. Sykes, *Dar ul Islam*, pp. 229–31.
44. Ibid., p. 236.
45. Ibid., p. 241.
46. Ibid., pp. 242–3.
47. M.S. to E.G., 21 September 1903, U DDSY/x2/1/2d/13.
48. M.S. to E.G., 22 September 1903, U DDSY/x2/1/2d/14.
49. M.S. to E.G., 27 September 1903, U DDSY/x2/1/2d/20.
50. *Yorkshire Herald*, 29 October 1903.
51. Leslie, *Mark Sykes*, p. 101.
52. *The Army and Navy Illustrated*, 14 February 1903.
53. *The Spectator*, 21 February 1903.
54. M.S. to E.S., U DDSY/2/1/2d.
55. M.S. to E.S., December 1903, U DDSY/2/1/2d.
56. Sykes, *Dar-ul-Islam*, p. 18.
57. Ibid., p. 18n.
58. Rudyard Kipling to M.S., 6 May 1904, from a press-cutting book in the Sledmere Library.
59. H. G. Wells to M.S., 7 May 1904, from a press-cutting book in the Sledmere Library.
60. Leslie, *Mark Sykes*, p. 161.
61. M.S. to E.S., 23 July 1904, U DDSY/x2/1/2d/34.
62. Lord Curzon, Viceroy of India.
63. M.S. to E.S., 23 July 1904, U DDSY/x2/1/2d/34.

Chapter 6: Return to the East

1. M.S. to E.S., 13 July 1904, U DDSY2/1/2d/29.
2. M.S. to E.S., 13 July 1904, U DDSY2/1/2d/34.
3. M.S. to E.S., 26 September 1904, U DDSY/2/1/2d/35.
4. Elizabeth Burgoyne, *Gertrude Bell: 1889–1914*, London, Ernest Benn Ltd, 1958, p. 197.
5. Lady Bell (ed.), *The Letters of Gertrude Bell*, London, Ernest Benn Ltd, 1927, p. 178.

6. Mark Sykes, 'Sir Nicholas O'Connor', *Dublin Review*, September 1913.
7. Ibid.
8. M.S. to E.S., 16 April 1905, U DDSY/2/1/2d/43.
9. J.S. to M.S., 6 September 1905, SP.
10. M.S. to H.C., 20 August 1905, U DDSY/2/1/1/35.
11. J.S. to M.S., 6 September 1905, SP.
12. M.S. to H.C., 2 September 1905, U DDSY/2/1/1.
13. Mark Sykes, *Report on the Petroliferous Districts of the Vilayets of Baghdad, Mosul and Bitlis*, FO/78/5398.
14. M.S. to H.C., 20 August 1906, U DDSY/2/1/1/35.
15. M.S. to E.S., 22 February 1906, U DDSY/2/1/2/47.
16. M.S. to H.C., 13 March 1906, U DDSY/2/1/1/50.
17. Ibid.
18. Ibid.
19. M.S. to E.S., 20 March 1906, U DDSY/2/1/1/52; 'I never would have believed that our Lady is as beautiful as that.'
20. M.S. to E.S., 20 March 1906, U DDSY/2/1/1/53.
21. Mark Sykes, *The Caliphs' Last Heritage: A Short History of the Turkish Empire*, London, Macmillan and Co., 1915, p. 303.
22. Ibid., p. 302.
23. M.S. to E.S., 5 April 1906, U DDSY/2/1/1/56a.
24. Sykes, *Caliphs' Last Heritage*, p. 317.
25. Ibid., p. 326.
26. Ibid.
27. Ibid., p. 333.
28. ibid.
29. M.S. to E.S., 28 April 1906, U DDSY/2/1/1/56b.
30. E.S. to M.S., 26 March 1906, S.P.
31. E.S. to M.S., 15 April 1906, SP.
32. M.S. to E.S., 28 April 1906, U DDSY/2/1/1/56b.
33. Ibid.
34. Sykes, *Caliphs' Last Heritage*, p. 338.
35. Ibid., p. 339.
36. A Lieutenant-General in the Ottoman army.
37. An Aide-de-Camp.
38. M.S. to F.M., 'May the somethingth, 1906', U DDSY2/1/3d/1.
39. M.S. to E.S., 28 April 1906, U DDSY/2/1/1/56b.
40. M.S. to E.S., May 1906, U DDSY/2/1/1/53.
41. Sykes, *Caliphs' Last Heritage*, pp. 354–5.
42. M.S. to E.S., May 1906, U DDSY/2/1/1/53.
43. M.S. to E.S., 11 May 1906, U DDSY/2/1/1/58.
44. E.S. to M.S., 12 May 1906, SP.

Chapter 7: Family Life

1. M.S. to E.G., 1902, U DDSY/x2/1/2c/8.
2. M.S. TO H.C., 1901, U DDSY2/1/1/27.
3. MS to ES. May 1906. U DDSY2/1/2d/59
4. *Hull Daily Mail*, 25 January 1907.
5. Ibid.
6. M.S. to H.C., 8 August 1905, U DDSY/2/1/1.
7. Ibid.
8. M.S. to E.S., 3 September 1907, U DDSY.
9. About £20,600 today.
10. M.S. to H.C., 1905, U DDSY2/1/1/33.
11. U DDSY/2/10/12. Fragment of ms. memorial for Mark Sykes by Lady Sykes, 1919.
12. A.H. to the author, October 1997, SP.
13. Interview with Christopher Sykes.
14. Ibid.
15. Interview with Freya Elwes.
16. Harold E. Gorst, *Much of Life is Laughter*, London, George Allen & Unwin, 1936, p. 270.
17. M.S. to E.B., 25 February 1907, U DDSY. Leslie, *Mark Sykes*, p. 208.
18. *Hull Daily Mail*, 5 October 1907.
19. *Things Political, IV*, Malton, 1909.
20. Adelson, *Mark Sykes*, p. 134.
21. Leslie, *Mark Sykes*, p. 213.
22. M.S. to E.S., 23 February 1911, U DDSY2/1/2e/49.
23. M.S. to E.S., February 1911, U DDSY2/1/2e/45.
24. M.S. to E.S., 26 February 1911, U DDSY2/1/2e/53.
25. Ibid.
26. M.S. to E.S., 23 February 1911, U DDSY2/1/2e/49.
27. M.S. to E.S., 28 February 1911, U DDSY2/1/2e/54.
28. Ibid.
29. M.S. to E.S., March 1911, U DDSY2/1/2e/57.

30. M.S. to E.S., March 1911,
    U DDSY2/1/2e/56.
31. M.S. to E.S., 11 March 1911,
    U DDSY2/1/2e/58.
32. M.S. to E.S., 17 March 1911,
    U DDSY2/1/2e/60.
33. H.C. to M.S., U DDSY2/1/16/94.
34. U DDSY2/1/16/460.
35. Ibid.
36. *Yorkshire Post*, 24 May 1911.
37. Adelson, *Mark Sykes*, p. 137.
38. U DDSY2/1/16/460.
39. H.C. to M.S., 23 May 1911,
    U DDSY2/1/16/93.
40. U DDSY2/1/16/460.
41. MSS account of her childhood by
    Everilda Smith. Property of Mrs Tessa
    Scott.
42. *Yorkshire Post*, 24 May 1911.

Chapter 8: A Seat in the House
1. M.S. to E.S., July 1911,
    U DDSY2/1/2e/68.
2. The PM's Private Secretary.
3. M.S. to E.S., July 1911,
    U DDSY2/1/2e/68.
4. Ibid.
5. M.S. to E.S., July 1911,
    U DDSY2/1/2e/69.
6. M.S. to E.S., 24 July 1911,
    U DDSY2/1/2e/70.
7. M.S. to E.S., 9 August 1911,
    U DDSY2/1/2e/74.
8. M.S. to E.S., 10 August 1911,
    U DDSY2/1/2e/76.
9. M.S. to W.B., January 1912, YAS MS
    729.
10. M.S. to W.B., 9 February 1912, YAS
    MS 729.
11. M.S. to W.B., 30 January 1912, YAS
    MS 729.
12. M.S. to E.S., 3 September 1911,
    U DDSY/2/1/2e/78.
13. M.S. to W.B., 18 October 1911, YAS
    MS 729.
14. M.S. to W.B., 23 October 1911, YAS
    MS 729.
15. M.S. to E.S., 9 August 1911, U
    DDSY2/1/2e/75.
16. Gorst, *Much of Life is Laughter*,
    p. 213.
17. An MS. account by a Mr Goulton, SP.
18. Leslie, *Mark Sykes*, p. 222.
19. Hansard, HC Deb. (series 5) vol. 32,
    col. 106 (27 Nov. 1911).
20. Gorst, *Much of Life is Laughter*, p. 214.

21. Leslie, *Mark Sykes*, p. 218.
22. Gorst, *Much of Life is Laughter*, p. 271.
23. Leslie, *Mark Sykes*, p. 228.
24. M.S. to E.S., July 1909, U
    DDSY2/1/2e/20.
25. Obituary, 'The Late Lady Sykes', SP.
26. *Daily Mail*, 4 June 1912.
27. M.S. to Lord Northcliffe, 5 June 1912,
    U DDSY2/1/41/414.
28. Ibid.
29. M.S. to E.S., March 1913,
    U DDSY2/1/2f/5.
30. M.S. to W.B., 3 July 1914, YAS MS
    729.
31. M.S. to W.B., 5 July 1914, YAS MS
    729.
32. M.S. to W.B., 6 July 1914, YAS MS
    729.
33. M.S. to W.B., 8 July 1914, YAS MS
    729.
34. Leslie, *Mark Sykes*, p. 222.
35. *Sunday Chronicle*, 20 April 1913.
36. Leslie, *Mark Sykes*, p. 19.
37. Leo Amery, *My Political Life*, London,
    Hutchinson, 1953, p. 426.
38. M.S. to E.S., 9 August 1911,
    U DDSY2/1/2e/74.
39. *The Saturday Review*, 28 March 1914.
40. Quoted in Leslie, *Mark Sykes*, p. 223.
41. Hansard, HC Deb. (series 5) vol. 60,
    cols. 1201–70 (1 Apr. 1914).
42. Ibid.
43. M.S. to E.G.B., 10 April 1914,
    U DDSY/2/1/3C.
44. *Daily Sketch*, 2 April 1914.
45. Ibid.

Chapter 9: War
1. Hansard, HC Deb. (series 5) vol. 56,
    cols. 2313–17 (12 Aug. 1913).
2. Sykes, *Caliphs' Last Heritage*, p. 507.
3. Ibid.
4. Ibid., p. 513
5. M.S. to his children, 13 September
    1913, U DDSY2/1/2f/10.
6. Sykes, *Caliphs' Last Heritage*, p. 513.
7. Ibid., p. 515.
8. E.S. to her children, October 1913,
    U DDSY2/1/2f/10.
9. Sykes, *Caliphs' Last Heritage*, p. 521.
10. M.S. to E.S., October 1913,
    U DDSY2/1/2f/17.
11. Sykes, *Caliphs' Last Heritage*, p. 532.
12. Ibid., p. 533.
13. Ibid., p. 541.
14. Ibid., p. 542.

15. M.S. to E.S., October 1913,
    U DDSY2/1/2f/13.
16. Ibid.
17. M.S. to E.S., January 1914,
    U DDSY2/1/2f/19.
18. M.S. to E.S., January 1914,
    U DDSY2/1/2f/20.
19. Anna Pavlova was a Russian prima
    ballerina of the early twentieth century
    who was a global star.
20. M.S. to E.S., February 1914,
    U DDSY2/1/2f/24.
21. Leslie, *Mark Sykes*, p. 233.
22. Hansard, HC Deb. (series 5) vol. 64,
    col. 67 (29 June 1914).
23. Hansard, HC Deb. (series 5) vol. 59
    (February 1914).
24. M.S. to E.S., 30 July 1914,
    U DDSY2/1/2f/26.
25. M.S. to E.S., August 1914,
    U DDSY2/1/2f/27.
26. M.S. to E.S., 30 July 1914,
    U DDSY2/1/2f/26.
27. Ian Sumner, *The Wolds Wagoners*,
    Sledmere Estate, 2000, p. 4.
28. Ibid.
29. Ibid., p. 10.
30. MSS account of trip by M.S. to the
    Western Front, September 1914, U
    DDSY2/5/103.
31. Ibid.
32. Ibid.
33. *The Times*, 29 October 1914.
34. *Yorkshire Post*, 2 December 1914.
35. Leslie, *Mark Sykes*, p. 19.
36. Sykes, *Much of Life is Laughter*, p. 230.
37. Leslie, *Mark Sykes*, p. 234.
38. Ibid.
39. M.S. to Winston Churchill, quoted in
    Adelson, *Mark Sykes*, p. 175.
40. Margaret Fitzherbert, *The Man Who was
    Greenmantle*, John Murray, London,
    1983, p. 143.

Chapter 10: Kitchener and the Middle East
1. Ronald Storrs, *Orientations*, London,
   Nicholson and Watson, 1945, p. 122.
2. Ibid., p. 148.
3. Ibid., p. 149.
4. Ibid., p. 152.
5. M.S. to E.S., 5 November 1914,
   U DDSY2/1/2f/29.
6. M.S. to E.S., 11 December 1914,
   U DDSY2/1/2f/30.
7. M.S. to E.S., 30 December 1914,
   U DDSY2/1/2f/32.
8. M.S. to W.C., 26 February 1915, in
   Martin Gilbert, *Churchill: Companion to
   Vol. 3*, London, Heinemann, 1972,
   pp. 581–3.
9. M.S. to E.S., February 1915,
   U DDSY2/1/2f/33.
10. M.S. to O.F., 4 March 1915,
    U DDSY2/1/3f/1.
11. M.S. to G.A., 12 September 1916,
    Kitchener Papers, PRO 30/57.91.
12. Aaron Klieman, 'Britain's War
    Aims in the Middle East', *Journal of
    Contemporary History*, vol. 3, no. 3, July
    1968, p. 241.
13. M.S. to G.A., 12 September 1916,
    Kitchener Papers, PRO 30/57.91.
14 Ibid., p. 250, n.25.
15. M. Sykes, 'The Proposed Maintenance
    of a Turkish Empire in Asia without
    Spheres of Influence', 3 May 1915,
    PRO Cab 27/1.
16. M.S. to A.H. in Fitzherbert, *Man Who
    was Greenmantle*, p. 147.
17. M.S. to G.A., 12 September 1916,
    Kitchener Papers, PRO 30/57/91.
18. The substance that gives certain types of
    tea its Muscatel flavour is called terpene,
    and many small insects are allergic to its
    smell.
19. M.S. to E.S., 18 July 1915,
    U DDSY2/1/2f/41.
20. *Orientations*, Storrs, pp. 195–6.
21. M.S. to E.S., 17 July 1915,
    U DDSY2/1/2f/43.
22. Storrs, *Orientations*, p. 196.
23. M.S. to E.S., 17 July 1915,
    U DDSY2/1/2f/43.
24. M.S. to E.S., 19 July 1915,
    U DDSY2/1/2f/44.
25. M.S. to E.S., 21 July 1915,
    U DDSY2/1/2f/45.
26. Despatch from M.S. to War Office,
    23 July 1915, U DDSY2/11/7.
27. Briton Cooper Busch, *Harding of
    Penshurst: A Study in the Old Diplomacy*,
    Hamden, Conn., Archon Books, 1980,
    p. 257.
28. Adelson, *Mark Sykes*, p. 189.
29. M.S. to E.S., 3 September 1915,
    U DDSY2/1/2f/49.
30. M.S. to E.S., 9 September 1915,
    U DDSY2/1/2f/50.
31. M.S. to E.S., 3 September 1915,
    U DDSY2/1/2f/49.
32. M.S. to E.S., 9 September 1915,
    U DDSY2/1/2f/50

33. Ibid.
34. A. T. Wilson, *Loyalties: Mesopotamia 1914–1917*, Oxford University Press, 1930, p. 152.
35. M.S. to E.S., 19 September 1915, U DDSY2/1/2f/51.
36. 'The Baghdad Advance', *Manchester Guardian*, 22 November 1915.
37. Briton Cooper Busch, *Britain, India, and the Arabs: 1914–1921*, Berkeley and London, University of California Press, 1971, p. 70.
38. Adelson, *Mark Sykes*, p. 193.

Chapter 11: The Sykes–Picot Agreement
1. Storrs, *Orientations*, p. 152.
2. George Antonius, *The Arab Awakening: The Story of the Arab National Movement*, London, Hamish Hamilton, 1938, p. 167.
3. Ibid., p. 416.
4. Ibid.
5. Ibid., p. 419.
6. Ibid.
7. Cambon to the Ministry of Foreign Affairs, 21 October 1915, quoted in 'France's Middle Eastern Ambitions', *The Journal of Modern History*, December 1994, p. 707.
8. Ibid., p. 708.
9. T. E. Lawrence, *Seven Pillars of Wisdom*, London, Cape, 1973, p. 464.
10. C. M. Andrew and A. Kanya-Forstner, *France Overseas*, London, Thames and Hudson, 1981, p. 67.
11. 'France's Middle Eastern Ambitions', p. 709.
12. Andrew and Kanya-Forstner, *France Overseas*, p. 89.
13. Ibid., p. 90.
14. Ibid., p. 91.
15. Minutes of War Committee meeting. 15 December 1915, National Archives. CAB/24/1.
16. Elie Kedourie, *Arabic Political Memoirs and Other Studies*, London, Frank Cass, 1974, p. 237.
17. Andrew and Kanya-Forstner, *France Overseas*, p. 93.
18. K. Bourne and D. C. Watt (eds.), *Studies in International History*, London, Longmans, 1967. p. 328.
19. Jonathan Schneer, *The Balfour Declaration*, London, Bloomsbury, 2010, p. 80.
20. He was probably referring to Anders Zorn (1860–1920).

21. M.S. to E.S., 3 March 1916, U DDSY2/1/2f/54.
22. *Letters from Tsar Nicholas to Tsaritsa Alexandra*, www.alexanderpalace.org/letters.
23. Andrew and Kanya-Forstner, *France Overseas*, p. 100.
24. Kedourie, *Arabic Political Memoirs*, p. 240.
25. M.S. to E.S., April 1916, U DDSY2/1/2f/55.
26. Adelson, *Mark Sykes*, p. 201.

Chapter 12: Zionism
1. Viscount Samuel, *Memoirs*, London, Cresset Press, 1945, p. 140.
2. Adelson, *Mark Sykes*, p. 226.
3. Herbert Samuel, 'The Future of Palestine', CAB 37/123/43.
4. Adelson, *Mark Sykes*, p. 207.
5. Schneer, *Balfour Declaration*, p. 165.
6. Ibid., p. 166.
7. Ibid., p. 167.
8. Adelson, *Mark Sykes*, p. 207.
9. L. Stein, *The Balfour Declaration*, London, Vallentine, Mitchell, 1961, p. 279.
10. Mark Sykes, 'The Problem of the Near East', 20 June 1916, U DDSY2/11/13.
11. Leslie, *Mark Sykes*, p. 23.
12. M.S. to E.S., 3 August 1916, U DDSY2/1/2f/61.
13. Ibid.
14. Extract from a memoir of her childhood by Angela Sykes, in the possession of the author.
15. MS account of her childhood, by Petsy Scrope, in the possession of her daughter, Tessa Scott.
16. Angela Sykes, memoir.
17. Letter to the author, SP.
18. David Fromkin, *A Peace to End All Peace: The Fall of the Ottoman Empire and the Creation of the Modern Middle East*, new edn, London, Phoenix, 2000, p. 233.
19. Adelson, *Mark Sykes*, p. 215.
20. Elizabeth Monroe, *Britain's Moment in the Middle East*, London, Chatto & Windus, 1963, p. 38.
21. D. Lloyd George, *Memoirs of the Peace Conference*, New Haven, Conn., Yale University Press, 1939, vol. 2, p. 722.
22. Memo of Downing St Conference, 3 April 1917, U DDSY2/12/6.
23. Adelson, *Mark Sykes*, p. 220.

24. Fromkin, *Peace to End All Peace*, p. 286.
25. Nahum Sokolow, *History of Zionism: 1600–1918*, London, Longmans, Green & Co., 1919, p. xxix.
26. M.S. to E.S., April 1917, U DDSY2/1/2f/62
27. Elie Kedourie, *In the Anglo-Arab Labyrinth*, Cambridge University Press, 1976, pp, 170, 171.
28. Schneer, *Balfour Declaration*, p. 211.
29. Ibid.
30. Schneer, *Balfour Declaration*, p. 212.
31. Sokolow, *History of Zionism*, p. xxx.
32. Schneer, *Balfour Declaration*, p. 213.
33. Christopher Sykes, *Two Studies in Virtue*, London, Collins, 1953, p. 198.
34. M.S. to E.S., 12 April 1917, U DDSY2/1/2f/62.
35. Ibid.
36. Ibid.
37. Ibid.
38. Schneer, *Balfour Declaration*, p. 215.
39. Ibid.
40. Christopher Sykes, *Two Studies in Virtue*, p. 200.
41. Ibid., p. 202.
42. Ibid., p. 203.

Chapter 13: The Balfour Declaration
1. M.S. to E.S., 15 April 1917, U DDSY2/1/2f/64.
2. M.S. to E.S., 23 April 1917, U DDSY2/1/2f/65.
3. Ibid.
4. M.S. to E.S., 28 April 1917, U DDSY2/1/2f/66.
5. Ibid.
6. Adelson, *Mark Sykes*, p. 229.
7. M.S. to E.S., 28 April 1917, U DDSY2/1/2f/66.
8. Kedourie, *In the Anglo-Arab Labyrinth*, p. 166.
9. Ibid.
10. Scott Anderson., *Lawrence in Arabia*, London, Atlantic, 2014, p. 309.
11. Schneer, *Balfour Declaration*, p. 334.
12. Stein, *Balfour Declaration*, p. 467.
13. Ibid., p. 419.
14. Chaim Weizmann, *Trial and Error*, London, Hamish Hamilton, 1949, p. 262.
15. Jehuda Reinharz, *Chaim Weizmann*, Oxford University Press, 1993, p. 205. '*Mazel tov*' means 'good luck'.
16. Stein, *Balfour Declaration*, p. 629.

17. Clayton to M.S., 15 December 1917, U DDSY2/11/83.
18. *Manchester Guardian*, 10 December 1917.
19. Weizmann, *Trial and Error*, p. 254.
20. Ibid., p. 256.
21. Sokolow, *History of Zionism*, p. xxxi.
22. Fromkin, *Peace to End All Peace*, p. 319.
23. Clayton to M.S., 15 December 1917, U DDSY2/11/83.
24. Fromkin, *Peace to End All Peace*, p. 322.
25. Ibid., p. 323.
26. *Manchester Guardian*, 26 November 1917.
27. *The Times*, 7 January 1918.
28. Adelson, *Mark Sykes*, p. 250.
29. Sokolow, *History of Zionism*, p. xxxii.
30. Ibid.
31. Ibid., p. xxxiii.
32. Weizmann, *Trial and Error*, pp. 268, 269.
33. Ibid., p. 292.
34. Ibid.
35. Fromkin, *Peace to End All Peace*, p. 324.
36. John Barnes and David Nicholson (eds.), *The Leo Amery Diaries*, London, Hutchinson, 1980, vol. 1, p. 206.
37. C. M. Andrew and A. S. Kanya-Forstner, 'The French Colonial Party and French Colonial War Aims, 1914–1918', *Historical Journal*, vol. xvii, 3 September 1974, p. 101.
38. Elie Kedourie, *England and the Middle East*, London, Mansell, 1987, p. 112.
39. C. M. Andrew and A. Kanya-Forstner, *The Climax of French Imperial Expansion, 1914–1924*, Stanford University Press, 1981, p. 157.
40. Ibid., p. 158.
41. Ibid.
42. Hansard, HC Deb. (series 5) vol. 109, col. 727 (1 Aug. 1918).
43. Walter Wilson to Hallmark, 1 August 1918, U DDSY2/1/38/92.
44. Andrew and Kanya-Forstner, *Climax of French Imperial Expansion*, p. 159.
45. The Cabinet Papers, TNA, CAB 23/14/35.
46. Antonius, *Arab Awakening*, p. 435.
47. Leslie, *Mark Sykes*, pp. 272–3.

Chapter 14: Worked to Death
1. Angela Sykes, memoir.
2. Adelson, *Mark Sykes*, p. 278.
3. M.S. to E.S., November 1918, U DDSY2/1/2f/75.

4. Major Ronald Gladstone, MS. 'Account of Trip to Middle East, October 1918–February 1919', U DDSY2/4/188.

5. Ibid. This refers to the massacres of Armenians that took place in 1894–6 and 1909, during which up to 100,000 or more Armenians were slaughtered by Moslem Turks.

6. M.S. to E.S. November 1918, U DDSY2/1/2f/75

7. Celebrated conductor, famous for his series of 'Proms' concerts that started at the Queen's Hall in the late 1890s.

8. M.S. to E.S., November 1918, U DDSY2/1/2f/77.

9. Gladstone, MS. account of trip to Middle East, p. 6, U DDSY2/4/188.

10. Matthew Hughes (ed.), *Allenby in Palestine: The M.E. Correspondence of Viscount Allenby, 1917–1919*, Army Records Society, 2004, p. 218.

11. Ibid., p. 221.

12. M.S. to E.S., 17 November 1918, U DDSY2/1/2f/78.

13. Gladstone, MS. account of trip to Middle East, p. 6.

14. Storrs, *Orientations*, p. 323.

15. Hughes (ed.), *Allenby in Palestine*, p. 218.

16. Ibid., p. 220.

17. Gladstone, MS. account of trip to Middle East, p. 7.

18. M.S. to E.S., 17 November 1918, U DDSY2/1/2f/76

19. Adelson, *Mark Sykes*, p. 282.

20. Gladstone, MS. account of trip to Middle East, p. 9.

21. Adelson, *Mark Sykes*, p. 284.

22. An inn with a large courtyard to accommodate caravans crossing the desert.

23. Gladstone, MS. account of trip to Middle East, p. 10.

24. Leslie, *Mark Sykes*, p. 280.

25. *The Times*, 12 December 1918.

26. Leslie, *Mark Sykes*, p. 278.

27. Adelson, *Mark Sykes*, p. 291.

28. Ibid.

29. 'You are my helper and my liberator.'

30. Edith's recollections of Mark, U DDSY2/16/12.

31. Gladstone, MS. account of trip to Middle East, p. 13.

32. Ibid., p. 14.

33. Ibid.

34. Ibid., p. 16

35. Hughes (ed.), *Allenby in Palestine*, p. 224.

36. Storrs, *Orientations*, p. 324.

37. Leslie, *Mark Sykes*, p. 299.

38. Memo by Edmund Sandars, 10 February 1919, p. 3, U DDSY2/9/38.

39. Adelson, *Mark Sykes*, p. 289.

40. Sandars, memo, 10 February 1919, p. 3.

41. Adelson, *Mark Sykes*, p. 289.

42. Leslie, *Mark Sykes*, p. 279.

43. Sandars, memo, 10 February 1919, p. 1.

44. Ibid., p. 4.

45. Ibid., p. 5.

46. E.S. to her children, 17 February 1919. Letter in the possession of the author.

47. Leslie, *Mark Sykes*, p. 292.

48. Ibid., p. 301.

49. H. Gorst, *Much of Life is Laughter*, p. 282.

50. Leslie, *Mark Sykes*, p. 298.

51. Ibid., p. 299.

52. 'You were my helper and my deliverer.'

53. *Eastern Morning News*, 26 February 1919.

54. 'Rejoice, O Jerusalem; and gather round, all you who love her; rejoice in gladness, after having been in sorrow; exult and be replenished with the consolation flowing from her motherly bosom. I rejoiced when it was said unto me: "Let us go to the house of the Lord."'

55. Antonius, *Arab Awakening*, p. 291.

Epilogue: The Legacy

1. 'Bulldozing the border between Iraq and Syria: the Islamic State (part 5)', *ISIL Says The End of Sykes–Picot*, Alhayat News, 17 September 2014. www.youtube.com/watch?v=tP4uwySxi-k.

2. Raja Shehadeh and Penny Johnson, eds., *Shifting Sands: The Unravelling of the Old Order in the Middle East*, London, Profile Books, 2015, p. 24.

3. Ibid.

4. Ibid., p. 28.

5. Fromkin, *Peace to End All Peace*, p. 5.

Index